Angela Carter:
New Critical Readings

Also available from Bloomsbury

Andrea Levy: Contemporary Critical Perspectives, Edited by Jeannette Baxter
and David James
Contemporary Women Writers Look Back, Alice Ridout
Ian McEwan: Contemporary Critical Perspectives, Edited by Sebastian Groes
J.G Ballard: Contemporary Critical Perspectives, Edited by Jeannette Baxter
Julian Barnes: Contemporary Critical Perspectives, Edited by Sebastian Groes
and Peter Childs
Kazuo Ishiguro: Contemporary Critical Perspectives, Edited by Sean Matthews
and Sebastian Groes
Salman Rushdie: Contemporary Critical Perspectives, Edited by Robert Eaglestone
and Martin McQuillan
Sarah Waters: Contemporary Critical Perspectives, Edited by Kaye Mitchell

Angela Carter:
New Critical Readings

Edited by
Sonya Andermahr and Lawrence Phillips

B L O O M S B U R Y
LONDON · NEW DELHI · NEW YORK · SYDNEY

Bloomsbury Academic

An imprint of Bloomsbury Publishing Plc

50 Bedford Square
London
WC1B 3DP
UK

1385 Broadway
New York
NY 10018
USA

www.bloomsbury.com

Bloomsbury is a registered trade mark of Bloomsbury Publishing Plc

First published in 2012 by the Continuum International Publishing Group Ltd
Paperback edition first published 2014 by Bloomsbury Academic

British Library Cataloguing-in-Publication Data
A catalogue record for this book is available from the British Library.

ISBN: HB: 978-1-4411-6928-0
PB: 978-1-4725-2852-0
ePDF: 978-1-4411-4111-8
ePUB: 978-1-4411-7776-6

Library of Congress Cataloging-in-Publication Data
Angela Carter: new critical readings/edited by Sonya Andermahr and Lawrence Phillips.
p. cm.
Includes bibliographical references and index.
ISBN 978-1-4411-6928-0 – ISBN 978-1-4411-4111-8
1. Carter, Angela, 1940-1992–Criticism and interpretation.
I. Andermahr, Sonya. II. Phillips, Lawrence (Lawrence Alfred), 1966–
PR6053.A73Z5285 2012
823'.914–dc23
2012011970

Typeset by Deanta Global Publishing Services, Chennai, India

Contents

Notes on Contributors

Sonya Andermahr is Reader in English at the University of Northampton, U.K. She has written widely on contemporary British and American women's writing. Her publications include *Jeanette Winterson* (Palgrave 2009), *Jeanette Winterson: A Contemporary Critical Guide* (Continuum, 2007) and, with Terry Lovell and Carol Wolkowitz, *A Glossary of Feminist Theory* (Edward Arnold, 2000). Her current research interest lies in female trauma narratives with a particular focus on narratives of maternal loss in contemporary women's writing.

Sarah Artt is Lecturer in English and Film at Edinburgh Napier University. Her work has appeared in the *Journal of Adaptation in Film and Performance*, and the edited collections *Reading Rocky Horror* (Palgrave Macmillan 2008) and *Translation, Adaptation and Transformation* (Continuum 2012). Her teaching and research interests focus on contemporary issues in screen adaptation, Hollywood cinema, women's writing and filmmaking and science fiction.

Sarah Gamble is Reader in English with Gender at Swansea University. She is a specialist in contemporary women's writing and gender theory, with a particular interest in the life and work of Angela Carter. She is the author of *Angela Carter: Writing from the Front Line* (1997) and *Angela Carter: A Literary Life* (2006), the editor of *Angela Carter: A Reader's Guide to Essential Criticism* (2001) and has also written numerous articles on Angela Carter and other contemporary women writers such as Sarah Waters, Pat Barker and Michele Roberts. She is currently engaged in a project funded by the British Academy focussing on Carter's early poetry, and is also writing a monograph on Carter's engagement with the Gothic.

Katie Garner is a PhD student and Postgraduate Tutor in English Literature at Cardiff University, Wales, UK. Her doctoral thesis looks at British women writers' responses to the medieval revival in the late eighteenth and early nineteenth centuries. She is the co-author (with Rebecca Munford) of an essay-length entry on 'Feminism' in *The Encyclopedia of Literary and Cultural Theory: Literary Theory from 1966 to the Present* (2010).

Simon Goulding studied for his PhD at the University of Birmingham, UK. He has written many articles for a variety of journals including Literary London and has work on Siegfried Sassoon to be published in 2012. He is currently completing work on his first book.

Susanne Gruss specializes in contemporary English literature and culture as well as in early modern drama. She has published a monograph on twentieth-century feminist writing (*The Pleasure of the Feminist Text: Reading Michèle Roberts and Angela Carter*), and written articles on film adaptation, questions of canonization, ecofeminism and the Gothic conventions in *Harry Potter*. Her research interests include gender studies, film and media studies, Neo-Victorianism and, more recently, the intersection of legal discourses and literature and Jacobean revenge tragedy.

Jane Hentgès is a Senior Lecturer at Pau University in the South of France. She specializes in twentieth-century English literature and women's writing in particular. She is interested in how women reinvent 'reality' through the gothic, surrealism and magic realism in order to express 'otherness'. She is also interested in the different ways women play with humour to transgress and create. Her doctoral thesis is on the double eye/I and playing with the double in Angela Carter's novels. She has published numerous articles, mainly on Angela Carter.

Kari Jegerstedt is Postdoctoral fellow at the Centre for Women's and Gender Research at the University of Bergen, Norway, with a project on reading and globalization. She has co-authored Kjønnsteori [Gender Theory] (with Ellen Mortensen *et al.* 2008) and published articles on feminist theory, postcolonialism, psychoanalysis and British, Norwegian and South African literature. She is working on a book on feminist resistance in the age of multiple identities.

Hope Jennings is an Assistant Professor at Wright State University-Lake Campus where she teaches British Literature and Women's Studies. She received her PhD from the University of St. Andrews for a thesis examining myth and gender in Angela Carter's fiction. Her essays and criticism have appeared in *Journal of Contemporary Literature, Michigan Feminist Studies, Margaret Atwood Studies* and *Interdisciplinary Humanities*. She recently completed a fictional biography of the Modernist poet, Mina Loy, and is currently writing a book-length study, *Beyond Apocalypse: Re-Visions of the End in 20th Century and Contemporary Women's Writing*.

Lorna Jowett is a Reader in Television Studies at the University of Northampton, UK, where she teaches some of her favourite things, including horror, science fiction and television sometimes all at once. Her research focuses on genre and gender across film, television and literature and recent publications include articles on *Heroes, Supernatural and the science fiction of Kurt Vonnegut. Her monograph, Sex and the Slayer: A Gender Studies Primer for the Buffy Fan*, was published by Wesleyan University Press in 2005 and she is on the editorial board of *Slayage: the Journal of the Whedon Studies Association*. She is currently co-writing with Stacey Abbott a book on TV Horror.

Anja Müller-Wood is Professor of English Literature and Culture at Johannes Gutenberg-Universität Mainz, Germany. She is the author of two monographs – *Angela Carter: Identity Constructed/Deconstructed* (1997) and *The Theatre of Civilized Excess: New Perspectives on Jacobean Tragedy* (2007) – and has published numerous articles on early modern English literature and culture as well as on twentieth-century and contemporary British fiction. Her further research interests include combining literary studies and linguistics and exploring the aesthetics and psychology of literary reception. She is currently developing a long-term project that will reconsider the latter from the angle of evolutionary psychology and the cognitive sciences.

Mine Özyurt Kılıç is an Assistant Professor of English Literature at Doğuş University, İstanbul, Turkey. She is the author of *Gender-Bending Fantasies in Women's Writing* which investigates the function of the fantastic in the works of Angela Carter and Jeanette Winterson.(VDM, 2009) She also co-edited *Winterson Narrating Time and Space* (Cambridge Scholars Publishing, 2009). She is a contributor of ABES Contemporary Literature section. Currently, she is currently writing a monograph provisionally *titled Maggie Gee: Writing the State of Britain* (Continuum, 2012).

Lawrence Phillips is Professor of English and Cultural Criticism at the University of Northampton, UK. He has written or edited six books including (with Anne Witchard) *London Gothic: Place, Space and the Gothic Imagination* (2010) and most recently *The South Pacific Narratives of Robert Lois Stevenson and Jack London* (2012). His research has three main strands: the representation of space and place; empire writing and Victorian and Edwardian literature; and post-war and contemporary British fiction.

Maria José Pires currently teaches at the Escola Superior de Hotelaria e Turismo do Estoril, in Portugal. She is a researcher at the Centre for English Studies at the University of Lisbon, where she worked on her MA thesis (how Angela Carter answers William Shakespeare in a post-modern context) and PhD thesis (studying Carter's work from a gastro-criticism perspective). Her published articles include 'Angela Carter's uncontaminated renegotiation and redefinition of values' and 'Facing Difference: Angela Carter's Petrified Harvest'.

Michelle Ryan-Sautour is Associate Professor at the Université d'Angers, France where she is a member of the short story section of the CRILA research group. Her research focus is the speculative fiction and short stories of Angela Carter and Rikki Ducornet with a special emphasis on authorship, reading pragmatics, game theory and gender. She has published articles in *The Journal of the Short Story in English, Etudes Britanniques Contemporaines, Marvels and Tales* and in several edited collections.

Anna Watz is currently completing her PhD in English Literature at Uppsala University, Sweden, on the influence of surrealism on Angela Carter's writing. She has published previously on Carter, most recently an article about her unknown translation of Xavière Gauthier's feminist polemic *Surréalisme et sexualité*.

Introduction

Sonya Andermahr and Lawrence Phillips

New Critical Readings

The year 2012 represents the twentieth anniversary of Angela Carter's death. In those twenty years her work has given rise to much critical debate, which has consolidated her reputation as a major British writer of the post-war period. She is taught widely across the UK, US and internationally on twentieth-century literature and contemporary women's writing courses. Indeed, according to Danielle M. Roemer and Cristina Bacchilega (2000), alongside Toni Morrison and Maxine Hong Kingston she is the most commonly taught woman writer on North American programmes. As befits her recent popularity, there have been a number of important surveys of her work. Monographic studies by Lorna Sage, Sarah Gamble, Linden Peach (2009), Nicola Pitchford (2002) and Aidan Day and essay collections (by Alison Easton and Rebecca Munford [2006]) have analysed her oeuvre in terms of literary experiment, iconoclasm, fantasy, radical politics, postmodernism and feminism. Biographical works by Sage (1994) and Gamble (2006) have linked her work to her life in illuminating ways; while Day calls for Carter's work to be seen in the context of longstanding debates about Enlightenment reason (1998). Yet, while critics have acknowledged Carter's versatility and hybridity, the dominant critical construction of Angela Carter is as a feminist and postmodern fabulist. Recent studies such as Gamble's *Angela Carter: A Literary Life* (2006) have begun to offer a corrective to this tendency by placing Carter in her historical context, in line with her own materialist emphasis. As Gamble states:

> Such a commitment to materialism made Carter an extremely astute observer of the cultural milieu within which she lived and worked. In both her fiction and her substantial body of non-fiction, she chronicled her times with a thoroughness which has sometimes been underplayed in studies of her work which concentrate on her as a fabulist, neo-Gothic or postmodernist writer. (Gamble 2006: 12)

In our view, too, Carter has been overly categorized as a postmodern folklorist. Just as we concur with Gamble that Carter's work needs to be located historically, we also think her work needs to be put in a broader genre context, given that her career encompassed such a variety of different genres. It is our contention that Carter be viewed, not simply as a major feminist fabulist, but as a major late twentieth-century writer *tout court*. She is sometimes seen as narrowly focused but Carter was ambitious and would try anything. For us, Carter is a writer who was not restricted by particular genres or particular political positions (notwithstanding her work's fierce political engagement). She was a public intellectual and the essays we have collected here reflect that emphasis. This volume therefore avoids the tendency to restrict discussion of Carter's narrative techniques to the demythologization of fairy tale discourse, to embrace the uniqueness of her approach to narrative as a whole. We have not felt obliged either to go over ground that has already been well covered, or to cover every aspect of Carter's substantial oeuvre; rather, we see this collection as an attempt to fill in some of the critical gaps and to re-evaluate earlier critical assessments of Carter. Our collection therefore needs to be read as a contribution to the development of Carter studies.

It is just this maturity in the Carter debate that signals the need for a critical revaluation covering the many recent new directions being taken by scholars and the broadening of the evaluation of her oeuvre. Writing about future possibilities for Carter Studies in 2000, Easton identified a number of areas for development: a more thorough historicization of Carter and her work including localized contexts; studies of her treatment of class; analyses of Carter's dialogue with key thinkers such as Foucault and Benjamin; and more detailed analysis of her poetics, especially close textual work on her sources and multi-layered meanings (Easton 2000: 16). This collection goes a long way towards fulfilling Easton's 'wish list'. The volume seeks both to evaluate Carter's critical legacy and provide richly detailed readings of her work. It draws together international scholars to provide new critical readings of Carter's work from a variety of innovative theoretical and disciplinary approaches. It both evaluates Carter's legacy as feminist provocateur and postmodern stylist, and broaches new ground in considering Carter as, variously, journalist, philosophical thinker, cultural critic, dramatist and 'naturalist'. In particular, the volume identifies a shift from the politics to the poetics of Carter's work, providing close readings of her use of myth, allegory and parody. It also seeks to interrogate the view of Carter as an 'anti-nature' social constructionist hostile to the biological sciences; rather, it argues that Carter's work engages constructively with naturalism and evolutionary theory. Other topics covered include new perspectives on Carter's relation to key art movements such as surrealism and the Pre-Raphaelites; her views on the politics of food, her mapping of the 1960s city, her 'staging' of the canon and Carter's legacy for women's writing. In offering a revisionary account of Carter's work, it pays close attention to her early novels, such as *Shadow Dance*, her journalism and her less well-known short stories such as 'Black Venus', 'Master', 'Alice in Prague *or* The Curious Room' and 'Penetrating to the heart of the Forest'. It therefore seeks to redress the critical neglect of aspects of Carter's oeuvre and provide a good balance between her more obscure and more canonical works.

This book therefore provides a timely reassessment of Carter's oeuvre, evaluating the development of Carter studies within that time frame and offering innovative ways of reading her work in the twenty-first century. It functions not only as an up-to-date study exploring recent trends in Carter criticism, but also provides a much needed historical perspective on the development of Carter studies, offering readers new perspectives on her work. It is divided into three sections, which reflect our re-evaluation of Carter and her work as cross-generic and traversing multiple canons; as a philosophical thinker and writer, engaged in an ad hoc but serious project of philosophical raiding and revisionism and, thirdly, as a figure who sought to engage in various ways with myth, both as (famously) demythologizer and as (a less-acknowledged) re-mythologizer of cultural narrative.

Genre and the Canon

In the first section, our contributors re-evaluate Carter's relationship to genre and the canon in a number of key ways. First, the essays argue forcibly for viewing Carter, not as a postmodern folklorist *tout court*, but as a writer whose work traverses multiple genres including journalism, film scripts, plays for stage and radio, as well as novels and short stories. Secondly, these essays explore Carter's relationship to the canon, both in terms of how she engages with and writes back to canons of various kinds, and in terms of how she herself is positioned in respect of canons of contemporary literature. The range and breadth of her output, we would contend, argues strongly for Carter's position as a writer, intellectual and cultural commentator of major standing. In the first essay, while acknowledging her substantial influence on contemporary writers of both sexes, Sonya Andermahr examines Carter's particular legacy for women writers and assesses her unique place in the canon of contemporary women's writing. She argues that Carter's work provides a model for subsequent generations of women writers in which politics and poetics are combined in a radical writing practice. In particular, Carter's work has licensed the confident conflation of fantasy and realism, the subversion of gender and sexual norms and a linguistic playfulness and excess that may be seen in the work of women writers who have been published since the 1980s including Jeanette Winterson, Kate Atkinson, Sarah Waters and Ali Smith. Above all, Carter provides an exemplum of how the writing of literary fiction may be combined with an astute political critique in post-feminist times. In 'Carter's Excessive Stagings of the Canon', Susanne Gruss demonstrates Carter's ongoing project of demythologizing the male Western canon and its historical and theoretical contexts. Focusing on three short pieces, 'The Cabinet of Edgar Allan Poe', 'Overture and Incidental Music for *A Midsummer Night's Dream*' and 'John Ford's "*'Tis Pity She's a Whore*"', Gruss examines how Carter both stages and appropriates 'the canon'. 'The Cabinet of Edgar Allan Poe' is a recreation of Poe's childhood (and an excavation of his mother) in explicitly Oedipal terms; Carter does not merely interrogate Poe, she also deconstructs the psychoanalytic discourse that has dominated readings of Poe's work. 'Overture and Incidental Music' gives a voice to 'Golden Herm', a marginalized figure in Shakespeare's original text while simultaneously and humorously writing against the way in which Shakespeare was canonized and bowdlerized by the Victorians by making Herm and the fairies playfully transgressive in their sexuality. Finally, 'John Ford's "*'Tis Pity She's a Whore*"' grafts the plot of the Jacobean play onto a fictitious screenplay for a film by the American director John Ford and thus transfers the revenge tragedy to what is arguably its twentieth-century equivalent – the Western. As Sarah Artt demonstrates, it is through these excessive and humorous (re)stagings of canonized authors, texts and contexts that Carter explores and explodes the canon.

Gamble revisits Carter's use of the gothic in her chapter, '"Isn't it *every* girl's dream to be married in white?": Angela Carter's Bridal Gothic', focusing on the complex symbolism of the wedding dress in her fiction. Tracing its evolution across *The Magic Toyshop, Heroes and Villains, The Passion of New Eve* and *Wise Children*, Gamble argues that this archetypal bridal symbol becomes in Carter's hands a gothic trope *par excellence*. Carter brings to the surface all the latent, suppressed meanings associated with the trope of the wedding dress, exploiting the tension between a series of binary oppositions: surface/depth, purity/putrefaction, life/death. Comparing Carter's use of the trope to that of Dickens in *Great Expectations*, Gamble demonstrates how the combination of the wedding dress and the 'wrong' body sets off a series of unsettling associations that operate to disrupt the marital narrative, displacing it from its central cultural position as the 'natural' culmination of female dreams and desires. Carter's fiction therefore works to expose the apparatus of power that underlies the institution of marriage, suggesting that, for women who permit themselves to be reduced to the level of an object, a 'sexual thing', the wedding dress is really a shroud, which signifies the death of autonomous female subjectivity. In 'Between the Paws of the Tender Wolf: Art, Authorship, and Adaptation', Lorna Jowett considers Carter's writing for film, in particular her screenplay based on her short story for Neil Jordan's *The Company of Wolves*. Comparing Carter's text to the popular genre of Dark Romance that emerged in the 1990s, Jowett argues that Carter's political contradictoriness as well as her gothic motifs find an echo in the contemporary genre and that neither should be dismissed as 'dumbing down'.

Addressing yet another genre that Carter made her own, Maria José Pires discusses Carter's journalism, focusing on her food writing from the 1970s. Pires provides a detailed analysis of two of her articles from *New Society* which, she argues, establish Carter not merely as having an interest in food, but as a keen cultural commentator and ideological critic of her day. Indeed, her writing can be seen to endorse the demythologizing cultural criticism of Barthes and Bourdieu. In 'The New Vegetarians' and 'Saucerer's Apprentice', Carter argues that the new-wave vegetarianism and the 'Elizabeth Davidisation' of food represent a means to regenerate man and as an antidote to rationing and the austerity of the post-war period, respectively – being products which exult food as a generous gift from nature or celebrate the opportunity of tasting Mediterranean food. Arguing that we use food as a way of establishing relationships and social positions, Carter debunks what some believe to be the *real* real by questioning its transcendence and establishes herself as an important critic of the relationship between food, morality and 'circuits of culture'. In 'The Alchemy of Reading', Michelle Ryan-Sautour explores how Carter's texts produce what she terms an 'alchemical transformation' in the reader. She focuses on one of Carter's most obscure short fictions, 'Alice in Prague *or* The Curious Room' which, as she points out, challenges the reader's understanding to the limits and, perhaps in consequence, has received very little critical commentary. Shifting the emphasis from thematics, Ryan-Sautour concentrates on the forces of interpellation at work in reading – on what Carter's fiction *does*. She argues that Carter's story is a conglomeration of speculative strands that provoke thought but withhold clear answers. When the characteristic didactic pull of Carter's work is counterbalanced as it is here by a series of multi-layered, intertextually saturated language games, the reader's subsequent vertigo becomes a 'laboratory' in which the alchemical processes of Carter's aesthetic occur, where the ideological forces of language momentarily surface and interpellate the reader. The essay points to what we see as a key Carter strategy, namely the importance of readerly unsettlement: Carter writes texts which get the reader to work, think and finally, perhaps, experience a kind of cognitive unravelling through the series of impossible contradictions she sets up. Finally, Mine Özyurt Kılıç considers Carter's foray into adaptation and drama in her 1988 stage adaptation of Frank Wedekind's Lulu plays. Noting both the difficulty of ideological as well as aesthetic issues inherent in adaptation and crossing of genre boundaries, Carter utilizes the modern myth of the *femme fatale* to draw out the ideological repression of women that underpins Wedekind's original character. Carter's play was rejected as unstageable by Richard Eyre who commissioned it for the National Theatre. The play is an important milestone in Carter's art and it is valuable to reflect on what appears to be one of her few generic failures. Like her preference for folktale over myth, this represents more of a commentary on the rigidity of the formal constraints of the theatre and the problem of adaptation as opposed to re-imagination which characterizes Carter's work. In a sense, the 'institutionalization' of a pre-existing ideologically informed work and the institution of the theatre in the form of the National Theatre kills the creativity of the liberation Carter was able to release through the figure of the *femme fatale* drawn from yet another genre, film. As Jowett's chapter suggests, as a form film was a more congenial genre for Carter's powerful demythologization of modern life.

Philosophies

In the second section of the book, Philosophies, the authors advance the view that Carter was more than an important writer of literary fiction, and seek to establish her as a major public intellectual, whose work explicitly engages with various philosophical ideas and traditions. Although Carter was not a trained philosopher (she read Medieval Literature at Bristol University) and did not study philosophy in any systematic way, she was nevertheless an avid, if eclectic, reader of philosophy. She was an intellectual magpie, a voracious and enthusiastic reader of (and writer back to) classical and unconventional thinkers. It is typical of Carter that she would choose the iconoclastic, morally problematic de Sade for her major work of non-fiction, *The Sadeian Woman*, which still, and rightly, divides and disconcerts humanist, feminist and other critics. Lawrence Phillips in 'Sex, Violence, and Ethics – Reassessing Carter's "Moral' Relativism" argues that the prevalence of, frequently extreme, violence across her oeuvre represents far more than a simple strategy to shock the reader into reflection. Instead Carter's discursive and aesthetic use of violence enters into a much broader debate about Western ethics, morals and Enlightenment reason by means of the acute defamiliarization of content and context that is part and parcel of her insistence on a materialist stance and the productive dialogue between myth and folklore. Equally as intriguing in relation to Carter's committed materialism is Anja Mueller-Wood's investigation of Carter's engagement with evolutionary science in 'Angela Carter, Naturalist'. Famous for arguing that the social construction of her 'femininity' had been palmed off on her, Carter's work also reveals that the influences on individual identity are not entirely cultural and against which some of her characters struggle in vain. In her work this material reality is not limited to the socio-economic conditions of human existence, but extends to its physiological and psychological dimensions. The categories of imagination and reality are also the subject of Anna Watz's chapter on the surrealist uncanny in *Shadow Dance* where she argues that Carter's adoption of an overwhelmingly male narrative perspective of the novel and the iconography of the largely male surrealist movement serves two subversive aims. The text seeks provocatively to mimic in order to expose misogynist patterns buried deep in the psyche, and in that way challenge traditional and proscriptive notions of femininity as either passive and virtuous or threatening and castrating. Carter's alignment with the historical avant-garde serves as a revolt both against what she perceived to be the contemporary British 'realist' literary scene and against static cultural conventions, including prescribed versions of 'feminine' behaviour.

Kari Jegerstedt calls for a reassessment of Carter's aesthetic stance and practice in the face of prevailing political readings of her work in 'The Art of Speculation: Allegory and Parody as Critical Reading Strategies in *The Passion of New Eve*'. Carter's politics and poetics are intrinsically intertwined, but the dominant critical approach to her work has focused on what her texts say rather then what they do. This encapsulates the prevailing ethos of this volume as a whole which seeks a renewed focus on Carter's texts, aesthetics and discourse rather than an over-emphasis on the author and politics. Jegerstedt takes on this issue in her reading of *The Passion of New Eve*: noted as one of Carter's allegorical novels there has been little attention focused on the poetics of allegory which is shown by a close textual reading of the novel to reveal a parodic allegory of Freudian psychoanalysis.

Carter's aesthetic range, skill and interests were broad and well-informed as is evident from the density and allusiveness of her writing style for which she is rightly celebrated. Whether subtly or vulgarly drawn, the result is always intellectually challenging and demands attention. Katie Garner explores the influence of the art of the Pre-Raphaelites in Carter's early novels *Shadow Dance* and *Love*. The French arts, notably surrealism, but also French film and cinema, exert a strong influence in Carter's early novels as Watz argues in her chapter. Less remarked upon, however, is how the works, muses and associates of the English Pre-Raphaelite Brotherhood mingle with trends from across the channel. The violence and fragmentation suffered by the female (muse) is all the more shocking in these novels due to their almost double interrogation of both surrealist and Pre-Raphaelite visions of the female body. The philosophical and aesthetic gulf between these two movements enables Carter to create an aesthetic 'in-betweenness' in these two novels through which she offers an important identification of the female artist's struggle for creativity. Indeed, each essay in this section explores the profoundly productive tension at the heart of Carter's philosophy and aesthetic engagement between materiality and creativity of self, text and culture that ensures her place in literary history.

Mythologies

The third section interrogates Carter's reputation as a cultural de- and re-mythologizer. While we acknowledge the significance of demythologizing as an explicit part of Carter's artistic project (see Andermahr's essay in this volume), we also view Carter as both consciously and unconsciously participating in a re-mythologizing of narrative modes and mythical discourses. In her essay, 'Mythic Appropriation in Carter's Short Stories', Hope Jennings explores how Carter's short story, 'Penetrating to the Heart of the Forest', challenges the myth of the Fall through providing an alternative male perspective that refuses to reduce the other's, or 'woman's', difference. By reading Carter alongside Kristeva and Cixous, Jennings demonstrates the ways in which the story focuses on the (female) flesh as representative of a feminine economy of desire that disrupts the repressive authority of the paternal law/word, and is aimed at providing an alternative discourse of sexual difference that seeks out a reciprocal relationship between the sexes. In 'Woman as "Ambulant Fetish"', Artt starts from Munford's assertion that Carter's adoption of the male-centred aesthetic of nineteenth-century art raises uncomfortable questions, to analyse two of Carter's less well-known short stories, 'Black Venus' and 'Master' which, she argues, attempt to rewrite male canonical discourse, giving presence and history to women who are seen by the men they encounter as 'ambulant fetish[es]' (Carter 1995: 241) while at the same time, mimicking and aestheticizing the exotic woman as object.

Simon Goulding reads Carter's 1967 novel *The Magic Toyshop* as an example of spatial/narrative dislocation as a representation of 1960s 'swinging' London from the peripheries of far-reaching social transformation that works against the grain of subsequent mythologizing of both period and place. The indeterminate location in London of the house/shop in which the characters live creates an 'abstract space' through which the novel reflects another city than the canonical history of the 1960s has suggested. Noting the foregrounding of the city as a rather ephemeral, empty space in iconic 1960s films like Michelangelo Antonioni's *Blow-Up* where people are distinctly background material, Goulding argues that the intersection of pithy, everyday life focused on relationships (however dysfunctional) and the transformation of everyday places and spaces into something fantastic and magical anticipates and inspires the work of Michael Moorcock and Iain Sinclair. As the chapter concludes, a text such as *The Magic Toyshop* offers a beginning, a first step, in connecting the individual and the local to their time, space and their future. This fascination with change and transformation is a recurring motif of Carter's oeuvre which produced an optimistic art that belies the frequent grimness of subject and content. In this respect, Jane Hentgès also focuses on the 1960s and returns us to Carter's first novel, *Shadow Dance*. Noting the preoccupation of critics to record Carter's debate with Freud, Hentgès points to the significant but largely ignored influence of R. D. Laing's *The Divided Self* on her thought and art and particularly how Carter manipulates time and space informed by Freud's theory of condensation, displacement and dramatization. By using *The Divided Self* as an intertext, Hentgès argues that Carter employs psychiatric illness to introduce a 'shadow dance', a new surrealist, subversive, inverted vision of the world that has the aesthetic aim shared with the surrealists of piercing the looking glass of reality to create new images of perception.

Works Cited

Carter, A. (1995), 'Black Venus', Burning Your Boats: Collected Short Stories. Toronto: Penguin. pp. 231–44.

Day, A. (1998), *The Rational Glass*, Manchester: Manchester University Press.

Easton, A. (ed.) (2000), *Angela Carter: Contemporary Critical Essays*, Basingstoke: Macmillan.

Gamble, S. (2006), *Angela Carter: A Literary Life*, Basingstoke: Palgrave Macmillan.

Laing, R. D. (1990) [1960], The Divided Self, London: Penguin Books.

Munford, R. (ed.) (2006), *Re-Visiting Angela Carter: Texts, Contexts and Intertexts*, Basingstoke: Palgrave Macmillan.

Peach, L. (2009) [1998], *Angela Carter*, Basingstoke: Palgrave Macmillan.

Pitchford, N. (2002), *Tactical Readings: Feminist Postmodernism in the Novels of Kathy Acker and Angela Carter*, Lewisburgh: Bucknell UP.

Roemer, D. M. and Bacchilega, C. (eds) (2000), *Angela Carter and the Fairy Tale*, Wayne State UP.

Sage, L. (2006) [1994], *Angela Carter*, London: Northcote House.

Part One

Genre and the Canon

2

Contemporary Women's Writing:
Carter's Literary Legacy

Sonya Andermahr

Since her death in 1992, Angela Carter's reputation has soared. She is one of the most widely studied contemporary writers in Britain and the US and is generally acknowledged to have transformed the character of British fiction. 'It is hard to imagine the literary landscape without Angela Carter', stated Christina Patterson on the reissue of Carter's major works: 'Hers is a legacy that extends way beyond the bounds of her own work' (Patterson 2006: 3). According to Richard Rayner, 'her brash brilliance helped crack open the middle-class conventions that had dominated the British novel. She played fairy godmother to younger generations of talent. Without her, Salman Rushdie and Jeanette Winterson wouldn't be the writers they are; likewise David Mitchell and Zadie Smith' (Rayner 2008: 1). Carter's work was inimical to the realist conventions that dominated the British novel in the 1960s and, in the rush to acknowledge her importance, it should not be forgotten that Carter was an outsider, a socialist and feminist who was writing against mainstream values. As Lorna Sage said of her: 'She is a splendid example of a woman writer who made it from the margins' (Sage 1992), albeit one who never received a major literary prize in her lifetime.[1] A number of contemporary women writers have freely acknowledged Carter's importance in relation to their own work. Ali Smith, who cites her as a major influence, states: 'I can't think of anyone who is at that pitch of intellectual commentary, fictional experimentation and fullness of expression' (Patterson 2006: 3). Sarah Waters confesses to having recognized Carter's influence on her work when she was re-reading *Nights at the Circus* (Patterson 2006: 2). Similarly, Helen Simpson, whose early work was compared to 'the young Angela Carter', describes Carter's writer as 'invigorating and inspiring', saying that 'She put steel in my spine' (Patterson 2006: 2).[2]

Of course, Carter's legacy is not restricted to women's writing. She is cited by literary admirers of both sexes as an influential figure in British literature since the 1960s. On her death in 1992, Ian McEwan and Salman Rushdie wrote obituaries acknowledging her literary importance and Kazuo Ishiguro, who was briefly taught by Carter at the University of East Anglia, stated: 'As a writer she changed the landscape' (Patterson 2006: 3).[3] Carter herself, always concerned about her literary reputation and public persona, would have hated to be pigeonholed simply as a woman writer, just as

Margaret Atwood and Jeanette Winterson reject the term as too limiting. Carter saw herself and is seen by many as writing back to a tradition of Western literature and art, and this is surely right. Nevertheless, despite its general reach and appeal, Carter's work consistently interrogated the social construction of femininity and frequently focused on female voices and experience. For this reason, I would argue she has a particular resonance for feminist readers and critics and a special place in the canon of contemporary women's writing.

Yet, in many ways of course, Carter went against the grain of post-1960s women's writing which, according to Rita Felski, has predominately adopted the mode of psychological realism.[4] In contrast to the confessional, autobiographical character of much women's writing, Carter's work foregrounds narrative irony, indeterminacy and play. And, rather than attempt to give fictional voice to an authentic female self, Carter explores subjectivity as contradictory and shifting. It could be argued that Carter's work of the 1960s and 1970s anticipated women's writing of the 1980s and 1990s in this respect, undertaking the fictional play with identity characteristic of postmodern writing and the work of Jeanette Winterson and others. For example, the tropes of drag and cross-dressing that get an early treatment in Carter's work arguably did not become common features of women's writing until the late 1980s and 1990s with novels such as *Sexing the Cherry* and more recently Sarah Waters' *Tipping the Velvet*. While, then, Carter's work has sometimes been at odds with the prevailing feminist current and, at other times, in advance of it, it has always in some sense been in dialogue with feminism.

In the rest of this chapter, I want to explore the nature of Angela Carter's 'influence', broadly defined as distinctive and recurring tropes, thematic preoccupations and literary devices, on subsequent women writers. As space is limited, I will focus on three of Carter's works, which happen to be her best-known and arguably most popular books: *The Bloody Chamber and Other Stories*, *Nights at the Circus* and *Wise Children*. I shall be tracing the aesthetic and political concerns that these works share with those by contemporary women writers who have been publishing since the 1980s including Jeanette Winterson, Kate Atkinson, Sarah Waters and Ali Smith, suggesting not that they are necessarily directly influenced by Carter, but that her work gives this later generation a certain licence to operate in particular ways. They clear the ground for the confident conflation of the magical and the real, the playful debunking of myths of gender, for exhilarating flights of linguistic fantasy and, in some cases, for a renewed political assertiveness in post-feminist times. There are, in my view, four main ways in which Carter's approach to writing survives in contemporary women's writing: first, in her anti-realism, which includes the use of the fantastic mode and magic realist allegory; secondly, through her deconstruction of identity, particularly gender identities; thirdly, in her linguistic playfulness and exuberant use of intertextuality; finally, and perhaps most importantly for Carter the socialist-feminist, through her political critique of capitalism, patriarchy and imperialism.

Whether viewed primarily as a fabulist – 'painting vivid pictures of fairy tale creatures and monsters in complex fusions of fantasy, gothic, science fiction and romance' (Patterson 2006: 1) – or as a novelist of ideas, writing 'feminist tracts about the social creation of femininity' (Carter 1998: 38), Carter's work is characterized by a distinctive and subversive use of magic realist allegory. In *The Bloody Chamber*, for example, which offers a radical reworking of the European fairy tale tradition with its cast of vampires, werewolves and animal–human hybrids, Carter's characters morph from women and men into beasts and vice versa, precisely in order to debunk myths about humanity and gender. Notwithstanding, the enormous impact Carter's work has had on the fairy tale genre,[5] it is the element of demythologizing that most concerned Carter herself and has been so fruitful for subsequent women writers. In Carter's texts, characters typically depart historical time and enter a different realm, one which is 'ahistorical, mythic and symbolic' (Gamble 2006: 34). Whatever its putative 'setting', be it fin-de-siècle London or late twentieth-century New York, Carter's work displays a tendency to veer off into magical realism, and a world governed by dreams, magic and fairytales. Yet, Carter's use of the fantastic is never a repudiation of historical reality. As Gamble writes of *The Magic Toyshop*, 'these "fairy tale" elements are being played off against a very precisely delineated historical moment' (Gamble 2006: 29), in this case her own teenage years of the 1950s.

This curious and distinctive narrative style, which moves continuously between historical actuality and magic realism, and seems unique to Carter, has in fact been adopted and adapted in different ways by a number of subsequent women writers. For example, in Kate Atkinson's *Behind the Scenes of the Museum*, events from the late nineteenth-century to the present day are viewed from the narrator Ruby's perspective of magical omniscience, which bizarrely begins in the womb, and gives her narrative free rein. From this vantage point, in 1951, the year of the Festival of Britain, she describes her sister Gillian in the following proleptic terms: 'Clean and new as a pin or an unwrapped bar of soap she represents everything they fought the war for – our Gillian, the promise of the future. (Not much of a future as it turned out, as she gets run over by a pale blue Hillman Husky in 1959 but how are any of us to know this?)' (Atkinson 1996: 19). The narrative speeds up, slows down and even freezes time at will, as in the moment of Ruby's apparent death, from an overdose of pills in the airing cupboard. At another point, she instructs us to 'dive into the picture' with her (Atkinson 1996: 29), which recalls Carter's technique in *Wise Children*, where she has Dora cry 'freeze-frame' (Carter 1992: 11) as if she were directing a film rather than telling a story.

Such magical narrative floating invokes the trope of aerialism. According to Mary Russo, the 'aerial sublime' describes an imaginary zone, which 'posits a realm of freedom within the everyday. For latecomers to the scene of political identity, freedom as expressed in boundless flight is still an almost irresistible image' (Russo 11). It appears repeatedly in women's writing but, as Russo warns, ' "women's liberation" as so imaged, is imbricated with the history and ideology of bourgeois exceptionalism which marks off categories of irregular bodies to leave behind' (Russo 11). In Carter's work aerialism functions as a metaphor for the subversion of the ontological status quo or as a form of risky tightrope walking between material reality and utopian idealism. No one is more aware of the risks run by the aerial sublime than Carter whose heroines, like Fevvers, always keep one foot on the floor and their tongue firmly in cheek. Walser's account of Fevvers' trapeze act emphasizes not the speed and elegance of her flight, but its very ungainliness and sense of defying the impossible:

What made her remarkable as an *aerialiste*, however, was the speed – or, rather the lack of it – with which she performed even the climactic triple somersault. When the hack *aerialiste*, the everyday, wingless variety, performs the triple somersault, he or she travels through the air at a cool sixty miles an hour; Fevvers, however, contrived a leisurely twenty-five, so that the packed theatre could enjoy the spectacle, as in slow-motion, of every tense muscle straining in her Rubenesque form. (Carter 1994: 17)

In Carter's version of aerialism, therefore, the body is anything but ideal; she overturns the reifying implications of the image and employs it rather to interrogate the boundary between fantasy and 'reality'.

Since Carter, numerous women writers have employed the trope in order to signify otherness and altered states, to unsettle binary oppositions between material/ bodily and non-material realities and to deconstruct gender and other stereotypes. In Atkinson's *Behind the Scenes*, a key moment of aerialism occurs in the narrative of Ruby's nineteenth-century forebear Alice who, in 'a cool rush of air' (Atkinson 1996: 34), finds herself floating thirty feet above her cottage:

'Why,' thinks my floating great-grandmother, 'I have been living the wrong life!'
    With these magic words she accelerates again, away from the ground, upwards into the thin brilliant air towards where it is darkening into indigo.' (Atkinson 1996: 35)

In fact, Alice escapes her life of drudgery only to be cast into another one, and lives to rue the day. In Atkinson's fictional world, aerial lift-off is no guarantee of freedom from oppression.

Jeanette Winterson's *Sexing the Cherry* makes extensive use of the aerial sublime in the form of Fortunata, the lightest of the twelve dancing princesses, who dances out of Grimm's fairy tale and into Jordan's narrative, and whose enigmatic identity dissolves into 'empty space and points of light' (Winterson 1990: 144). Images of flight have been a consistent feature of her subsequent work from the 'flight' of Picasso in *Art & Lies*, who hurls herself off a parapet to avoid the incestuous rape by her brother but is saved by 'the resolution of wings' (Winterson 1995: 155), to the literal and metaphorical flights that make up the stories in her collection, *The World and Other Places*. In the latter, characters are in flight from the rat race and social conformity, from disappointment in love and from themselves. While Winterson's use of aerialism is more than a little tinged with romanticism, for her, as for Carter, the trope signifies the imaginative going-beyond of the 'here and now' in all its ramifications of common-sense logic, gender ideologies and bourgeois-capitalist system.

Written for the Canongate Myth series, Ali Smith's *Girl Meets Boy* is a reworking of Ovid's account of the Iphis myth in *Metamorphosis*. Smith's approach to myth recalls Carter's methodology of 'putting new wine in bottles . . . to make the old bottles explode' (Carter 1998: 37). Like Carter, Smith uses myth to explore political themes, in this case sexism, homophobia and corporate greed. The novel opens in a first person voice, which introduces a paradox around identity reminiscent of the opening of Carter's *Wise Children*: 'Let me tell you about when I was a girl, our grandfather says' (Smith

2007: 3). The narrator's grandfather is a kind of Scottish Tiresius who once worked in a circus and walked a tightrope across the Thames. The novel foregrounds the clash between realism and the fantastic in a similar way to *Nights at the Circus* with Midge, the narrator's sister, representing the rational voice of Walser questioning the veracity of Fevvers' wings. After one of Grandad's stories about cross-dressing suffragists, she tells him:

> Grandad, you're like insane. ... Because if you work it out, even if you *were* a girl, that story would make you born right at the beginning of the century, and yeah, I mean you're old and everything, but you're not that old. (Smith 2007: 16)

In *Girl Meets Boy*, magic realism functions as a means to deconstruct patriarchal myths, just as it does in the stories that make up *The Bloody Chamber*. Myth can be a regulatory and oppressive regime of discourse – 'extraordinary lies designed to make people unfree' (Carter 1998: 38) – but it can also offer possibilities for re-imagining and subverting the 'real'. At one point, Smith asks a crucial question that Carter's fiction may also be seen to explore: 'Do myths spring fully formed from the imagination and the needs of a society . . . as if they emerged from society's subconscious? Or are myths conscious creations by the various money-making forces?' (Smith 2007: 89). Both writers provide literary responses to this question which foreground simultaneously its liberatory and oppressive potential.

Carter, as Roz Kaveney observes, 'wrote one of the most decorated proses of the twentieth-century' (Kaveney 2006). Her work is noted for its high level of intertextuality and the sources she drew on are famously wide ranging: a single scene in 'The Bloody Chamber' contains numerous references to everything from the myth of Pandora to de Sade's Justine and Red Riding Hood ('All the better to see you' (Carter 1995: 17)). However, Carter always combines literary erudition with an emphasis on storytelling; all her characters are self-conscious fashioners of narrative whose aim is to entertain, seduce and, not infrequently, bamboozle. When, for example, Walser comes to interview the Cockney Venus in *Nights at the Circus*, he finds her tale literally captivating: 'Fevvers lassooed him with her narrative and dragged him along with her' (Carter 1994: 60). Later, flicking through his notes, he thinks: 'What a performance! Such style! Such vigour!' (ibid., 90). Indeed, style as performance is an apt description of Carter's own narrative technique. Her narrators are larger than life, full of gusto, frequently apostrophizing their words like Dora Chance in *Wise Children* who declares 'I've got a tale and a half to tell, all right!' (Carter 1992: 227) and is often to be found 'drunk in charge of a narrative' (ibid., 158).

Jeanette Winterson and Ali Smith are obvious inheritors in this respect, foregrounding the poetic, playful aspects of language and simultaneously articulating a critique of heteropatriarchy. Winterson, like Carter, uses grotesque and bawdy language to debunk myths of gender. Her description of Dogwoman, who can outweigh an elephant, explodes conventional ideas of femininity, just as Fevvers and the Chance twins do. Dogwoman's rhetorical question, 'How hideous am I?' (Winterson 1990: 24) forces the reader to reassess their definition of ugliness and abjection in the light of Dogwoman's bravery and devotion to her son Jordan, just as Walser reassesses his view of Fevvers from one of discomfiture to love. Winterson's writing career began in 1985 while Carter was still alive. By the time of Carter's death, Winterson was an established writer with three novels in print. The two authors near contemporaneity is reflected in their work in a number of ways, as Jeffrey Roessner suggests: 'Reveling in elements of fantasy and grotesquerie and foregounding a complex intertextual lineage, the fiction of Jeanette Winterson and Angela Carter reveals a host of common stylistic traits and thematic preoccupations' (Roessner 2002: 1). For example, the grotesque scene in *Sexing* in which Dogwoman unwittingly bites off a male lover's member deflates the phallic imperative as effectively as the raucous guffaws of Carter's heroine in 'The Tigers' Bride'. Winterson's work evinces a similar commitment to the blending of storytelling, sexual politics and narrative playfulness as Carter's work.

For Ali Smith, Carter's work is characterized by outlandishness, rich language and artifice. Smith has repeatedly acknowledged Carter's influence on her work and her novels evince a similar linguistic inventiveness. Her debut *Hotel World* is characterized by a joyful and energetic approach to language even as it critiques the alienation of modern life. Its exhilarating opening cry of 'Wooooooo-hoooooo what a fall what a soar what a plummet' (Smith 2001: 3) belies the fact that a young woman has just plunged to her death. While the novel explores the alienation of life in post-Thatcher Britain, its language encapsulates utopian possibilities. In *Girl Meets Boy*, Smith makes use of intertextual references, puns and plays on meaning, revelling in the power of the storyteller to invent new worlds. At one point, Smith's narrator wittily puns on the Lacanian idea that 'woman does not exist': 'A lass and a lack, I say' (Smith 2007: 76). Smith represents the way in which lesbian existence is rendered invisible through the use of linguistic gaps: 'I also remember, we all always called . . . that word behind her back at school' (Smith 2007: 55). In order to signify sexual difference, Smith incorporates a language of sexual metamorphosis and ambiguity: 'She had the swagger of a girl. She blushed like a boy. She had a girl's toughness. She had a boy's gentleness' (Smith 2007: 84); and her prose performs a series of grammatical gender inversions and substitutions: 'I was a she was a he was a we' (Smith 2007: 103). Smith's reworking of Ovid involves myriad transformations of people, animals and plants, which recalls Carter's description of becoming animal in 'The Tiger's Bride' in which the narrator shrugs off 'skin after successive skin' of human femaleness to join her tiger lover (Carter 1995: 67):

> . . . then I was a tree whose branches were all budded knots, and what were those felty buds, were they – antlers? Were antlers really growing out of both of us? Was my whole front furring over? And were we the same pelt? Were our hands black shining hooves? (Smith 2007: 102–3)

As in Carter's work, this merging and blurring of animals, people and forms act 'as a knife that could cut through myth' (Smith 2007: 103), in order to create a utopian fantasy of transformation and disguise.

In *Angela Carter: A Literary Life*, Gamble argues that Carter's literary technique is characterized by disguise and self-crafting and testifies to the problematic process of life writing. Indeed her work evinces a fascination with masks, masquerade, spectacle and dressing-up, and the final impossibility of defining a self. As Ali Smith points out,

'Carter's work is full of divided selves, women regarding their mirror-images with suspicion' (Smith 2006: 2). The recognition of this process of self-crafting as disguise reaches its apotheosis at the end of *Nights at the Circus* when Fevvers, with her peroxide roots gone brown and her broken wing, is unable to maintain the feminine masquerade, and contemplates her reflection in dismay: 'she felt as though her heart was breaking when she looked in the mirror and saw her brilliant colours withering away' (Carter 1994: 273). In Carter's final work, *Wise Children*, the Chance twins are reconciled to the diminishment of their looks that age inevitably brings. Describing the process of getting made up for their father's one hundredth birthday party, Dora admits: 'It took an age but we did it; we painted the faces that we always used to have on to the faces we have now' (Carter 1992: 192). Paraphrasing Oscar Wilde, Nora opines: 'It's every woman's tragedy . . . that, after a certain age, she looks like a female impersonator' (Carter 1992: 192). While both novels foreground the feminine masquerade as constitutive of female identity, they also destabilize it through the deployment of the grotesque and carnivalesque modes. These ideas resonate strongly with the post-Carter generation of women writers, many of whom are preoccupied in their fiction with issues of disguise and self-crafting. Atkinson's unreliable narrator, attempting to narrate her life story; Winterson's motherless protagonists striving to assert an 'I' through literary artifice; Ali Smith's multiple and gender-blurring narrators, and Waters' cross-dressing picaresque heroines are all engaged in a similar project of simultaneously asserting and deconstructing their identities. Doubleness, it seems, becomes a defining feature not just of Carter's work but of women's writing in general. If in Carter's life and work, nothing is ever unified, the same can be said about the generation of women writers who followed her.

While it is clear that Sarah Waters does not use the fantastic mode in the way that Winterson and Atkinson do, her work draws generically on that of Carter. Like Carter, Waters makes extensive use of the gothic mode, a genre predicated on the notion of duality; *Affinity*, *Fingersmith* and *The Little Stranger* rewrite the gothic novel in queer and innovative ways. Her first novel, however, borrows not so much from the gothic – although there are gothic interludes – as from the picaresque genre and, in this respect, *Tipping the Velvet* resembles Carter's picaresque fictions, particularly *Nights at the Circus*. Both novels are Victorian pastiches whose first person narratives recount a series of extraordinary adventures in the sentimental education of their respective heroines. This structure allows Waters to explore similar themes of identity, feminism and socialism interwoven with a variety of historical and literary intertexts. Just like Fevvers, Nan Astley is a performer; in her case, a music hall act specializing in male impersonation. *Tipping* also shares the comic momentum, the storytelling brio, and the political desire to deconstruct patriarchal historiography of Carter's novel. The first person voice immediately situates the narrator as a working class girl: 'I was raised an oyster-girl, and steeped in all the flavours of the trade' (Waters 1998: 4). Nan becomes her music hall heroine's dresser and then a male impersonator or 'masher' herself. Her career on the stage allows her to escape her destiny as an oyster-wife, but also represents a disguise which conceals her lesbian desire. *Tipping the Velvet* both historicizes queer performance, providing a social history of cross-dressing in music hall acts, and also presents identity as essentially performative. The pleasure of performance is vividly described by Nan: 'it was my new *capacity* for pleasure – for pleasure in performance, display and disguise, in the wearing of handsome suits, the singing of ribald songs – that shocked and thrilled me most' (Waters 1988: 126; italics original). This approach mirrors Carter's credo that life itself is a performance and there is ultimately no distinction between authentic and inauthentic selves. In this respect Carter's representation anticipates the work of Judith Butler, whose influential work *Gender Trouble* was published towards the end of Carter's life. Butler's notion of gender performativity resonates with Carter's many masquerading, shape-shifting selves and with the cross-dressing protagonists of Carter's successors like Waters, Smith and Winterson.

Mother-daughter relations are a key aspect of the exploration of female identity in women's writing. In Carter's work the role of the mother is an extremely ambiguous if not absent one: Fevvers is apparently an East End foundling discovered by Lizzie and the Chance twins are brought up by Grandma after their mother dies in childbirth. However, in some works the mother figure is rehabilitated: she has, for example, a starring role in 'The Bloody Chamber', 'telepathically' intuiting her daughter's danger and riding to the rescue. Some critics also see *Wise Children* as Carter's attempt to draw a more positive role for the maternal, in which she conflates the figures of mother and grandmother. According to Gamble, 'Grandma is another indication that Carter is forging a link with a maternal, rather than paternal, past by filling in the gap usually left by the absent mother in her work' (Gamble 2006: 187). In *Wise Children* Carter interweaves her own family history, especially that of her mother and grandmother, with the public history of Shakespeare and Empire, enabling her to reclaim a maternal history. Atkinson uses a similar technique in *Behind the Scenes*, charting the lives of the 'women lost in time' (Atkinson 1996: 38) by recording their marginal and 'magical' lives. Both writers ponder the question of the maternal bond, Carter stating that 'a mother is a biological fact, while a father is a moveable feast' (Carter 1992: 216), only to undermine the binary. Atkinson debunks the myth of maternal bonding by producing an array of unsuitable and frequently grotesque mothers. This maternal ambivalence continues in the post-Carter generation: Winterson in *Oranges* and *The PowerBook* conjures some distinctly unmaternal, monstrous, implicitly 'Thatcherite' mother figures thereby melding autobiographical and political discourses.

Like Carter in *Wise Children*, Atkinson in *Behind the Scenes* rewrites the Freudian family romance. Whereas Carter shows every family relationship to be an assumed or constructed one, so that there is ultimately no certainty about maternal and paternal identity, Atkinson explores just how unnatural biological families can sometimes seem. As Ruby states early on in her relationship with her mother: 'I do not believe Bunty is my real mother' (Atkinson 1996: 42). She hopes that the situation will soon be rectified and that her real mother 'the one who dropped the ruby-red blood onto a snow-white handkerchief' (ibid., 43) will return to claim her. In the Snow White fairy tale, the good mother never does return of course, a point that women writers from Carter onwards have been at pains to acknowledge. Carter gave the tale a grotesque treatment in 'The snow child', distilling it into one traumatic scene in which the daughter is sacrificed to the father-king's lust and the mother-queen's jealousy.

If anything may be said to direct Carter's use of the fantastic, her linguistic experiment and questioning of selfhood, it is her critique of social reality and her commitment to political change. As she riposted to one interviewer who asked about her interest in fairy tales: 'I'm a socialist, damn it!' And, in 'Notes from the Frontline' she insisted, 'I'm in the demythologising business' (Carter 1998: 38). Echoing Matthew Arnold, Carter famously described the aim of *Nights at the Circus* as being 'to entertain and to instruct' (Haffenden: 36). Gamble describes it as at once a 'burlesque fantasia' and a 'deadly serious satire' (Gamble 2006: 174) on *inter alia* the abuses of power, nationalism and empire-building using the circus as metaphor. At its heart is the figure of Buffo the clown, 'a great patriot, British to the bone' (Carter 1994: 118), whose 'violent slapstick' (ibid., 117) represents the declining British Empire: jingoistic, farcical and grotesque. As Gamble observes, 'Carter's flights of fantasy are always wedded to an astute awareness of place, time, and social context' (Gamble 2006: 200).

To a greater or lesser extent, contemporary women writers follow Carter in allying storytelling with social critique. For example, Atkinson's *Behind the Scenes* couples domestic melodrama with a careful delineation of the First and Second World Wars, and events such as the Festival of Britain. Similarly, Winterson's *Sexing the Cherry* is set in the English civil war and represents an oblique attack on Western capitalism in its late, Thatcherite guise. Like Carter, Winterson historicizes the patriarchal and national forces that shape their characters, thereby exposing 'the contingency of supposedly universal values, including the naturalness of heterosexuality and the father's authority in a patrilineal culture' (Roessner 2002: 1). And, just as Carter's novels from 1979 onwards 'can be viewed as positioning themselves in ironic relationship to the Thatcherite return of "Victorian values" ' (Gamble 2006: 166), Winterson's historiographic metafictions of the late 1980s may be viewed as an attack on Thatcherism from the space of fantasy. Her carnivalesque treatment of Civil War Puritans and Royalists may be seen, like *Nights at the Circus*, as a satire on 'patriotism as theatre' (ibid., 163) in which the political target is turned into spectacle.

Ali Smith is the most politically engaged of Carter's successors. *Girl Meets Boy* links the Ovidian myth of Iphis (in which a mother disguises her daughter as a boy to avoid its death at the hands of her father), to the contemporary phenomenon of female infanticide. In Chapter 4 we are told that 60 million girls annually are aborted or killed at birth (Smith 2007: 133). Smith's modern day Iphis becomes a graffiti artist reminiscent of 1990s feminist art collective 'The Guerilla Girls' who inserted feminist slogans into advertising copy or visual art. Smith incorporates an explicitly radical feminist critique of gendered power relations, which goes further than that of Carter, whose own critique remained alive to women's collusion in their own oppression. The novel ends like a classical comedy or romance with a wedding: 'The music and dancing went on late into the night. In fact, there was still dancing going on when the night was over, the light coming back and the new day dawning' (Smith 2007: 159). However, this distinctly romantic and utopian ending is subsequently undercut by the narrator's ironical admission that 'Uh-huh. Okay. I know. In my dreams' (ibid.).

According to Gamble, there is a 'dichotomy between personal fulfilment and public disillusionment' (Gamble 2006: 177) in Carter's late works. While delivering trenchant critiques of social and political values, Carter delivers a 'happy ending' in both *Nights*

(Fevvers gets Walser) and *Wise Children* (the twins get their babies) in tune with the comedic structure of the texts. Usually seen as an insistently anti-romantic writer, in *Nights* Carter allows herself to privilege love only following a period of reconstruction for the two protagonists. Having experienced her own existential crisis ('Am I fact? Or am I fiction? Am I what I know I am? Or am I what he thinks I am?' (Carter 1994: 290), Fevvers finds Walser irrevocably changed by his encounter: 'And then she saw he was not the man he had been or would ever be again; some other hen had hatched him out' (ibid., 291).

Like Carter, contemporary women writers often evince a contradiction between personal and public realms, and between utopianism and ideological scepticism, which is particularly evident in the resolutions to their novels. Sarah Waters and Ali Smith both attempt to wrest love for another individual from their fictional indictments of patriarchal and class oppression. Waters and Smith work hard to reward their queer marginal subjects with a measure of personal happiness in the midst of the world's homophobic hostility and rejection. In *Tipping the Velvet*, Nan has to learn about social responsibility as well pursuing her own romantic desires. Like Carter, Waters insists that her heroine learns the value of sisterhood and community, and her personal happiness is made conditional on these wider social perspectives. The end of the novel brings together performance and politics as Nan gives a rousing speech on the need for socialism and collective action. She becomes a self-in-relation, and learns that she is not alone in her difference but part of a collective of radical men and women: 'I belong here, now: these are my people. And, as for Florence, my sweetheart, I love her more than I can say; and I never realised it, until this moment' (Waters 1998: 467). Waters' utopian vision recalls Carter's ironic invocation of the dawn of a new century in *Nights*, although significantly Carter chooses to conclude her novel, not with a millenarian or romantic gesture, but with a giant peel of laughter at the human comedy. There is the sense in *Tipping* that Nan is moving through a series of inauthentic selves until she attains a truer self at the novel's end. Despite the novel's playful gender-bending and collectivist finale, Waters appears to be working with a more stable, humanist model of identity than Carter's work allows.

Winterson and Atkinson offer distinctly ambivalent endings, which frequently eschew comedy and relationship for autonomy and a certain amount of isolation. *Behind the Scenes* evinces an ambivalence about the redemptive power of love; it is absent in the family relationships of generations of Lennoxes, and at the novel's end the narrator is a divorced poet who lives alone on a Scottish island. Winterson celebrates romantic love yet her novels' endings are quite frequently occluded and leave the heroine ambivalently positioned in respect of others. In *The PowerBook*, for example, the love affair between the writer protagonist and the lover who reads her emailed stories may or may not survive; the reader (both addressee and us) is given the choice between two endings. These, however, are followed by another 'resolution' in which the narrator resolves to 'Go home and write the story again. Keep writing it because one day she will read it' (Winterson 2000: 243), thereby deferring romance and displacing events into the realm of metafiction.

Anti-realist, fantastic, political, subversive, allusive, allegorical and anti-romantic: these are the watchwords for readers of Carter's oeuvre and the writers it has inspired.

In her obituary, Lorna Sage identified the cultural relevance of Carter's writing to her generation of writers:

> She interpreted the times for us with unrivalled penetration: her branching and many-layered narratives mirrored our shifting world of identities lost and found, insiders versus outsiders, alternative histories and utopias postponed. (Sage 1992, n.p.)

As this suggests, the model of women's writing that Carter's work represents incorporates astute social and political commentary, an understanding of identity as provisional, contradictory and shifting and a commitment to articulating, through complex intertextual and metafictional narratives, the subjugated histories of women, the working class and other marginal subjects. In her *Literary Life*, Sarah Gamble identifies a structuring paradox in Carter's work between 'the excessive, ornate and fabulous and the pragmatic issues of the real world, such as class and political allegiance' (Gamble 2006: 15). While this tension between aesthetic and the material realms exists in different ways in every work of literature, its significance in Carter's work lies in the extent to which she pushed the artificiality of language on the one hand and her commitment to political critique on the other. Her work exhibits a fearless blending of fictional artifice and material reality, which is a key feature of her legacy for subsequent writers. It seems to me that the women writers who followed her have been licensed to pursue either or both routes, choosing to foreground aesthetic or political issues or to attempt to combine both with Carteresque panache.

Notes

1 *The Magic Toyshop* (1967) won the Somerset Maugham Award but none of Carter's books were ever even shortlisted for the Booker Prize.
2 Waters, Simpson and Smith have all written introductions for Vintage editions of Carter's novels, respectively: *Nights at the Circus*; *The Bloody Chamber* and *Wise Children*.
3 At a celebration of her work at the London South Bank Centre in 2006, writers who gathered to discuss her influence included her friend Tariq Ali, a political writer, as well as novelists Ali Smith and Sarah Waters.
4 This claim may be more valid in relation to US and European literature; as Patricia Waugh argues, British women's writing has been characterized by irony and ontological uncertainty in the whole post-war period (Waugh 2005).
5 The journal *Marvels and Tales* recently published a special issue based on papers presented at a conference on 'The Fairy Tale After Angela Carter' held to coincide with the thirtieth anniversary of the publication of *The Bloody Chamber*. As the editors state: *The Bloody Chamber* has had 'a profound and pervasive impact on our understanding of and engagement with the fairy tale' and '[c]onsideration of the work of contemporary writers who have, like Carter, used fairy tale as a springboard for imaginative invention has been one of the most buoyant areas of academic research in the field over the last thirty years' (Benson and Teverson 2011: 13–14).

Works Cited

Atkinson, K. (1996), *Behind the Scenes at the Museum,* London: Black Swan.

Benson, S. and Teverson, A. (2011), 'Preface to the Special Issue on the Fairy Tale After Angela Carter', *Marvels and Tales* 24.1: 13–15.

Butler, J. (1990), *Gender Trouble,* London and New York: Routledge.

Carter, A. (1981) [1967], *The Magic Toyshop,* London: Virago.

—(1992) [1991], *Wise Children,* London: Vintage.

—(1994) [1984], *Nights at the Circus,* London: Vintage.

—(1995) [1979], *The Bloody Chamber And Other Stories,* London: Vintage.

—(1998) [1983], 'Notes from the Front Line', in Jenny Uglow (ed.), *Shaking a Leg: Collected Writings,* New York and London: Penguin, 36–43.

Felski, R. (1989), *Beyond Feminist Aesthetics: Feminist Literature and Social Change,* London: Hutchinson Radius.

Gamble, S. (2006), *Angela Carter: A Literary Life,* Basingstoke, Hampshire: Palgrave Macmillan.

Haffenden, J. (1984), 'Magical Mannerist', The Literary Review (November), pp. 34–8.

Kaveney, R. (2006), 'Angela Carter Remembered', *Time Out,* 30 May. http://www.timeout. com/london/books/features/1472/Angela_Carter_remembered.html. Accessed on 12 October, 2011.

Patterson, C. (2006), 'Angela Carter: Beauty and the beasts', *The Independent,* 18 January. http://www.independent.co.uk. Accessed on 12 October, 2011.

Rayner, R. (2008), 'Giving Angela Carter her due.' *LA Times,* 3 February, http:// www.latimes.com/features/la-bkw-rayner3feb03,0,1996005.story. Accessed on 12 October, 2011.

Roessner, J. (2002), 'Writing a history of difference: Jeanette Winterson's *Sexing the Cherry* and Angela Carter's *Wise Children', College Literature,* 29(1), Winter: 102–22.

Russo, M. (1997), The Female Grotesque: Risk, Excess and Modernity. London & New York: Routledge.

Sage, L. (1992), *The Guardian,* 17 February, www.guardian.co.uk. Accessed on 12 October, 2011.

Smith, A. (2001), *Hotel World,* London: Hamish Hamilton.

—(2006), 'Book choice: *Wise Children.' The Telegraph,* 9 April, www.telegraph.co.uk. Accessed on 12 October, 2011.

—(2007), *Girl Meets Boy,* London: Canongate.

Waters, S. (1998), *Tipping the Velvet,* London: Virago, 1998.

—(1999), *Affinity,* London: Virago.

—(2002), *Fingersmith,* London: Virago.

—(2009), *The Little Stranger,* London: Virago.

Waugh, P. (2005), 'The woman writer and the continuities of feminism', in James English (ed.), *A Concise Companion to Contemporary British Fiction,* Malden: Blackwell: 188–208.

Winterson, J. (1985), *Oranges Are Not the Only Fruit,* London: Vintage.

—(1990), *Sexing the Cherry,* London: Vintage.

—(1995), *Art & Lies,* London: Vintage.

—(1999), *The World and Other Places,* London: Vintage.

—(2000), *The PowerBook,* London: Jonathan Cape.

3

'Isn't it *Every* Girl's Dream to be Married in White?': Angela Carter's Bridal Gothic

Sarah Gamble

In her essay 'Consuming Pleasure on the Wedding Day: The Lived Experience of Being a Bride' Sharon Boden observes that the wedding dress has a pivotal role to play in the marriage process: 'regarded as the most "sacred" artifact in the bridal ensemble', the moment when it is put on is 'the start of the wedding day proper . . . the defining moment in the transformation of the bride' (Boden 2007: 114). That the wedding dress possesses 'its own magical, transformatory powers' (ibid., 115) in marital mythology is one upheld in Carter's fiction; but it does not present this as a positive metamorphosis for the female subject. Carter herself made her opinion of the traditional white wedding dress quite clear in an essay published in 1967, 'Notes for a Theory of Sixties Style', in which she theorizes fashion as a complex sign system. She argues that while we may 'think our dress expresses ourselves . . . in fact it expresses our environment . . . almost at a subliminal, emotionally charged, instinctual, non-intellectual level' (Carter 1997a: 105). Thus, the romantic glamour surrounding the 'tulle and taffeta bride in her crackling virginal carapace, clasping numinous lilies' only disguises her real function, which is as 'the supreme icon of woman as a sexual thing and nothing else whatever' (ibid., 108). It was a view she enlarged upon in an interview she gave in 1977, where she opined that:

> [A] wedding dress is like a gift-wrapped girl. It's as though the wearer is only existing in transition. It's the greatest day of her life, and she's gift-wrapped for it, and she's passing from her father to her husband, and only at the moment of passage is she allowed any being at all, in this completely artificial manner. (Bedford 1977: no page no.)

Carter went on to trace back the prevalence of wedding dresses in her fiction to a fascination with the figure of the jilted bride Miss Havisham in Charles Dickens' *Great Expectations*, whom she summarizes as an 'awful image of the condition of women' (Bedford 1977 no page no.). Deserted by her prospective husband at the altar, Miss Havisham refuses to adopt any alternative identity other than that of a bride, freezing both time and herself at the moment of her abortive marriage. Angela Carter's reference to such a figure is meaningful within any discussion of her portrayal of the wedding dress in her fiction, since it gives us the key to understanding the way in which it works as a specifically Gothic trope.

In *Great Expectations*, Pip's first view of Miss Havisham is of a conventional bride, 'dressed in rich materials – satins, and lace, and silks – all of white' (Dickens 2010: 49). But as he draws closer, he sees this is a dress put on a very long time ago, and on a very different body:

> [E]verything within my view which ought to be white had been white long ago, and had lost its luster, and was faded and yellow. I saw that the bride within the bridal dress had withered like the dress, and like the flowers, and had no brightness left but the brightness of her sunken eyes. I saw that the dress had been put upon the rounded figure of a young woman, and that the figure upon which it now hung loose, had shrunk to skin and bone. (ibid., 50)

Pip is unable to draw an analogy between this spectacle and anything living; instead it brings to mind two disturbing memories: a 'ghastly waxwork at the Fair', and 'a skeleton in the ashes of a rich dress, that had been dug out of a vault under the church pavement' (ibid.). While she may have stopped all the clocks in the house, Miss Havisham cannot stop time itself – dress and body decay together, transforming the iconic image of the beautiful bride into an object of Gothic horror. Sara Thornton has described the paradoxical sight that Miss Havisham thus represents – decaying body contained within a dress that symbolizes virginal purity – as 'a fleshly oxymoron' (Thornton 2010: 84), but this does not correspond with Carter's reading. Rather than seeing the emergence of an incongruity between body and dress, in her reworking of the Miss Havisham trope Carter's focus on the decayed or aged dress (the wedding dresses in her fiction are never new) suggests that its inability to resist decomposition is a necessary precondition of its existence. While the positive, life-affirming symbolism of the wedding dress seems self-evident, for Carter it acts as the carrier for an alternative set of suppressed and antonymic meanings suggestive of death and contamination. In her work she excavates these taboo connotations and brings them to the surface level of the narrative.

The resulting tension between surface/depth, life/death and purity/putrefaction can be aligned with Eve Kosofsky Sedgewick's argument in *The Coherence of Gothic Conventions* that the Gothic operates through a system of metonymical correspondence, whereby meaning spreads through proximal relations between images and bodies. One of Sedgwick's particular areas of interest is the recurring trope of the veil, which she identifies as possessing the 'function of spreading . . . extending by contiguity a particular chain of attributes among the novel's characters' (Sedgwick 1980: 149). The veil does not disguise the body over which it is draped, but becomes the surface upon which the body is written. As Sedgwick argues, 'When the flesh assumes the veil's "dazzling whiteness", the veil in turn can, like flesh, become suffused with blood' (ibid., 146).

It can be argued that, with regard to both Carter and Dickens, the veil assumes a metonymical function, standing in for the dress as well, and the stress on disguise and concealment that this association produces is what allows the wedding dress, too, to acquire its Gothic effects. *Great Expectations* exemplifies this tendency, for Miss

Havisham's wedding dress changes its meaning by means of movement through a number of synonymous associations with the word 'veil', both as noun and verb. The 9th edition of *The Concise Oxford Dictionary* defines the verb 'to veil' thus: 'a disguise; a pretext; a thing that conceals', and the noun as 'a piece of usu. more or less transparent fabric attached to a woman's hat etc., esp. to conceal the face'. On the *right* bride, the veil (as a noun) conforms with its function as verb, as a result becoming a complex and titillating sign; modestly baffling the – implicitly male – gaze while at the same time carrying an erotic charge (for the outcome of any veiling is, after all, an eventual *un*veiling). In the words of Eve Kosofsky Sedgwick, 'the veil that conceals and inhibits sexuality comes by the same gesture to represent it' (Sedgwick 1980: 256).

Yet Miss Havisham's bridal apparel acquires very different associations, as a direct result of its placement on the 'wrong' body. Pip's observation that the 'withered bridal dress on the collapsed form' looks 'like grave-clothes', and 'the long veil like a shroud' (Dickens 2010: 52) demonstrates a linguistic shift that merges the verb 'to veil' into the very similar verb 'to shroud'. As a verb, 'shroud' carries an almost identical dictionary definition to 'veil': 'to cover, conceal or disguise'. But as a noun, a shroud performs a completely different function, as a winding-sheet or garment clothing a dead body. On an unsuitable or unapproved bride, both veil and wedding dress become just that: a shroud clothing something repellent; what Julia Kristeva identifies in *Powers of Horror* as 'the utmost of abjection. . . . death infecting life' (Kristeva 1982: 4).

In her presentation of the bride in her fiction, Angela Carter employs very much the same devices used by Dickens, and achieves similar effects. Taking her cue from *Great Expectations*, Carter persistently associates bridal apparel with the shroud, and the body of the bride with that of a corpse, in narratives that play in various elaborate ways with the conventions of female Gothic. While the trope of the wedding dress appears in her work repeatedly, it never quite coincides with the 'right' body, and its placement on the 'wrong' one sets into circulation all kinds of unsettling associations that work to disrupt the marital narrative and displace it from its central position in culture as the 'natural' culmination of female dreams and desires. For Carter, marriage is a myth sold to women through the apparatus of romance, and the wedding dress the glamorous package in which they willingly 'gift-wrap' themselves in order to become a desirable object of exchange between men. As a writer who viewed herself as being 'in the demythologising business' (Carter 1997b: 38), Carter uses her fiction to expose the apparatus of power that underlies the institution of marriage, demonstrating that, for women who allow themselves to be reduced to the level of an object, a 'sexual thing', the wedding dress really is a shroud, since its assumption signals the death of an autonomous female subjectivity.

The first notable appearance of a wedding dress in Carter's writing is in her 1967 novel *The Magic Toyshop*. Its main protagonist, Melanie, is a fifteen year old girl who, in the midst of puberty, is just beginning to see herself as a potentially desirable sexual object, future bride to 'a phantom bridegroom' (Carter 1981a: 2). She and her siblings are left at home for the summer while her father, who is a successful writer, goes on a lecture tour to the United States and takes her mother with him. In their absence, Melanie explores their bedroom and pores over her parents' wedding photograph, fascinated by the elaborate nature of the display: 'On her mother's wedding day, she had an epiphany of clothing. So extravagantly, wholeheartedly had she dressed herself that her flying hems quite obscured Melanie's father. . . . her mother exploded in a pyrotechnic display of satin and lace' (ibid., 10–11).

Full of burgeoning sexual curiosity as she is, Melanie is not wholly seduced by superficial appearances. In fact, caught up as she is in a pubescent preoccupation with sexuality, she is only too well aware of the nature of the contract that is being celebrated. She reflects, while engaged in a close examination of the wedding dress, that 'It seemed a strange way to dress up just in order to lose your virginity' (ibid., 13). Melanie comes very close here to identifying a paradox central to any reading of the wedding dress as Gothic. Insofar as the white dress signifies the sexual purity of the bride, it acquires meaning only in the context of its imminent defilement, thus becoming emblematic of endings rather than beginnings:

> Symbolic and virtuous white. White satin shows every mark, white tulle crumples at the touch of a finger, white roses shower petals at a breath. Virtue is fragile. It was a marvelous wedding dress. Did she, Melanie wondered for a moment, wear it on the wedding night? (ibid., 13)

Viewed from this perspective, the wedding dress carries strong intimations of mortality, which are foregrounded by the wedding photograph, which, in its very attempt to freeze-frame 'this fragment of her mother's happy time' (ibid.), can only capture it in the act of its passing away. The photograph may hint at immortality, but it is actually a coffin containing a corpse preserved for permanent display, an analogy Carter drives home with brutal, forensic directness: 'Her smiling and youthful mother was as if stabbed through the middle by the camera and caught forever, under glass, like a butterfly in an exhibition case' (ibid., 12–13).

The association between death and display – seductive veiling and sinister shrouding – is preserved in the transition from the photographic image to the real thing. Melanie feels 'wicked, like a grave-robber' (ibid., 15) for disinterring her mother's bridal outfit from the trunk in which it has been carefully preserved. When she lifts the creaking lid, it is as if she has disturbed a phantom when a 'great deal of loose tissue paper packed in the top rose up . . . and hovered a few inches in the air, momentarily levitated, an emanation' (ibid.). And the mass of fabric contained in this coffin-like space possesses sinister characteristics too – the extravagant veil appears bent on stifling Melanie, 'blinding her eyes and filling her nostrils', and when she puts on the dress 'It slithered over her, cold as a slow hosing with ice-water' (ibid.).

It is at this point that the 'wrong body' narrative comes to the fore. Although Melanie feels momentarily transfigured by her donning of the dress, it soon becomes very apparent that she is 'too young for it' (ibid., 18). When – in an episode which makes no attempt to hide its heavy symbolism – she leaves her father's house and goes out into the garden in her stolen bridal regalia, she panics and, finding she has accidentally locked the front door behind her, is forced to climb an apple tree in order to reach her bedroom window. In the process, the dress is ruined; torn to ribbons, 'filthy, streaked with green from the tree and her own red blood' (ibid., 22).

Melanie has already noted (and subsequently definitively proved) that white dresses are particularly vulnerable to becoming stained, but because, as Carter has argued in 'Notes for a Theory of Sixties Style', clothes are *always and already* texts that bear the inscriptions of culture, they are also pages intended to convey a particular kind of meaning. To read the whiteness of the wedding dress as a blank page awaiting inscription is a *mis*reading, for it has already been written on – even if it is with invisible ink. When Melanie puts on the wedding dress at the wrong time and in the wrong place, her act of transgression results in the meanings embedded in the wedding dress rising to the surface of the fabric – that these 'acres of tulle' and 'sliding satin' (ibid., 15) are representative of an institution set up to regulate female sexual activity and reproduction – signified by the shedding of hymenal, and menstrual blood, as well as the blood shed in childbirth – and to discipline the female tendency towards transgression, exemplified in the belief in Eve as the agent of original sin. The value culture places on female purity is gained from the enduring belief in woman as an abject agent of pollution, the possessor of an abjected, leaky and innately sinful body, which is disguised by the superficial glamour of the white wedding dress.

In its despoiled state, the wedding dress also merges, as in *Great Expectations*, with its Gothic mirror image of the shroud. Torn and stained with dirt and blood, it could be the dress of a murder victim, or a revenant. When Melanie looks at her mother's wedding photograph, she wonders whether her mother will take her wedding dress to the grave, asking herself: 'Would she be laid out in it or wear it up to heaven?' (ibid., 13–14). This is a more ironic question than she could know, since the image she is contemplating at this moment is indeed that of a dead woman. The day after Melanie's abortive visit to the midnight garden, she receives the news that both of her parents have been killed in a plane accident; a tragedy that she immediately attributes to her appropriation of the dress: ' "It is my fault," she told the cat. . . . "It is my fault because I wore her dress. If I hadn't spoiled her dress, everything would be all right" ' (ibid., 24).

The fate suffered by Melanie's mother constitutes a cautionary tale warning of the dangers of regarding marriage as the purpose of one's life. Because she never appears in the novel directly (we do not even know her name), Melanie's mother's only real identity *is* that of a bride; she is defined to the point of over-determination by this 'piece of her . . . best and most beautiful time' (ibid., 12). She cannot survive the destruction of the wedding dress because her very being is contained within it: with it gone, she is, quite literally, nothing.

Carter revisited the wedding dress trope in *Heroes and Villains*, published in 1969. She claimed this book as her first properly Gothic novel, saying in 1977 that she had become 'very irritated at the Gothic tag' that reviewers habitually attached to her work and, as a retort, decided to show them what a Gothic novel really was: 'owls and ivy and ruins and a breathtakingly Byronic hero' (Bedford 1977). Yet the similarity of the wedding dress imagery in *Heroes and Villains* to that contained within *The Magic Toyshop* indicates that this novel is not so much of a departure from her past work as Carter might have us believe.

Heroes and Villains is a post-apocalyptic novel, set in a future where the survivors of a nuclear war are struggling to live among the ruins of former civilization. Some live in villages that strive to preserve a sense of social order; they are centred upon the Professors, who dedicate their lives to recovering the knowledge lost in the holocaust. These villages are constantly under threat from raids conducted by the nomadic tribes they call Barbarians, who live a hand-to-mouth existence on what they can scavenge or steal. The heroine of the novel is a girl called Marianne, a Professor's daughter who is kidnapped by a Barbarian boy called Jewel, and taken back to his tribe. He rapes her and then marries her in a bizarre ceremony conducted by the tribal shaman Donally, a former Professor. Inspired by his reading of Thomas Hobbes's *Leviathan*, Donally is in the process of setting up a new system of 'ritual and tradition' (Carter 1981b: 63) in order to consolidate his control over the tribe. This is a marriage, therefore, that serves a very specific political and social function, which the bridal paraphernalia does nothing to disguise. Whereas Melanie's own actions cause the destruction of the dress in *The Magic Toyshop*, this is a dress that is already on the verge of disintegration:

> The dress had a satin bodice, now fissured with innumerable fine cracks; long, tight, white sleeves that came to a point over the backs of the hands and an endless skirt of time-yellowed tulle. There was a vast acreage of net veil and a small garland of artificial pearls. . . . Marianne screwed up a handful of the hem and watched the fabric shiver to dust between her fingers. . . .There were shadows of mildew in every fold of the voluminous skirt and all smelled musty and stale. (ibid., 67–8)

In the world after the bomb, the wedding dress has lost its significance – but does this mean that it has lost its power to entrap the female subject? Marianne's first impulse when she sees it is to laugh, and to dismiss it as 'perfectly ludicrous' (ibid., 68); and, unlike Melanie, she is astute enough to know that '[i]t's far too big for me' (ibid.). But Marianne's initial mockery is soon replaced by a sense of disquiet as in her mind the dress becomes imbued with attributes of contagion: 'As the room grew dark, the dress took on a moon-like glimmer and seemed to send out more and more filaments of tulle, like a growth of pale fungus shooting out airy spores, a palpable white infection' (ibid.). The longer Melanie is exposed to the dress, the more she becomes enmeshed in its symbolic functions, and as a consequence the whiteness of purity becomes transformed into the polluting whiteness of mould or fungus. As a result, Marianne's reaction to it changes dramatically: she becomes 'menaced . . . by this crumbling anachronism' (ibid., 69). Friable and fragile though it is, the dress becomes inextricably associated with death, and the day the world ended: 'Some young woman had worn it before her for a wedding in the old style with cake, wine and speeches; afterwards, the sky opened an umbrella of fire' (ibid., 68–9).

Just as in *Great Expectations*, the wedding dress in *Heroes and Villains* gains its significance through its contradictory ability to both transcend time and act as a reminder of time's effects, thus functioning as a disturbing point of overlap between past and present. '[F]orced to impersonate the sign of a memory of a bride' (ibid., 72), Marianne becomes a substitute or stand-in for the dress's previous owner, and thus a 'corpse bride' in the most literal of ways. Yet that former bride was herself only the temporary occupant of a one-size-fits-all role passing down the generations, each bride an identikit of the one that has gone before. Whereas the wedding dress in *The Magic Toyshop* offers itself up for interpretation, this dress is an empty signifier, each level of meaning revealing only another vacant space.

Carter's use of the wedding dress trope reaches the height of audacity in her 1977 novel *The Passion of New Eve*. Melanie and Marianne subvert the romantic ideology of marriage from opposite ends of the spectrum, as it were, in that Melanie puts the dress on too early, and Marianne too late, but in this novel the 'wrong body' narrative is taken to its extreme. The novel is narrated in the first person by a figure who is initially male – the masculine Evelyn – but who subsequently undergoes an enforced sex change at the hands of the radical feminist Mother, who transforms him into the feminine Eve. On escaping from Mother, Eve is kidnapped by the misogynistic survivalist Zero and made to join his harem of oppressed women. They then go on a quest into the desert to find the glass mansion of a former Hollywood movie star, Tristessa, the most beautiful and most famous actress of her generation, whom Zero believes has performed a 'spiritual vasectomy' (Carter 1982: 92) on him. Yet when Zero and his group invade her house, they discover 'the best kept secret in the whole world' (ibid., 128): that Tristessa is in fact a man masquerading as his own vision of idealized femininity.

Zero then performs a savagely satirical marriage ceremony uniting Eve and Tristessa, in which Eve (a woman who was once a man) is the groom and Tristessa (a man who wishes with all his heart he were a woman) the bride. In preparation, the women of Zero's harem dress Tristessa in an old movie prop, 'the white satin bridal gown he'd last worn thirty years before in, God help me, coming events . . . that dreadful marriage scene in *Wuthering Heights*' (ibid., 133). But in spite of the fact that this is the most brutal of shotgun marriages, Tristessa is nevertheless seduced by the image of femininity he assumes in his role as bride – for after all, his ultimate ambition is to fulfil all the criteria required of the 'perfect' woman:

> He leaned forward and scrutinized the romantic apparition in the mirror with eyes filled with an obscure distress and also a luminous pride.
>
> 'Isn't it *every* girl's dream to be married in white?' the virgin bride demanded rhetorically of the company in her heroic irony. (ibid., 134)

Clearly, we are not meant to agree with Tristessa here: marriage is not every girl's dream, nor, more importantly, can it be his. Yet Tristessa is, ironically, the most Miss Havisham-esque bride in Carter's writing, a recluse who lives entirely in a fiction of his own devising, 'cheat[ing] the clock in her castle of purity, her ice palace, her glass shrine' (ibid., 119). Marriage is the culmination of all of Tristessa's assumed feminine fantasies, but this wedding is no more real than any of his many famed on-screen unions. Not only does Eve recall Tristessa's role as Catherine in *Wuthering Heights*, but also an unnamed film in which Tristessa plays the part of a nurse in a leper colony who becomes infected herself. Consequently, 'the missionary she loved . . . married her as soon as it was too late. She wore a veil thick enough to hide the ravages of the disease at the ceremony, but they could not touch, of course. So she died and he was sorry' (ibid., 122). As in *The Magic Toyshop* and *Heroes and Villains*, the body of the bride is also the body of a corpse: the wedding dress is worn both at the altar and in the coffin. What the veil – and the wedding dress – disguise is a Gothic horror: not the virginal modesty of the blushing bride, but the leprous signs of infection, or the face of madness and delusion.

Nevertheless, this does not quite constitute Carter's final word on the wedding dress. She revisits the trope in her last novel *Wise Children*, where she writes it out of the Gothic mode of abjection and into the world of light-hearted farce. Here the literary referent is not the nineteenth-century literary Gothic exemplified by Dickens and Brontë, but the comedies of Shakespeare. Catherine Bates has summarized these plays as dramas that tell and retell a single 'eternal story' of the various ways in which 'Men and women meet, match, marry and mate' (Bates 2002: 102), and in *Wise Children* Carter takes this formula to absurd extremes.

The novel centres upon the identical twins Nora and Dora who are the illegitimate and unacknowledged children of Melchior Hazard, head of a famous Shakespearean acting dynasty. Despite their father's theatrical eminence, they earn their living as music hall performers and vaudeville girls. As young women, they travel to America in order to play the roles of Peaseblossom and Mustardseed in a Hollywood film version of *A Midsummer Night's Dream* directed by their father. Filming culminates with a triple marriage between Daisy Duck, the actress playing Titania, and Melchior (who as well as directing the film, also plays the part of Oberon); Nora and Tony, an Italian gangster and Dora and Genghis Kahn, the film's producer. As Carter has done before in *The Passion of New Eve*, an analogy is drawn between marriage and performance: the ceremony takes place on set in an imitation wood, and the brides' 'wedding veils and orange blossom wreaths' are provided from the costume store by the 'girls from wardrobe' (Carter 1992; 158).

The important difference between this representation of marriage and those seen in *The Magic Toyshop*, *Heroes and Villains* and *The Passion of New Eve* lies in Carter's manipulation of the trope of veiling. While she does not quite cut it loose from its association with the shroud, in Dora Carter presents a narrator who differs from her predecessors in the ease with which she slips from beneath its enveloping drapery. To begin with, the very fact of a multiple marriage undermines the fiction of the uniqueness of one's wedding day by foregrounding its cultural ubiquitousness; and romantic notions of uniqueness are further undermined by the interchangeability of the brides themselves. Dora constitutes another variation on the 'wrong body' theme, for Genghis' first choice of wife is actually Nora, who blithely instructs her twin to accept his proposal in her stead on the grounds that '[h]e'll never tell the difference' (ibid., 148). However, the substitute bride is herself substituted when Genghis's discarded first wife turns up at the eleventh hour. So desperate is she to have her former husband back that she has had extensive plastic surgery 'to turn herself into a rough copy of his beloved' (ibid., 155), and while the operation has achieved only 'a blurred photocopy or an artists' impression' (ibid.) of the Chance sisters, in this case the assumption of 'the thickest veil' (ibid., 158) facilitates the deception by concealing the bruising and scars that no amount of makeup can hide.

Insofar as it disguises the Frankenstein identity of the bride, the veil's intimations of mortality remain but, as is typical of *Wise Children*, it serves a comedic rather than a Gothic function. Realizing that 'it wouldn't do to have *three* Chance sisters walking around, under the circumstances' (ibid., 156), Dora steals the costume of Bottom the Weaver in order to attend her own wedding undetected. As she remarks, 'It isn't every day you see yourself get married' (ibid., 157), and her position on the periphery of the ceremony in which she herself is supposedly participating enables her to commentate on her bridal role from one remove: 'I couldn't help it, I started crying. I made a lovely bride. I looked quite radiant' (ibid., 159). At this point, Dora is an invisible observer – a ghostly presence from 'beyond the veil' in the most literal of ways – yet the Gothic implications of her position are detracted from by the exchange of her wedding veil for a donkey's head, an ironic commentary on marriage itself as an asinine institution.

Dora's sentimental tears do not signify regret so much as conscious self-dramatization, which is heightened by her use of the first person in reference to both herself and the bride. The universality of the veil's symbolism creates a blank space into which Dora can for a moment imaginarily insert herself, but she differs from her predecessors from previous novels in that she faces no risk of being forced to do so in actuality. Indeed, in *Wise Children* as a whole marriage represents little danger to the female subject, a fact Carter stresses by replaying *The Magic Toyshop*'s scenario of the bloodstained wedding dress. But here Dora's dramatic cry of 'Blood on the bridal veil!' (ibid., 160) is a gleeful exaggeration, for it is actually only tomato sauce that has been thrown over Nora by Tony's vengeful mother. This bloody veil (which is, in fact, not bloody at all) signifies the definitive severing of the link between the veil and the body. Traditional bridal apparel no longer signifies the purification of an abjected feminine which is always threatening to breach its disguise and rise up to defile its sanctifying draperies. Instead, it is shown to be a fabrication, a costume, and any significance it may have is imposed upon it from the outside rather than spreading up from underneath.

In *Wise Children* Carter definitively deprives the wedding dress of any association with depth. It exists as nothing but surface, and there is no authenticity to be found beneath its white satin drapery. Yet this is not a departure from her previous representations so much as a comic apotheosis. This essay has throughout distinguished between the 'wrong' body and the 'right' one, and argued that the wedding dress acquires different meanings within these opposing contexts – yet one of the things that Carter is suggesting through her manipulation of the image of the wedding dress in all her fiction is that the body it clothes is *never* quite the 'right' one, for no woman can live up to the idealized myth of femininity that traditional bridal apparel represents. Furthermore, *all* wedding dresses make *all* brides potentially Gothic subjects in that they are costumes that manufacture women purely as sexual objects, as 'sexual things'. Although veiling hints at the concept of depth – at something 'underneath' – Carter's wedding dresses accumulate their meanings on the surface, thus making subjectivity itself, in the words of Judith Halberstam, 'a surface effect' (Halberstam 1995: 64). In Carter's fiction, therefore, every veiling is a Gothic act in that it is also simultaneously an enshrouding, signalling a terrifying descent into 'nothingness' for the female subject. Miss Havisham, whose life effectively comes to an end at the moment she dons her wedding dress, is indeed – to reiterate Carter's words – 'an awful image of the condition of women', because she suggests that, for women for whom marriage is the ultimate life ambition, the wedding dress really is the garment in which they will both live and die.

Works Cited

Bates, C. (2002), 'Love and Courtship' in Alexander Leggett (ed.) *The Cambridge Companion to Shakespearean Comedy*, Cambridge: Cambridge University Press.
Bedford, L. (1977), 'Angela Carter: An Interview'. Sheffield University Television.

Boden, S. (2007), 'Consuming Pleasure on the Wedding Day: The Lived Experience of being a Bride' in Emma Casey and Lydia Martens (eds), *Gender and Consumption: Domestic Cultures and the Commercialisation of Everyday Life*, Aldershot: Ashgate, 109–21.

Carter, A. (1981a) [1967], *The Magic Toyshop*, London: Virago Press.

—(1981b) [1969], *Heroes and Villains*, Harmondsworth: Penguin.

—(1982) [1977], *The Passion of New Eve*, London: Virago Press.

—(1992) [1991], *Wise Children*, London: Vintage.

—(1997a) [1967], 'Notes for a Theory of Sixties Style', in *Shaking A Leg: Collected Journalism and Writings*, London: Chatto & Windus, 105–8.

—(1997b) [1983], 'Notes from the Front Line', in *Shaking A Leg*, 36–43.

Dickens, C. (2010) [1860–1], *Great Expectations*, London: Harper Press.

Halberstam, J. (1995), *Skin Shows: Gothic Horror and the Technology of Monsters*, Durham & London: Duke University Press.

Kristeva, J. (1982), *Powers of Horror: An Essay on Abjection*, New York: Columbia University Press.

Sedgwick, E. K. (1980), *The Coherence of Gothic Conventions*, New York & London: Methuen.

Thornton, S. (2010), 'The Burning of Miss Havisham: Dickens, Fire, and the "Fire Baptism" ' in Harold Bloom (ed.), *Charles Dickens' Great Expectations* [new edn] New York: Chelsea House Publishers, 79–98.

4

Between the Paws of the Tender Wolf: Authorship, Adaptation and Audience

Lorna Jowett

The time seems ripe for a re-evaluation of the ways Angela Carter's 'The Company of Wolves' has been adapted. Carter's story challenges male authorship of horror, the predominance of male protagonists and the assumption of male audiences. The current boom in so-called Dark Romance across fiction, film and television also contests the framing of horror as masculine. Drawing on a tradition of mass market female gothic, the commercial success of Dark Romances as diverse as the *Twilight* saga (novels 2005– 2008, films 2008–), the *Anita Blake: Vampire Hunter* novels (1993–), Charlaine Harris's *Southern Vampire Mysteries* novel series (2001–) and their television incarnation *True Blood* (2008–), emphasizes how important horror-fantasy is to women consumers.

Gina Wisker argues that Carter's horror fiction does not 'simply reveal the limiting ways in which horror writing makes women into either bloodthirsty vampires or quaking violets,' rather it 'sets out to redefine the genre altogether' (Wisker 1997: 116). Wisker is, however, one of the few who acknowledge that horror as a genre might be capable of such reinvention. Feminist critics have been wary of Carter's negotiation of horror, sexuality and violence, especially their close association in stories from *The Bloody Chamber* collection in which 'The Company of Wolves' appeared. It is hardly surprising, then, that opinion on the film version, *The Company of Wolves* (1984, directed by Neil Jordan), is also divided. Carole Zucker argues that it is 'one of the rare films of the horror genre that chose a female character as its main subject, and displayed a genuine concern for a woman's problems from a decidedly feminist perspective' (Zucker 2000: 66) yet scholars, viewers and readers might even be confused as to whether Carter's stories, or Carter and Jordan's film can be defined as horror. Responses to horror are often contradictory, perhaps because unlike other popular genres (usually taken to be 'pleasurable escapist entertainment') horror is designed 'to elicit negative emotions from its viewers,' as Brigid Cherry points out (Cherry 2009: 12). This chapter examines *The Company of Wolves* in relation to horror, to contemporaneous werewolf films, and to Dark Romance, examining its negotiations of gender and sexual identity.

There has been much less written on adaptations of Carter's work than on her fiction. Several scholars who discuss the film get mired in judgements about the relative value of literature and film. Some lament the way Carter's 'feminist' stories are dumbed down for a more mainstream audience, or her 'sophisticated mythology' is co-opted by the 'grubby stereotypes' (Bristow and Broughton 1997: 4) of the, by implication, conservative, sexist horror genre. Yet recent developments in adaptation studies open up new ways of reading the text/s. Rather than a process from 'original' to inferior copy, adaptation is now considered as a complex and nuanced process of translation, reimagining or appropriation. Foregrounding the fidelity of an adaptation usually serves to valorize literature above film or television or at least to award status to the 'original'. Now that adaptation traffic of all kinds is acknowledged (from stage show to TV show, from comics to movies, from historical events to fictionalizations, from film to film remake) the very notion of the 'original' is in question.

Stories from *The Bloody Chamber* are a case in point: many adapt or appropriate well-known fairy tales such as Bluebeard, Beauty and the Beast or Little Red Riding Hood. The majority of critics mention Charles Perrault's late seventeenth-century edition of fairy tales (translated by Carter prior to the publication of *The Bloody Chamber*) as a major (patriarchal) revision of existing folk stories when discussing Carter's fiction. 'Perrault's version was itself a falsification of the dynamics of the original folk tale,' states Maggie Anwell (Anwell 1988: 77), implying that Carter's rewriting is closer to the tale's origins. Zucker points out that *The Company of Wolves* 'screenplay appropriates a variety of different folk-legends, fairy tales, and myths' (Zucker 2000: 66), rather than a single source text. 'Colonizing adaptations,' suggests Thomas Leitch, 'see progenitor texts as vessels to be filled with new meanings' (Leitch 2007: 109) and Carter scholars view 'The Company of Wolves' (and *The Bloody Chamber*) in exactly this way, with almost all major analyses repeating her comment about putting old wine into new bottles ('most intellectual development depends upon new readings of old texts. I am all for putting new wine in old bottles, especially if the pressure of the new wine makes the bottles explode' (Gamble 1997: 4). Far fewer scholars have been conscious of the same mechanisms of adaptation when examining the translation of Carter's stories into radio or film, however.[1]

This is a curious omission, since Carter herself was obviously aware of the possibilities of different media. She notes that, 'because of the absence of the visual image, radio drama need not necessarily be confined to the representations of things as they are' (Carter 1997: 500), lending itself to the fantastic and to the metamorphoses that abound in *The Company of Wolves*. Crofts observes that Carter sees radio as an aural space which could 'disrupt the unities of character, time and place' (Crofts 2003: 35). Given how *The Company of Wolves* radio and screenplays weave together different times and places, as well as different sets of characters and their stories, this disruption of standard unities is essential to the way the piece works in either medium.

'The Company of Wolves' is a retelling of Little Red Riding Hood and the act of telling stories is integral to the story, radio play and film. The centrality of voice in radio drama is particularly appropriate for Carter's rewriting of the oral tradition, as Crofts also observes (ibid., 25). The integration of several stories into the radio play and then the screenplay ensures that multiple voices are heard and even compete with each other, not just through dialogue and character interaction, but through the very structure of the narrative and the nature of the medium. The story, for example, switches between third and first person narrators. The radio play is largely structured around Granny telling tales to Red Riding Hood, so that different stories are introduced via the first person narrator and, in this case, sometimes questioned or interrupted by the narratee (and perhaps also the listener outside the diegesis).[2] In the film, the different stories emerge through stories exchanged between characters and through dramatization (extending what the radio play does), and the film uses conventional cinematic techniques to shift between the different frames. Indeed, 'This film also deals centrally with the image of the frame,' as Lucie Armitt observes (Armitt 1997: 97), and director Jordan refers to the film's 'Chinese box' structure (Jordan 2005). Laura Mulvey sees cinema as ideally suited to rendering the 'different layers of story-telling and belief' in *The Company of Wolves* since 'In the cinema, worlds can open up and shift from one to another without verbal explanation' (Mulvey 1995: 241). This idea is echoed in Jordan's comment on the use of mirrors as visual transitions (Jordan 2005), reflected images leading us into new worlds.

Moreover, this emphasis on telling different stories refers back to the perceived function of fairy stories. Such tales are often assumed to have a didactic purpose, setting out social norms and behaviours, and Jack Zipes' analysis of their social function is regularly mentioned by Carter scholars. Some critics also see the horror genre as revamped cautionary tales for young adults (see Twitchell 1985: 7), suggesting why Carter draws on its imagery when rewriting fairy tales. This is most apparent in Granny's warnings to Red Riding Hood/Rosaleen about the dangers of straying from the path when walking in the woods.

However, the multiple voices within each adaptation detract from Granny's authority: her warnings are not privileged as the only or the most important way to see things. Crofts notes, for example, that although Granny functions as a 'voice of interdiction' (Crofts 2003: 54), this is seen to provoke 'back talk' from Red Riding Hood in *The Company of Wolves* radio play (ibid., 56), as when she laughs at Granny's notion of meeting a naked man in the woods ('In *this* weather? He'd have his thingumajig's frozen off, Granny!' (Carter 1997: 72)). Likewise, Jordan notes that Granny's cautionary tales are 'counterproductive' in the film and although the scenario depicted in Carter's story 'The Werewolf' where Granny is revealed to be the wolf never comes to pass in the film, as played by Angela Lansbury, Granny's 'benignly sinister' air is visualized (Jordan 2005).[3] For Granny, argues Zucker, 'the sexual is the demonic, given a real existence in the film that is brutal, fearful, and evil' (Zucker 2000: 67), yet a different view comes from Rosaleen's mother, who tells her daughter that the beast in men 'meets its match in women too' (screenplay, Carter 1997: 205) as well as from Rosaleen herself. Granny demonstrates that women can accede to their traditional roles by replicating its models and passing them onto future generations. Thus Carter's reproduction of the oral tradition, including both tale-teller and listener not only offers 'unmediated access to female subjectivity' as Crofts notes of the radio production (Crofts 2003: 49), but also foregrounds reception and audience.

As several of these examples demonstrate, the film version of *The Company of Wolves* exploits the possibilities of its medium by telling through showing. Armitt describes both the stories and the film as 'an endlessly destabilizing series of images which encode the metamorphoses that are their thematic concerns into the very fibre of both works' (Armitt 1997: 98). Certainly the film provides some arresting images, from the final transformation scene where a wolf emerges snout-first from the huntsman's mouth, to the strange egg Rosaleen finds in a treetop nest. The visuals in *The Company of Wolves* are not restricted to the 'Spectacular body-horror special effects' (Hutchings 2004: 165) that form expectations of a werewolf film after the success of *An American Werewolf in London* (directed by John Landis) and *The Howling* (directed by Joe Dante, both 1981), which each feature ground-breaking effects sequences in their set piece transformations. Yet similar scenes inevitably position the film as a kind of horror film, if not a traditional example.

One reason for critical neglect of Carter's adaptations may be that she generally adapted her own work, and scholars may assume that authorship remains with Carter for radio versions of *The Company of Wolves*, *Vampirella* (later adapted into the story 'The Lady in the House of Love'), and *Puss in Boots*. Even Crofts, who clearly signals adaptation as a process involving distinct media, tends to ignore Carter's collaboration with others on these projects. Even with a script by Carter herself, a finished radio production receives input from producers, actors, directors and many others. While film authorship is generally assumed to reside with the director rather than the writer, the screenplay for *The Company of Wolves* film was co-written by Carter and Jordan, demonstrating how 'as both procedure and process, adaptation and appropriation are celebratory of the cooperative and collaborative model' (Sanders 2006: 4).

The Company of Wolves does not just adapt Carter's story: in the same way that Carter appropriates fairy tales for her own purposes, remaking them, the film appropriates conventions and modes of horror and fantasy. Jordan is not primarily a horror director and his range as a director proves broad, including social realism, in films like *Mona Lisa* (1986), *The Crying Game* (1992) and *The Butcher Boy* (1997), as well as fantasy and romance in *Interview With the Vampire* (1994) or *Ondine* (2009). The films Jordan directs often twist genre, and there is also an ongoing theme of unconventional sexuality or relationships in his work – both evident in *The Company of Wolves*, his second film. The film plays with the surreal and fantastic, in what Jordan sees as a direct contrast with social realism and the politics of the Thatcher years during which it was produced (Jordan 2005). Some scholars compare it to Hammer horror films but *The Company of Wolves* is closer to the richly coloured AIP movies (many of them adaptations of Edgar Allen Poe stories) directed and produced by Roger Corman, as Jordan points out. When discussing influences, Jordan cites Gustav Doré's engravings, as well as Samuel Palmer's expressionist paintings and the cinema of F. W. Murnau. Such 'art' influences, like the more 'trashy' AIP movies, privilege an expressionist rather than a realist style. Music and imagery establish a level of realism in the opening of *The Company of Wolves*, set in the contemporary world, but this soon yields to a more theatrical, non-naturalistic look and sound that includes surrealism and symbolism. Thus Louise Watson comments that 'Red dominates the palette of *The Company of Wolves*, representing preening (lipstick), temptation (red apples), and menstruation and death (blood)' (Watson 2003–10). The theatricality and outright fantasy of certain scenes mitigates the werewolf transformation scenes, situating them too as 'fantasy violence'. Jordan, for instance, describes Granny's death, where she smashes to pieces like a china doll, as 'one of those moments you realise you're looking at a story' (Jordan 2005), and clearly both Carter and Jordan played with levels of fantasy and surrealism in writing the screenplay and realizing it for the film.

Anwell criticizes the special effects used in the werewolf scenes, arguing that 'The blood and the violence of the transformations are linked to sexuality in a way that recalls the standard horror movie, in which the girl is seen as victim' (Anwell 1988: 84) and citing 'the gratuitous violence of the physical man/wolf transformations' (ibid., 85). Taking issue with this, Crofts argues that while the graphic nature of these transformations is not included in the short story, it is evident in the radio play, as Carter's script offers 'minute, juicy detail' appropriate to the medium (Crofts 2003: 113), detail visualized equally juicily in the film version. Here I offer a rather different way of reading the transformation scenes and their effects-driven spectacle.

Crofts is one of the few scholars who notes Carter's work on masculinity (ibid., 71), pointing out that her work, in seeking to challenge gender norms for women, inevitably challenges masculine roles and representations too. *The Company of Wolves* does this by contrasting an assertive female protagonist with images of male abjection, as well as masculine power and violence. Peter Hutchings notes, 'Frankenstein's monster and the werewolf . . . are defined as much through the pain they themselves experience as the pain they cause others' (Hutchings 2004: 162): the male werewolf is an object of pathos as well as of horror. In werewolf movies, and particularly the contemporaneous *An American Werewolf in London* and *The Howling*, the show-stopping transformations from human to wolf emphasize affect as well as effects.

Transformation scenes do inscribe physicality and sexuality, as Anwell observes, but they also present the male body as abject, eliciting sympathy for the (graphically detailed) pain of the transformation, as well as emphasizing the male werewolf's alienation from mainstream society. It is the latter as much as the former that causes the female protagonists of *The Company of Wolves* and *An American Werewolf in London* to sympathize with a werewolf 'monster'. In *American Werewolf* nurse Alex Price is not fazed by protagonist David's 'delusions' of being attacked by a werewolf, nor by seeing him as a wolf in a London alley before he is shot and killed. Moreover, David, in a version of the werewolf film that goes back to Universal Pictures' 1941 *Wolf Man* (directed by George Waggner), is presented as a victim: following the werewolf attack he is helpless to control the changes that affect his body and his sense of identity. Ken Gelder points out that, as in possession or zombie narratives, a werewolf attack is frequently shown to result in 'the struggling moral subject actually becoming the frenzied subject of excess' (Gelder 2000: 3). The werewolf's position as conflicted, reluctant monster and helpless victim further blurs traditional gender roles. The emphasis on horror in *The Company of Wolves*' transformation scenes foregrounds the abject male body, not female terror. Director Jordan recalls his desire to find an actor who could convey both 'physicality' and an 'animal quality,' causing him to select a dancer (Micha Bergese) with a high degree of physical control and expressiveness to play the huntsman/wolf (Jordan 2005). Crofts even suggests that *The Company of Wolves* film presents an image of male birth as the wolf emerges from the huntsman's mouth in the final transformation (Crofts 2003: 119).

Thus the inherent appeal of these monsters is their combination of hypermasculinity with feminized abjection and vulnerability. Cherry's research into female audiences of horror discovers substantial 'sympathy or empathy with monstrous creatures' (Cherry 2002: 173), perhaps precisely because of the way such monsters destabilize gender distinctions. 'The phantasy of a mutilated male creature,' as Barbara Creed observes, 'is central to representations of the male monster in myth, legend, fairy story, the horror film and Gothic literature' (Creed 1993: 115) and the male werewolves in *The Company of Wolves* are no exceptions. In addition, female power and resistance to expectations, especially in terms of gender roles, is foregrounded. During neither of the transformation scenes do female characters respond with fear alone, and Rosaleen never screams during the final transformation. In presenting abject males and mostly unshrieking females the story, the radio play and the film are each a 'deliberate engagement with the existing sado-masochistic power relations exhibited in the traditional tales' (Crofts 2003: 36).

When Carter's stories were published, the horror genre was changing. The 1970s saw a wave of horror films that rejected the reassuring endings common to earlier films (in which monsters are defeated), instead often deliberately allowing their monsters to escape (as in *The Texas Chain Saw Massacre* 1974, directed by Tobe Hooper or *Halloween* 1978, directed by John Carpenter). The rise of the slasher film consolidates the figure Carol Clover dubs 'the final girl', a female protagonist who survives the attacks of the (almost always) male monster (Clover, 1992). Carter, a long-time fan of cinema, may not have seen these particular films, but she cannot have been unaware that female characters were taking on new roles in popular culture. Her own female protagonists in *The Company of Wolves*, like these characters, challenge the conventions of gender in genre fiction and these developments are apparent in other werewolf movies of the 1980s.

Prior to *The Company of Wolves*, *An American Werewolf in London* featured a confident female character, Alex; *The Howling* went further, with two female protagonists, Karen and Terri, eventually connecting a series of brutal killings with strange events at The Colony, an exclusive resort. *The Howling* also includes a female werewolf, Marsha Quist. Sue Short argues that Carter's female characters experience 'tremendous freedom in their bestial transformations' (Short 2006: 100) and this is also embodied by Marsha, who attempts to seduce Karen's husband Bill, attacks him when he rejects her, and then enjoys sex with him in the woods. While in the film *The Company of Wolves*, Rosaleen's mother allows the wolves to escape, knocking up a gun about to be fired at them, Marsha from *The Howling* receives no such sympathy from other characters and is narratively positioned as a monster to be executed. It is worth remembering, however, especially given the ending of *The Company of Wolves* film (which shows the 'real' Rosaleen screaming as wolves break into her world), that pleasure in such fictions is often in the disruptive middle, rather than the end. If endings evict the monster, catering to conventional morality and narrative resolution, 'the very existence of the monster reveals that [social] categories can be breached, that they – for all their apparent "naturalness" – are fragile, contingent, vulnerable,' as Hutchings puts it (Hutchings 2004: 37). Looked at in this way, the werewolf story can be disruptive as well as, or instead of, conservative, whatever its ending.

Horror movies in the 1970s also replaced Gothic trappings with more contemporary, often suburban settings, bringing horror home until 'the domestic space has become *the* locality for the worst of horror' (Wells 2000: 18). The various adaptations of *The Company of Wolves* also negotiate the domestic as part of gender roles. Mulvey notes that the film heroines of *The Company of Wolves* and *The Magic Toyshop* are 'established within the security of a bourgeois home' yet in both films are 'thrown into the insecurity of a radically reversed story space' (Mulvey 1995: 238). Certainly all versions of *The Company of Wolves* suggest a contrast between the safety of home and the danger of the forest, yet even supposedly safe spaces are disrupted in the Red Riding Hood tale that forms the concluding episode, when the wolf enters Granny's house and kills her. This merely makes clear what earlier parts of Carter's story imply, and the boom in suburban horror renders too: there is no such thing as a safe place. Life, including sexuality, is risky. Such insecurity is reinforced at the end of the film when the fairy tale world intrudes into the 'real' world of the 'bourgeois home' as wolves leap through windows and corridors are overtaken by forest plants.

Women's roles as wives, homemakers and mothers loom large in *The Company of Wolves*, whether it is through the story of the new bride whose handsome husband leaves her on their wedding night, only to return after she has married again and is a wife and mother, or through the interactions between Rosaleen, her mother and grandmother. Wisker suggests that Carter explores 'domestic horror . . . putting the spotlight on the werewolf in the kitchen' (Wisker 1997: 120). As the story of Bluebeard signals, the home can be a threatening and dangerous space for a woman. In the story of the new bride and the travelling man, horror enters the home, disrupting the family not only through violent excess, but by reminding the wife how handsome and young her first intended husband was. This episode is elaborated in the film to give a more ambivalent picture of the bride's subsequent life as wife and mother. 'In a multitrack medium,' Linda Hutcheon argues, 'everything can convey point of view' (Hutcheon 2006: 55). In the story, we are told that the wife 'gave him a pair of bonny babies and all went right as a trivet' (Carter 1996, 214), while the radio play has the wife herself describe 'bouncing babies, merry as grigs' (Carter 1997: 69). The film, however, offers visual cues (not in Carter's screenplay) that home and family may not be blissful, with an impatient mother who snaps, 'Oh, don't start!' at her crying baby and who struggles with household tasks at the same time as minding her three children. Granny's voice-over talks of happiness but the images tell a different story. Rosaleen's own tale of the pregnant witch woman (only present in the screenplay and film) who turns her ex-lover, his new bride and all their wedding guests into wolves reverses the gender of intrusion into the home, and gives it an extra twist of social class, as the discarded peasant takes her revenge on the gentry. Such episodes contribute to *The Company of Wolves'* challenge to the roles of wife, mother, housekeeper and caregiver, showing how domestic horror 'continually addresses the dysfunctional and antithetical aspects of the romantic and the domestic, collapsing all received notions of predictable gender identities and social formations' (Wells 2000: 18). Focusing on marriage in two of these stories also makes explicit the link between apparently 'natural' roles for women and the patriarchal social structure they uphold.

The Company of Wolves' appropriation of horror conventions is developed through the current boom in Dark Romance. Cherry's study of women consumers of horror film finds that 'Sexual and erotic themes . . . were important to many of the participants' (Cherry 2002: 173), hinting at the popularity of the Dark Romance, which stems from established tropes of the reluctant monster and the female gothic. *Twilight, The Vampire Diaries, True Blood*, the *Anita Blake: Vampire Hunter* novels and many others narrate the pleasures of a dark romance, wherein a female protagonist engages in a dangerous relationship with a potentially violent male 'monster' (often a vampire or werewolf). Rochester, Heathcliff and Dracula are all precursors of the Dark Romance hero and Cherry describes the 1992 film *Bram Stoker's Dracula* (directed by Francis Ford Coppola) as 'Gothic Romance with a Byronic monster who is conflicted rather than wholly evil and who is sexually appealing to female characters and female audience members alike' (Cherry 2009: 15).

While a phenomenon labelled Dark Romance might seem unlikely to subvert gender stereotypes, the range and complexity of its (usually serial) fictions allows substantial play with constructions of gender and sexuality. Like the Dark Romance, 'The Company of Wolves' and other stories from *The Bloody Chamber* match an assertive female protagonist with a violent male partner, seeking to rewrite the gender typing of classic horror through the examination of power dynamics. While each version of *The Company of Wolves* is more art than mass culture, its reworking of standard tropes and roles foreshadows their renegotiation across horror fictions from *Twilight* to the *Southern Vampire Mysteries*. Cherry describes not-quite-horror films like *Bram Stoker's Dracula* as 'culturally sanctioned forms of horror-romance that allow more casual female audiences . . . to watch and enjoy horror without calling the prescribed gender roles into question' (Cherry 2009: 51). Yet Tania Modleski's description of mass market female gothic as a way to 'deal with women's fears of and confusion about masculine behaviour in a world in which men learn to devalue women' (Modleski 1998: 60) is a useful one, suggesting that gender roles can be called into question even by apparently conventional romances. Modleski identifies the trajectory of female gothic as a 'transformation from love into fear' (ibid., 60): most twenty-first century Dark Romance fictions transform fear into love. As a vampire or werewolf the Dark Romance male is 'naturally' positioned as an aggressor and the human female protagonist as his prey or victim, yet both resist this. *Twilight* can be read as a cautionary tale for the twenty-first century, advocating celibacy and positioning its female protagonist, Bella, as relatively passive. However, as Nickianne Moody's study demonstrates, *Twilight*'s consumers do not necessarily accept its intended or dominant reading: young adult readers are capable of seeing vampire love interest Edward as a controlling male and discussing toxic relationships (Moody 2010).

Crofts' analysis of *The Company of Wolves* film ascribes the violence of its werewolf transformations to perspective, suggesting that their violence is indicative of Granny's collusion in patriarchal myths of gender. This may be a viable reading, yet it potentially ignores the attractions of violent sexuality in fantasy. Carter's story gives voice to forbidden desire. In the radio play, Granny's description of the huntsman as having a body 'the colour of goatcheese, and nipples black as poison berries' (Carter 1997: 7) suggests fascination as well as disgust and Rosaleen, in all three versions, freely expresses her desire for the wolf. Representations of vampires and werewolves have long combined sexuality with violence, since one often overlays or collapses into the other. Laurell K. Hamilton, author of the *Anita Blake* novels, blends erotica with genre fiction, stating that the series is 'overtly sexual' and 'sometimes violently sexy' (quoted in Veldman-Genz 2011: 50). Queering heterosexuality and traditional gender roles are key elements of many top-selling Dark Romances, overtly in the *Anita Blake* novels (which include male strippers, female aggressors, threesomes and multiway sex) but are also discernible subtextually in fictions aimed at young adult audiences such as *The Vampire Diaries* or *Twilight* (both eminently slashable[4]). Dark Romance often suggests that heterosexual romance is itself 'darkened' by traditional patriarchal power relations. Like Carter's stories and adaptations, it explores how to rewrite such dynamics.

As Modleski notes of mass market romance, 'women writers have always had their own way of "evening things up" between men and women, even when they seemed most fervently to embrace their subordinate status' (Modleski 1998: 16). Similar strategies are taken by the contemporary Dark Romance. Hamilton presents Anita Blake as a dominant, violent 'alpha' who collects a harem of male monsters willing to be her sex slaves, thus exploring the pros and cons of gender role reversal. Other stereotypes from the busty waitress (Sookie Stackhouse of the *Southern Vampire Mysteries* and *True Blood*) to the blonde cheerleader (television show *Buffy the Vampire Slayer*'s title character, 1997–2003) or the popular high school It girl (Elena from *The Vampire Diaries* novels and TV series) are rewritten in Dark Romance. Following the lead of Carter's *The Company of Wolves*, these examples seek to foreground female agency and female desire, to rework familiar conventions (of genre, of gender) and in doing so risk attracting criticism for reproducing traditional dynamics.

For Carter, as Gamble observes, *The Bloody Chamber* collection 'provided her with work that could be transposed into other media, thus bringing her name to the attention of people who might not necessarily read her books' (Gamble 1997: 131). While some Carter scholars have questioned whether feminism can successfully intervene in mainstream popular culture without being co-opted or diluted, subsequent creators of female horror and Dark Romance argue that this is the only way to change perceptions about gender and sexuality. Joss Whedon, creator of *Buffy the Vampire Slayer*, states

> If I made 'Buffy the Lesbian Separatist,' a series of lectures on PBS on why there should be more feminism, no one would be coming to the party, and it would be boring. The idea of changing the culture is important to me, and it can only be done in a popular medium. (quoted in Lavery 2002: 15)

Carter's stories sketch what the later films, novels and TV series mentioned here explore at length: challenging combinations of violence and heterosexuality. Changes instigated by Carter have become a key element in horror, especially as constructed for female audiences. Culture may not be entirely changed, but it is changing. While the ending of Carter's story, where Red Riding Hood falls asleep 'between the paws of the tender wolf' (Carter 1996: 220) was too radical for a commercial film in 1984, *Twilight* consumers have long rooted for Team Jacob (the werewolf love interest) over Team Edward (the vampire love interest); Sookie Stackhouse's lovers include werewolf Alcide Herveaux as well as more than one vampire and Anita Blake regularly sleeps between the paws of assorted tender wolves and monsters.

Notes

1 As Crofts points out, the radio performance is not readily available as a recording, so it is understandable that it might be neglected.
2 The narrator by necessity emerges again at the end of the radio play after Granny is killed by the huntsman/wolf.
3 Crofts notes that sound effects suggest Granny's beastliness in the radio play (Crofts 2003: 55).
4 Slash fan fiction extrapolates relationships between characters. It is often written by heterosexual women depicting erotic encounters between male characters (though all kinds of slash fiction exist and writers are not necessarily female or straight). The name derives from the typographical slash pairing the characters: slash fiction about Stefan and Damon Salvatore from *The Vampire Diaries* would be Stefan/Damon stories.

Works Cited

Anwell, M. (1988), 'Lolita Meets the Werewolf', in Lorraine Gamman and Margaret Marshment (eds), *The Female Gaze: Women as Viewers of Popular Culture*, London: The Women's Press, 76–85.

Armitt, L. (1997), 'The Fragile Frames of *The Bloody Chamber*', in Joseph Bristow and Trev Lynn Broughton (eds), *The Infernal Desires of Angela Carter: Fiction, Femininity, Feminism*, London: Longman, 88–99.

Bristow, J. and Broughton, T. L. (eds) (1997), 'Introduction', *The Infernal Desires of Angela Carter: Fiction, Femininity, Feminism*, London: Longman, 1–23.

Carter, A. (1996), *Burning Your Boats: Collected Short Stories*, London: Vintage.

— (1997), *The Curious Room: Plays, Film Scripts and an Opera*, London: Vintage.

Cherry, B. (2002), 'Refusing to refuse to look: Female Viewers of the horror film', in Mark Jancovich (ed.), *Horror: The Film Reader*, London: Routledge, 168–78.

—(2009), *Horror*, London: Routledge.

Clover, C. (1992), *Men, Women and Chain Saws: Gender in the Modern Horror Film*, London: BFI.

Creed, B. (1993), *The Monstrous Feminine*, London: Routledge.

Crofts, C. (2003), *Anagrams of Desire: Angela Carter's Writing for Radio, Film, and Television*, Manchester: Manchester University Press.

Gamble, S. (1997), *Angela Carter: Writing from the Front Line*, Edinburgh: Edinburgh University Press.

Gelder, K. (ed.) (2000), *The Horror Reader*, London: Routledge.

Hutcheon, L. (2006), *A Theory of Adaptation*, London/NY: Routledge.

Hutchings, P. (2004), *The Horror Film*, Harlow: Pearson Longman.

Jordan, N. (2005), DVD commentary, *The Company of Wolves: Special Edition* DVD, Granada Ventures Limited.

Lavery, D. (2002), '"A Religion in Narrative": Joss Whedon and Television Creativity', *Slayage: The Journal of the Whedon Studies Association*, 2(3), http://slayageonline.com/PDF/lavery2.pdf. Accessed 9 September 2011.

Leitch, T. (2007), *Film Adaptation and its Discontents*, Baltimore: Johns Hopkins University Press.

Modleski, T. (1998), *Loving With a Vengeance: Mass Produced Fantasies for Women*, New York: Routledge.

Moody, N. (2010), 'Interview with the Postfeminist: Researching the Paranormal Romance', conference paper, Vegetarians, VILFs and Fang-bangers Conference, De Montfort University, 24 November 2010.

Mulvey, L. (1995), 'Cinema Magic and the Old Monsters: Angela Carter's Cinema', in Lorna Sage (ed.), *Flesh and the Mirror: Essays on the Art of Angela Carter*, London: Virago, 230–42.

Sanders, J. (2006), *Adaptation and Appropriation*, The New Critical Idiom series, London: Routledge.

Short, S. (2006), *Misfit Sisters: Screen Horror as Female Rites of Passage*, Houndmills: Palgrave.

Twitchell, J. B. (1985), *Dreadful Pleasures: An Anatomy of Modern Horror*, Oxford University Press.

Veldman-Genz, C. (2011), 'Serial Experiments in Popular Culture: The Resignification of Gothic Symbology in *Anita Blake: Vampire Hunter* and the *Twilight* series', in Giselle Liza Anatol (ed.), *Bringing Light to Twilight*, New York: Palgrave Macmillan, 43–58.

Watson, L. (2003–10), *The Company of Wolves*, BFI Screen Online. http://www.screenonline.org.uk/film/id/515281. Accessed 25 September 2011.

Wells, P. (2000), *The Horror Genre*, London: Wallflower.

Wisker, G. (1997), 'Revenge of the Living Doll: Angela Carter's horror writing', in Joseph Bristow and Trev Lynn Broughton (eds), *The Infernal Desires of Angela Carter: Fiction, Femininity, Feminism*, London: Longman, 116–31.

Zipes, J. (1995), *Breaking the Magic Spell: Radical Theories of Folk and Fairy Tales*, London: Routledge.

Zucker, C. (2000), 'Sweetest Tongue has Sharpest Tooth': The Dangers of Dreaming in Neil Jordan's *The Company of Wolves*', *Literature Film Quarterly*, 28(1), 66–71.

5

Angela Carter's Excessive Stagings of the Canon: Psychoanalytic Closets, Hermaphroditic Dreams and Jacobean Westerns

Susanne Gruss

One of the most widespread and pervasive critical opinions about Angela Carter was given by herself – the notion that she is 'in the demythologising business' (Carter 1998a: 38). In critical readings, Carter's attempts to demythologize are still predominantly located in her feminist revisions of literary and cultural 'myths' perceived as patriarchal: in her deconstructions of gender relations, the creation of sexually ambivalent or transgressive characters, and her decadently sensual fairy tales. Carter was, however, also an untiring demythologizer of the (male) Western canon and its historical and theoretical contexts and writes against the nostalgia for canonical texts as 'authoritative in our culture' (Bloom 1994: 1) as propagated in Harold Bloom's infamous *The Western Canon: The Books and School of the Ages* (1994). In this chapter, I will make use of three of Carter's short stories, 'The Cabinet of Edgar Allan Poe', 'Overture and Incidental Music for *A Midsummer Night's Dream*', and 'John Ford's *'Tis Pity She's a Whore'* in order to trace how Carter both stages and appropriates 'the canon' in these texts, and analyse how she explores and explodes the canon through excessive and humorous (re)stagings of canonized authors, texts and contexts.

Hyperbolic Psychoanalysis: 'The Cabinet of Edgar Allan Poe'

That Carter was fond of both Poe and the Gothic mode is a commonplace of Carter criticism – as is her much-quoted 'Afterword to *Fireworks*', in which she proclaims her predilection for Poe and 'Gothic tales, cruel tales, tales of wonder, tales of terror, fabulous narratives that deal directly with the imagery of the unconscious' (Carter 1995a: 459). 'The Cabinet of Edgar Allan Poe' (in *Black Venus*, 1985) takes a literary bow to Poe in language and content; at the same time, the text creates a seductively coherent psychoanalytic version of Poe's biography, a psychobiography which mirrors the psychoanalytic academic discourse on the author's work. Poe holds a unique position in psychoanalytic criticism: through the intense scrutiny of psychoanalytic critics, Poe's life has been transformed 'into a literary *oeuvre* in its own right' (Kokoli 2002: 57); or, as Maggie Tonkin puts it, '[f]ew authors are as undead as Edgar Allan Poe' (Tonkin 2004: 1). Psychoanalytic criticism of Poe 'as a biographical "myth" figure', Clive Bloom notes, 'has continually suffered from his tales being treated as hidden autobiographical confessions' (Bloom 1988: 5). While the most infamous Freudian reading of Poe's psychobiography is certainly Marie Bonaparte's *Life and Works of Edgar Allan Poe* (1933), which, as Shoshana Felman criticizes, treats 'Poe's works as nothing other than the recreation of his neuroses' (Felman 1988: 141), Jacques Lacan's 'Seminar on "The Purloined Letter" ' (1966, translated 1972) is probably the most productive psychoanalytic reading in terms of the discussions it has sparked in literary theory. It is, as Felman has argued, also more innovative than previous readings in providing not merely an analysis of the principle of repetition in Poe's text, but also an '*allegory of psychoanalysis*' (Felman 1988: 147; italics original).[1]

Carter's text is sprinkled with a generous dose of Freud: the theatre's changing room becomes the closet of her oedipal couple, the infant Edgar and his mother, actress Elizabeth Poe. Poe's mother is not merely Gertrude to Edgar's Hamlet – her theatrical penchant for tragic young women such as Ophelia overtly invites a reading of Poe's personality both Freud and Ernest Jones[2] would have revelled in; apart from making him a worthy 'Oedipus', Poe's fixation on the 'beautiful corpse' of his un/dead mother as Ophelia also readily explains his necrophilic tendencies. Additionally, the text includes Carter's version of the 'primal scene' of Poe's psychopathology; it is through the birth of his sister that young Edgar is so thoroughly traumatized that the mere evocation of female sexuality is forever tainted by the threats of the *vagina dentata*: 'The midwife had to use a pair of blunt iron tongs to scoop out the reluctant wee thing; the sheet was tented up over Mrs Poe's lower half for modesty so the toddlers saw nothing except the midwife brandishing her dreadful instrument and then . . . something bloody as a fresh-pulled tooth twitched between the midwife's pincers' (Carter 1995b: 264). The scene prefigures Poe's 'Berenice' – which is re-enacted by Poe's child-wife Virginia later in the story – but, more importantly, it also allows Carter's psychoanalytic Poe to recognize (and at the same time to repress) the uncanny origin of his tales of horror in the fact that 'women possess within them a cry, a thing that needs to be extracted . . . but this is only the dimmest of memories and will reassert itself in vague shapes of unmentionable dread only at the prospect of carnal connection' (ibid., 266). Kleinian psychoanalysis explicitly figures in the depictions of Elizabeth Poe withdrawing her 'good breast' ('he would retain only the memory of hunger and thirst endlessly unsatisfied') (ibid.), and Lacanian elements such as desire as well as the notion of the mirror stage can easily be read into the text. The story is so full of obvious psychoanalytic explanations of Poe's pathological character and tales that it can, as Tonkin notes, be analysed as both a literalization of psychobiographical readings and 'a parody of Bonaparte's work which foregrounds the relationships at the heart of Bonaparte's analysis: Poe's relation with his dead mother' (Tonkin 2004: 3). 'The Cabinet of Edgar Allan Poe' thus imitates and ridicules the fate of Poe, the author, in literary criticism.

A second significant aspect of this short story is Carter's emphasis on the theatricality of both Poe's autobiography and his tales. She specifically focuses on Poe's mother, who becomes a 'maternal haunting compulsively performed on and off stage' (Kokoli 2002: 64). Elizabeth Poe is imagined in intensely theatrical terms – she is an actress to her very last breath, remains 'in character' as Ophelia (her signature role) until her death, and even her funeral is 'ritualized, stage-managed' (Sanders 2006: 113). At the same time, the story's originality and effect cannot be located in the plot alone, which revises psychoanalytic Poe through an excessive parody of psychoanalytic discourse in the manner of a historiographic metafiction, a text that constantly alludes to its own fictional status. The main effect can be detected in the heightened artificiality and decadent sensuality of Carter's language, a (self-conscious) imitation of Poe that foregrounds his art – as Carter notes, Poe's style is both ornate and unnatural (Carter 1995a: 459) and thus operates 'against the perennial human desire to believe the word as fact' (ibid.). In 'Through a Text Backwards: The Resurrection of the House of Usher', she points out that the 'elements in Poe's voluptuous tales of terror . . . are over-determined, so that it is very difficult to find out what is going on. That is, to find out what is *really* going on, what is going on under the surface. Because at first it looks as if *everything* is on the surface; there is a grand theatricality about Poe, the true child of strolling players'. (Carter 1998b 482; italics original)

Because the latent content of his stories is so obvious, Poe's stories simultaneously are and are not what they claim to be – and Carter thus 'asserts that far from being a terrible secret, as Bonaparte would have it, Poe's necrophilia proclaims itself unselfconsciously on every page' (Tonkin 2004: 11); in defiance of the wave of psychoanalytic appropriations of Poe's psychobiography, she states that Poe's stories are like a mask that 'tells us nothing about the writer, only about itself' (Carter 1998b: 490). Consequently, her Poe is both 'excessive, and unstable' (Tonkin 2004: 12), a cleverly staged version of the psychoanalytic Poe that is intriguing because it defies easy interpretation despite its seeming obviousness. Through her deconstruction of the psychoanalytic Poe, Carter also recovers Poe's tales as more than mere reflections of his pathologically neurotic mind.

Soggy Fairies: 'Overture and Incidental Music for *A Midsummer Night's Dream*'

Carter's work is, as Julie Sanders has shown, characterized by a persistent appropriation of Shakespeare, the author one might easily call *the* personification of the British literary canon, and a motif of Carter's writing which reaches its climax with *Wise Children* (1991). Not surprisingly, Carter distances herself from Bloom's notion of Shakespeare as the epitome of the 'universal canon, multicultural and multivalent' (Bloom 1994: 38) – she is fond of a popular, pre-canonized Shakespeare, 'the intellectual equivalent of bubble-gum' (Sage 1992: 186). For her, *A Midsummer Night's Dream* holds an exceptional position within the Shakespearean canon, 'because it's beautiful and funny and camp – and glamorous, and cynical' (Carter in Sage 1992: 187).[3] With 'Overture and Incidental Music for *A Midsummer Night's Dream*' (*Black Venus*, 1985),

Carter follows an objective that is similar to her theatrical staging of Edgar Allan Poe: she writes against a petrified version of the Bard in general and, more specifically, against the Victorian version of Shakespeare and his fairies.

In the course of the nineteenth century, Shakespeare became 'a standard of immortality to aim at' (Stedman 1986: 181) for Victorian dramatists, and it is in his fairies that Victorian painters, composers, directors and writers found much of their inspiration: 'The *Dream*, Mercutio's Queen Mab speech from *Romeo and Juliet* . . . and *The Tempest* . . . made use of most of the earlier fairy literature and contemporary folkloric beliefs and provided an endless source of inspiration' (Beddoe 1997: 23).[4] The 1860s, in particular, saw an outpouring of fairy fictions such as Christina Rossetti's *Goblin Market* (1862), Jean Ingelow's *Mopsa the Fairy* (1869) or George MacDonald's *The Princess and the Goblin* (1872) (ibid., 27–30). While most productions of Shakespeare's 'fairy plays' between the 1830s and early 1900s 'typically combined music, dance, scenic display and spoken drama' (Jackson 1997: 39), the Victorians also felt that 'Shakespeare (as a national talisman of artistic probity) had to be protected from the taint of such lower entertainments as pantomime, ballet and extravaganza' (ibid.). In an essay, Carter notes sarcastically (and with a sly nod towards notorious fairy painter Richard Dadd, one of Bethlem Hospital's most famous patients) that the 'realm of faery has always attracted nutters, regressives and the unbalanced, as though a potential audience of children granted absolute licence' (Carter 1998c: 451).[5] As in *Wise Children*, she re-infuses her Shakespeare with the burlesque elements that the Victorian theatre stage tried to excise or control, and (re)creates Shakespearean fairies that might attract 'nutters, regressives and the unbalanced' instead of the orderly and conservative stereotypical Victorian audience. Consequently, and not very surprisingly, the fairies in 'Overture and Incidental Music' are no 'gauzy child-fairies' (Sanders 2006: 114), and Carter's narrator Golden Herm – the mute Indian boy from Shakespeare's original – is bored by the landscape which, countering the customary Victorian habit of providing a cityscape and country scenes identifiable as Athenian (see Jackson 1997: 40), is clearly a not so picturesque English scene, 'all soggy and floral as William Morris wallpaper in an abandoned house' (Carter 1995c: 275). The fairies are plagued by the cold – the English climate makes this *Midsummer Night's Dream* a 'midsummer nightmare' (ibid., 273). The title of the story alludes to Felix Mendelssohn Bartholdy's music for *Dream* (1826) – Carter's civilized wood is, the text points out, 'Mendelssohn's wood' (ibid., 277) and, as Sanders notes, for Carter 'Mendelssohn's music represents the harnessing of Shakespeare to a false Victorian ideal' (Sanders 2002: 55). This wood is therefore clearly marked as a construction of the nineteenth century which does not bear much resemblance to Shakespeare's original: 'This is the true Shakespearian wood – but it is not the wood of Shakespeare's time, which did not know itself to be Shakespearian, and therefore felt no need to keep up appearances' (Carter 1995c: 276).

The text's spirited disassembly of the Victorian fairies works on more levels than that of the English weather and setting: Carter also focuses on voices and aspects that were commonly marginalized in Shakespeare. Through the narrator Golden Herm, the story gains both a post-colonial impetus and a new gender twist: famously, the Indian boy in *Midsummer Night's Dream* does not speak, but was frequently used as an exotic stage presence, and Carter comically emphasizes Herm's status as an imperial commodity when she enumerates the spices that seem to emanate from her narrator's skin ('black pepper, red chilli, yellow turmeric, cloves, coriander, cumin, fenugreek, ginger, mace, nutmeg, allspice, khuskhus, garlic, tamarind, coconut, candlenut, lemon grass, galangal and now and then you get – phew! – a whiff of asafoetida. Hot stuff!)' (Carter 1995c: 281). Unlike the Indian boy, Carter's Herm is very eloquent, especially when it comes to the description of her/his sexual ambivalence: hermaphrodite Herm boasts both 'veritable reproductive erectile tissue, while the velvet-lipped and deliciously closable aperture below it is, I assure you, a viable avenue of the other gender' (ibid., 274). It is through this playfully transgressive sexualization that Carter defies the ethereal and miniscule Victorian fairies most effectively, a narrative strategy that is also applied to Titania, who echoes Mother's abundant fecundity[6] and prefigures Fevvers' earthy materiality[7] – she is 'Titania, she, the great fat, showy, pink and blonde thing, the Memsahib, I call her, Auntie Tit-tit-tit-ania (for her tits are the things you notice first, size of barrage balloons), Tit-tit-tit-omania' (ibid., 272). While the Indian boy becomes an outspoken hermaphrodite, 'polymorphously perverse' Puck comically fails in his attempts to transform his own genitals into an inverted copy of Herm's. The grotesque erotic of Carter's Puck can also be read as an obeisance to some of the more explicit Victorian fairy paintings, such as the 'grotesquely erotic in Fuseli' (Maas 1997: 21). Jeremy Maas argues that '[p]rim-lipped prudery was only too ready to stalk the corridors of the Victorian consciousness. But it was a prudery that was inconsistent and easily disarmed by a change of context' (ibid.). In Carter's tale, the continuous and explicit sexualization of her fairy folk is one of its most consistent features.

The text thus invokes a variety of themes, each of which is only briefly explored and staged: from the bowdlerization of Shakespeare to the censorship of sexuality this entails,[8] from the denigration of the overly civilized Englishness of Victorian Shakespeare's fairy world to the boisterous and transgressive sexuality of Carter's fairies, the text creates a dense pattern of parodic allusions and intertexts that serve to reintegrate burlesque elements into the canonical plays which Victorian stagings had attempted to suppress. It is through these variable readings of *Midsummer Night's Dream* that Carter writes against the Victorian attempt to ossify Shakespeare's works into 'one rigid and unchanging interpretation' (Sanders 2006: 115). She also taps into the generic hybridity of early modern drama as a means to restage the canon – her text is thus comparable to a pre-canonized early modern theatre, which 'consciously juxtaposed the tragic with the comic, and the grittily realistic with the magical and fantastic' (ibid., 117). Simultaneously, Carter counters the attempts of critics such as Harold Bloom to 'universalize' Shakespeare in making abundantly clear that 'our' Shakespeare is always already a construct and reflection of our time – be it the Victorian Age or the twenty-first century.

From the Margins of the Canon: 'John Ford's *'Tis Pity She's a Whore*'

It is to the early modern stage that Carter returns in the last text I want to discuss, 'John Ford's *'Tis Pity She's a Whore*' (*American Ghosts and Old World Wonders*, 1993). Her rewriting of a Caroline play in the tradition of the Jacobean revenge tragedy seems to defy my focus on the canon as both the Jacobean and Caroline plays – with the notable exception of Shakespeare's Jacobean plays – have frequently been ignored by critics until the more recent critical renaissance of Shakespeare's contemporaries and their bizarre gory tragedies. It is therefore a relatively recent development that plays which were still quite obscure at the time when Carter wrote her story have (re)entered the canon of Renaissance drama. The story is, however, not only an indication of Carter's continued interest in the early modern stage and its cultural politics, it can also be seen as a logical consequence of her appropriations of the canon – an attempt to re-canonize what has been marginalized by literary criticism – as well as a continuation of her interest in Poe and the decadent Gothic excesses his texts entail. As Gina Wisker points out, Poe's 'sensation horror' is linked to Jacobean revenge plays in his 'concern with perversions of power, spectacles of violence and themes of delusion, insanity and retribution' (Wisker 2006: 179). Carter's text is, as a footnote explains on the first page, an extended pun on the coincidence that the early modern playwright John Ford bears the same name as the famous American Western director – she restages Ford's play as a Western[9] and creates 'a multilayered text which masquerades as a John Ford movie adaptation of a John Ford play: as envisaged, of course, by Angela Carter' (Gamble 2007: 35).[10] Ford's Italianate incestuous siblings Giovanni and Annabella are turned into the equally incestuous but American Johnny and Annie-Belle, and Carter focuses strongly on that element of the play which she had already been drawn to in some of her earlier work: incest.[11]

As in both 'The Cabinet of Edgar Allan Poe' and 'Overture and Incidental Music', it is the narrative voice that creates much of the impact of the text. With reference to *American Ghosts and Old World Wonders* in general, Sarah Gamble has highlighted how far an intrusive narrative voice that cannot clearly be identified is 'an emphatic presence, who is always too well aware of the existence of an audience' (ibid., 31). In 'John Ford's *'Tis Pity She's a Whore*', the narrator quickly ironizes and thus debunks each attempt to romanticize both the love affair of brother and sister and their status as 'New Americans' and ironically marks the story's Western-setting as a self-conscious hybrid construct by introducing stage directions that come complete with a Hollywood score and stereotypical Western set pieces (see Carter 1995d: 334). The text itself is a clever montage that juxtaposes chunks of Ford's original Renaissance text and the narrator's Western stage directions – as in the film script's final showdown which culminates in Johnny/Giovanni shooting his sister: 'Johnny: He shan't have you. He'll never / have you. Here's where you belong, with / me. Out here. / *Giovanni*: Thus die, and die by me, and by my hand! / Revenge is mine; honour doth love command! / . . . / Bang, bang, bang' (ibid., 347). It is through this witty combination of film script and theatrical convention that Carter manages to integrate a humorous dimension into her version of Ford's play, which balances the fact that she has left out the original's comic subplot. The tale also shares a post-colonial emphasis with 'Overture and Incidental Music' – in her story, Death is a Native American, an Other who 'retains the ability to exercise a disruptive power from the margins of the dominant narrative' (Gamble 2007: 38). At the same time, Death functions as a double signifier which can easily be read as a reference to the medieval mystery play, the foundation of early modern drama.

The story itself is haunted by this most persistent myth of the American West, the frontier, which is evoked by the prairies of the story, a landscape, Gamble notes, 'on which an enduring myth of American identity has been founded, an identity defined by reference to a macho code of hardy individualism and pioneering spirit' (ibid., 34). The Western is probably *the* most characteristic American art from, and thus allows Carter a paradigmatic shift from the early modern stage to the canon of twentieth-century cinema. The notion of the West as 'a touchstone of national identity' (O'Connor and Rollins 2005: 2) is increasingly questioned in Westerns from the 1960s onwards, and even though director John Ford is the creator of the quintessential Western character, the 'John Wayne persona' (Redding 2007: 317), Ford's late Westerns (such as *The Man Who Shot Liberty Valance*, 1962) expose 'a kind of ideological exhaustion: not only can the old myths no longer sustain us, we would be foolish to suppose that they ever could' (ibid., 320). In analogy to Ford's late Western, the other Ford's plays can also be read as weary of their time – as decadent plays. It may therefore not come as a surprise that Carla Dente's brief definition of literary decadence also reads like an enumeration of many of the aspects that critics have identified in Carter's fiction: 'The diseases most commonly associated with the idea of decadence are sensationalism, egocentricity, an insistent search for the bizarre, artificiality, flippancy and sometimes even perversity' (Dente 1999: 27). She reads *'Tis Pity She's a Whore* as a transitional work which is notable for its exploration of transgression, especially for its (rhetorical) transgression of Renaissance cultural codes.

Like late Jacobean and Caroline tragedy or late Ford Westerns, Carter's tale is weary of myths and cultural legacy. While her narrator tries to stage Johnny in terms of the frontiersman, she has to concede that the youth does not live up to Western conventions – 'No cowboy, he, roaming the plains' (Carter 1995d: 336). The fragility of the frontier myth becomes even more obvious when Annie-Belle pragmatically instrumentalizes it to explain her scandalous pregnancy and makes the father's child a 'stranger from the west' (ibid., 340, 343). The myth of the frontier and the West is thus deconstructed and debunked at the same time as it is evoked. Carter's tale elaborates on the element of decadence as a concept that links the myth of the West, which has lost its cultural currency in Ford's late Westerns, to the decadence of Jacobean and early Caroline tragedy. At the same time, even though film would appear to be the medium closer to her readers, the narrator drily points out that Jacobean Ford could be more sensationalist and excessive in his depictions of violence than the Hollywood director. The 'final note' of the story highlights that

> [t]he Old World John Ford made Giovanni cut out Annabella's heart and carry it on stage; the stage direction reads: *Enter Giovanni, with a heart upon his dagger.* The New World John Ford would have no means of representing this scene on celluloid, although it is irresistibly reminiscent of the ritual tortures practised by the Indians who lived here before. (ibid., 348; italics original)

Ironically, the film's greater realism limits its visual representation of violence.

It is in the topic of incest that the story finds its most persuasive restaging of the Renaissance play. Generally speaking, incest threatens the purity of society. Russell West argues convincingly that within the context of Ford's play, what is dramatized is an early modern anxiety generated by the evolving place of women within the social exchange, and consequently the instability of patriarchal relations. He states that the 'intrusive eruption of feminine self-determination rehearsed in the figure of incest would thus be built onto a new gender configuration through a recuperating adjustment well-fitted to the emergent merchant capitalist society' (West 2004: 159). Carter's changed setting naturally involves a new ideological framework; in the West as she describes it, the politics of the marriage marketplace are subordinated to those of the emergent American identity which remains, as Sarah Gamble has pointed out, intrinsically tied to its European origins. Incest becomes 'a failure of the imagination, a self-absorbed narcissism' (Gamble 2007: 37). At the same time, and similar to its treatment in *The Magic Toyshop*, incest does have the potential to challenge oppressive patriarchal power structures; in the words of Gina Wisker, it is 'the sickness of society, the oppressive nature of patriarchy, which is threatened by incest' (Wisker 2006: 193). In the play, Giovanni and Annabella can be seen as both the products and the victims of an immoral society that is 'beyond all political or moral control, without a common code of behaviour' (McCabe 2006: 314) – and the same is true for their Western counterparts, whose relationship is doomed to fail because it is unable to 'break out of the multilayered cycle of story in which it is so firmly embedded' (Gamble 2007: 37).

Conclusion

All three texts privilege female or sexually ambivalent voices that are buried in the original texts – quite literally so in the case of Poe and Ford. This notion of feminist revision allows Carter to reinscribe Elizabeth Poe into her son's work, to re-sexualize the fairies, and, possibly, to make Annabella's fate at least a little easier: while she has to carry the complete weight of moral censure in Ford's play, Carter's Annie-Belle seems to have found a way out – her husband is willing to raise her unborn child as his own and offers her a fresh start, and while Annabella's body is melodramatically mutilated in the Jacobean text while her brother is granted a respectable burial, Johnny's body in Carter's Western does not fare any better than his sister's.[12] Carter therefore also appropriates the Western as a drama of masculinity for her own complex explorations of gender politics.

In 'Notes from the Front Line', Carter emphatically declared that she felt

> free to loot and rummage in an official past, specifically a literary past. . . . This past, for me, has important decorative, ornamental functions; further, it is a vast repository of outmoded lies, where you can check out what lies used to be à la mode and find the old lies on which the new lies have been based. (Carter 1998a: 41)

It is characteristic of her work in general, but specifically of the texts that I have analysed, that Carter does not merely 'rummage' in the past; rather, she consciously chooses to playfully and subversively re-stage specific authors, texts and contexts. At the same time, the exaggerated and amusing theatricality of all three tales can be seen as a deliberate attempt to control reader reactions. With reference to Poe's 'Fall of the House of Usher', Carter notes that his 'theatricality ensures we know all the time that the scenery is cardboard, the blade of the axe is silver paint on papier maché, the men and women in the stories unreal, two-dimensional stock characters, yet still we shiver' (Carter 1998b: 482). The same is true for Carter's tales: by denying her readers the possibility to immerse themselves in these tales or to fully identify with any of the characters, she forces them to think about the ideology that informs the more traditional receptions of Poe's tales, Shakespeare's fairies, the early modern canon and the American Western. At the same time, Carter's texts certainly also make their readers shiver: it is due to their insistent use of allusions that all three texts open up a powerful ideological field of contexts and connotations that allows – and sometimes even forces – readers to explore multiple readings of texts and contexts.

Carter's staging of canonical texts also reinforces an approach that she had already used for her fairy tale revisions in *The Bloody Chamber*: in arguing against the seemingly universal validity of fairy tales, Carter emphasized a notion of fairy tales as unique and individual products, shaped by historical and cultural contexts and their authors: 'Is there a definitive recipe for potato soup?', she asks. 'Think in terms of the domestic arts. "This is how *I* make potato soup" ' (Carter 2005: xii). The theatricality of Carter's appropriations of canonical material opens up multiple readings without ever exploring them fully. By multiplying the canon, by giving a voice to the marginal or by reinscribing a text into the canon via the popular visual currency of the Western, Carter effectively unhinges the canon. All three texts are characterized by an awareness of literary constructions created by the canon as overly simplistic, and expose the ideological agenda inherent in these constructions. Carter's 'un-canonized' canon forces us to think about our own attempts to frame and control the literary past, and gives us license to create our own access to this past. This is, in short, how *Carter* makes potato soup – and her version of the canon.

Notes

1 Famously, Jacques Derrida responded to Lacan's text by pointing out reductive aspects of Lacan's reading of Poe. A whole collection of essays, *The Purloined Poe: Lacan, Derrida, and Pschoanalytic Reading* (1988) is devoted to their debate. For a discussion of the 'dispute' between Lacan and Derrida, see Harvey's 'Structures of Exemplarity in Poe, Freud, Lacan, and Derrida' (1988) in this collection or Stockholder's 'Is Anybody at Home in the Text?: Psychoanalysis and the Question of Poe' (2000).
2 Ernest Jones's *Hamlet and Oedipus* (1949) continues and elaborates on Freud's 'diagnosis' of Hamlet's Oedipus complex in 'Psychopathic Characters on Stage' (1904) and has become one of the most well-known examples of Freudian literary criticism.
3 For a similar argument see Douglas Lanier's more recent *Shakespeare and Modern Popular Culture* (2002): Lanier highlights that '[o]ne of a very few literary figures who have a double life in contemporary culture, Shakespeare is recognizable to highbrow and lowbrow audiences . . ., and serves important iconic functions in both canonical and popular culture' (Lanier 2002: 18).
4 For a detailed analysis of Victorian fairies on the stage see J. W. Stedman, 'Victorian Imitations of and Variations on *A Midsummer Night's Dream* and *The Tempest*' (1986).

5   It is more than mere coincidence that Richard Dadd has played a central role in Carter's writing – she even produced an 'artificial' biography of him in her radio play *Come Unto These Yellow Sands* (1979). 'Come unto these Yellow Sands' (1842), which draws on Shakespeare's *Tempest*, is also one of Dadd's most famous fairy paintings.

6   In *The Passion of New Eve*, Mother is the personification of the overwhelming fertility of the female body. In a similar fashion, Titania's fecundity is overwhelming: 'She is like a double bed; or, a table laid for a wedding breakfast; or, a fertility clinic. In her eyes are babies. When she looks at you, you helplessly reduplicate' (Carter 1995c: 280).

7   Although the 'Cockney Venus' (Carter 1994: 7) sports wings and a carefully bleached hair-do, she is neither fragile nor ethereal – as her appetite and table manners prove: 'She gorged, she stuffed herself, she spilled gravy on herself, she sucked up peas from the knife; she had a gullet to match her size and table manners of the Elizabethan variety' (ibid., 22).

8   When Titania calls him 'boy', Golden Herm notes that 'She's censoring me, there, she's rendering me unambiguous in order to get the casting director out of a tight spot' (Carter 1995c: 272).

9   The story was first written and published in 1988, a year in which Carter's lifelong interest in film (see, for example, her depiction of Hollywood diva Tristessa in *The Passion of New Eve*) also resulted in a review on publications about classical Hollywood cinema (see Carter 1998d: 384–6).

10 In his monograph *Early Modern Tragedy and the Cinema of Tragedy* (2006), Stevie Simkin also points out the close proximity of Jacobean drama and film when he notes that a number of critics refer, almost always in passing, to the common elements of revenge tragedy and contemporary violent cinema, and suggests an 'affinity between the frequently explicit and inventive violence of early modern tragedy . . . and the graphic violence that finds its way into a number of different genres of popular film' (Simkin 2006: 3–4).

11 See, most notably, *The Magic Toyshop*.

12 See Wisker, who maintains that, in contrast to Edgar Allan Poe's female characters, 'many of Carter's beautiful dead, un-dead, or near dead women refuse to lie down forever. Her protagonists are feistier, empowered, twentieth-century women who narrowly escape incarceration, deification, reification and death' (Wisker 2006: 196).

Works Cited

Beddoe, S. (1997), 'Fairy Writing and Writers', in Jane Martineau (ed.), *Victorian Fairy Painting*, London: Merrell Holberton, 23–31.

Bloom, C. (1988), *Reading Poe, Reading Freud: The Romantic Imagination in Crisis*, New York: St. Martin's Press.

Bloom, H. (1994), *The Western Canon: The Books and School of the Ages*, New York, San Diego and London: Harcourt Brace.

Carter, A. (1994) [1984], *Nights at the Circus*, London: Vintage.

—(1995a) [1974], 'Afterword to *Fireworks*', in *Burning Your Boats: The Collected Short Stories*, London: Chatto & Windus, 459–60.

—(1995b) [1985], 'The Cabinet of Edgar Allan Poe', in *Burning Your Boats: The Collected Short Stories*, London: Chatto & Windus, 262–72.

—(1995c) [1985], 'Overture and Incidental Music for *A Midsummer Night's Dream*', in *Burning Your Boats: The Collected Short Stories*, London: Chatto & Windus, 273–83.

—(1995d) [1988], 'John Ford's *'Tis Pity She's a Whore*', in *Burning Your Boats:The Collected Short Stories*, London: Chatto & Windus, 332–48.

—(1998a) [1983], 'Notes from the Front Line', in Jenny Uglow (ed.), *Shaking a Leg: Collected Writings*, New York et al.: Penguin, 36–43.

—(1998b) [1988], 'Through a Text Backwards: The Resurrection of the House of Usher', in Jenny Uglow (ed.), *Shaking a Leg: Collected Writings*, New York et al.: Penguin, 482–90.

—(1998c) [1976], 'The Better to Eat You With', in Jenny Uglow (ed.), *Shaking a Leg: Collected Writings*, New York et al.: Penguin, 451–5.

—(1998d) [1988], 'Hollywood', in Jenny Uglow (ed.), *Shaking a Leg: Collected Writings*, New York et al.: Penguin, 384–6.

—(2005) [1990], 'Introduction', in Angela Carter (ed.), *Angela Carter's Book of Fairy Tales*, London: Virago, xi–xxiv.

Dente, C. (1999), 'Reading Symptoms of Decadence in Ford's *'Tis Pity She's a Whore*', in Michael Saint John (ed.), *Romancing Decay: Ideas of Decadence in European Culture*, Aldershot: Ashgate, 27–38.

Felman, S. (1988), 'On Reading Poetry: Reflections on the Limits and Possibilities of Psychoanalytical Approaches', in John P. Muller and William J. Richardson (eds), *The Purloined Poe: Lacan, Derrida and Psychoanalytic Reading*, Baltimore and London: Johns Hopkins University Press, 138–56.

Gamble, S. (2007), 'History as Story in Angela Carter's *American Ghosts and Old World Wonders*', in Ann Heilmann and Mark Llewellyn (eds), *Metafiction and Metahistory in Contemporary Women's Writing*, Basingstoke and New York: Palgrave Macmillan, 30–44.

Harvey, I. (1988), 'Structures of Exemplarity in Poe, Freud, Lacan, and Derrida', in John P. Muller and W. J. Richardson (eds), *The Purloined Poe: Lacan, Derrida and Psychoanalytic Reading*, Baltimore and London: Johns Hopkins University Press, 252–67.

Jackson, R. (1997), 'Shakespeare's Fairies in Victorian Criticism and Performance', in Jane Martineau (ed.), *Victorian Fairy Painting*, London: Merrell Holberton, 39–45.

Jones, E. (1949), *Hamlet and Oedipus*, London: Gollancz.

Kokoli, A. M. (2002), '"The Cabinet of Edgar Allan Poe": Towards a Feminist Remodelling of (Meta)History', in *In-between*, 11.1, 55–70.

Lacan, J. (1988) [1966], 'Seminar on "The Purloined Letter"' in John P. Muller and William J. Richardson (eds), *The Purloined Poe: Lacan, Derrida and Psychoanalytic Reading*, Baltimore and London: Johns Hopkins University Press, 28–54.

Lanier, D. (2002), *Shakespeare and Modern Popular Culture*, Oxford: Oxford University Press.

Maas, J. (1997), 'Victorian Fairy Painting', in Jane Martineau (ed.), *Victorian Fairy Painting*, London: Merrell Holberton, 11–21.

McCabe, R. A. (2006), '*'Tis Pity She's a Whore* and Incest', in Garrett A. Sullivan, Patrick Cheney and Andrew Hadfield (eds), *Early Modern English Drama: A Critical Companion*, Oxford: Oxford University Press, 309–20.

O'Connor, J. E. and Rollins, P. C. (2005), 'Introduction: The West, Westerns, and American Character', in John E. O'Connor and Peter C. Rollins (eds), *Hollywood's West: The American Frontier in Film, Television, and History*, Lexington: University Press of Kentucky, 1–34.

Redding, A. (2007), 'Frontier Mythographies: Savagery and Civilization in Frederick Jackson Turner and John Ford', in *Literature/Film Quarterly*, 35.4, 313–22.

Sage, L. (1992), 'Angela Carter Interviewed by Lorna Sage', in Malcolm Bradbury and Judy Cooke (eds), *New Writing*, London: Vintage, 185–93.

Sanders, J. (2002), *Novel Shakespeares: Twentieth-Century Women Novelists and Appropriation*, Manchester and New York: Manchester University Press.

—(2006), 'Bubblegum and Revolution: Angela Carter's Hybrid Shakespeare', in Rebecca Munford (ed.), *Re-Visiting Angela Carter: Texts, Contexts, Intertexts*, Basingstoke and New York: Palgrave Macmillan, 110–34.

Simkin, S. (2006), *Early Modern Tragedy and the Cinema of Violence*, Basingstoke and New York: Palgrave Macmillan.

Stedman, J. W. (1986), 'Victorian Imitations of and Variations on *A Midsummer Night's Dream* and *The Tempest*', in Richard Foulkes (ed.), *Shakespeare and the Victorian Stage*, Cambridge: Cambridge University Press, 180–95.

Stockholder, K. (2000), 'Is Anybody at Home in the Text?: Psychoanalysis and the Question of Poe', in *American Imago*, 57.3, 299–333.

Tonkin, M. (2004), 'The "Poe-etics" of Decomposition: Angela Carter's "The Cabinet of Edgar Allan Poe" and the Reading-Effect', in *Women's Studies*, 33.1, 1–21.

West, R. (2004), 'Realigning Desire in Early Modern Social Exchange: Feminine Sexuality, Incest and Gender Coercion in Ford's *'Tis Pity She's a Whore*', in Stephan Laqué and Enno Ruge (eds), *Realigning Renaissance Culture: Intrusion and Adjustment in Early Modern Drama*, Trier: WVT, 149–60.

Wisker, G. (2006), 'Behind Locked Doors: Angela Carter, Horror and the Influence of Edgar Allan Poe', in Rebecca Munford (ed.), *Re-Visiting Angela Carter: Texts, Contexts, Intertexts*, Basingstoke and New York: Palgrave Macmillan, 178–98.

6

The Moral Right of Food: Angela Carter's 'Food Fetishes'[1]

Maria José Pires

Alluding to V. S. Pritchett who said that he swallowed Dickens whole at the risk of indigestion, Guido Almansi states that he swallows Carter whole, and then rushes to buy Alka Seltzer. I cannot but agree with him and Emma Parker, who are not satisfied with the 'minimalist' *nouvelle cuisine*, but who need a 'maximalist' writer (Almansi 1994: 217; Parker 2000: 141). Carter's narratives evoke *so much*, through extreme and surreal events, flamboyant and outlandish characters, intense and heightened emotions, superb and appalling obscenities and through astonishing, highly decorated language. Carter raises myriad social and political issues in her fiction and non-fiction works, but when reading her journalism, it is interesting to note how frequently she performs the role of a daring tourist surveying the idiosyncrasies of both Western and Eastern cultures. Food itself permeates Carter's oeuvre, through references to diet, which are visible both in her fictional texts, in terms of what and how her characters eat, and in her non-fiction work, particularly her essays about her time abroad and her little known food writing.

Bearing in mind that Carter's oeuvre is a continuous source of moral thinking, her journalism should be understood as part of this ongoing process of writing and not as an independent category. Her somehow neglected collection of journalism and shorter writings *Shaking a Leg* (1998) may be read as an illustration of Carter's mind at work. In the introduction, Joan Smith points out the way in which the articles and reviews approach a subject from diverse angles and focal points, almost like conducting an experiment. Yet, this is not done in a hesitant way, but in a fervently engaged manner which encourages the reader not only to consider Carter's perspectives but to argue back. These short texts from the late 1960s to the very early 1990s show a writer who is a persistently acute observer of the social world and they act, simultaneously, as pointers that can chart a course along the fiction work – from the description of a pub scene in the first lines of *Shadow Dance* (1965), setting the camp tone and preparing the reader for the moment when the monstrously-scarred Ghislaine reappears and accosts an appalled Morris, to the celebration of life in *Wise Children* (1991), which joyously evokes the odds and ends of a lifetime spent on both sides of the tracks by the Chance sisters.

If Brecht said he would be remembered for his line in *The Three Penny Opera*: 'Food is the first thing, morals follow on' (1928), in which he satirized his German bourgeois audience, and its sizeable respect for both religion and money, Carter is not especially remembered for writing about food. However, Brecht's implication that our first priority is to be fed because we are nothing more than animals, is not far from some of Carter's inferences. Indeed, if diet has become a matter of morality, Angela Carter's two articles 'The New Vegetarians' and 'Saucerer's Apprentice', both originally published in *New Society* and collected in *Shaking a Leg*, may attest to that. These articles, which provide evidence of Carter's interest in food-related issues, are the first ones in the selection entitled 'Food Fetishes' and were published just a month apart from each other, on the 4 March and 8 April, 1976 respectively.

When we think of food, the well-known saying 'tell me what you eat . . . and I'll tell you who you are' comes to mind.[2] This has always been taken as a truism in an individual sense, but, more and more it is used when characterizing the identity of a country at a global level, as well as at the regional level through the different cultural and geographical resources of the country. Still, the important factor here is not so much *what* you eat – 'you are what you eat' – but *how* you eat. Food, without which man cannot survive, is an unquestionable protagonist in the social, political and economic evolution of history. As Sceats argues, it is a basic social signifier, a holder of interpersonal and cultural meanings:

> It is, and has been, constructed as symbolic in all sorts of ways, either intentionally (Passover, the Eucharist), through custom (harvest suppers and hot cross buns) or by commerce (the 'ploughman's lunch'); the resonances are, initially at least, culture-specific. (Sceats 2000: 125)

Accordingly, many of the important questions about food habits are moral and social. The ethical dimensions of foodways, agricultural practice and cultural meaning are undeniably central to several pedagogies.[3] Yet, we can also flip this assertion around to suggest that many moral and social questions can be answered by examining food. Our consumption of food takes place within a wider framework in which foods are produced, regulated, represented and associated with specific identities (Ashley *et al.* 2004: 60). From a historical perspective, the main fields associated with food consumption have been those concerned with diet, nutrition and health. Furthermore, even tastes of certain quantities, qualities and types of food are often taken as signs of the moral and cultural worth of different social groups' lifestyles. Also, tastes are related to broader aesthetic and moral classification, legitimatizing some tastes more than others.[4] A person's attitude towards food can therefore reveal not just personality traits but an entire *food ideology*, as well; a set of beliefs that encompasses a whole way of thinking about the world, and usually an ideal way of being in that world. Most food ideologies promise the individual that if s/he eats in this special way s/he will become a better, happier, more successful and more moral individual. This is definitively something that Carter challenges in her piece on 'The New Vegetarians'. The article describes the way an activist aesthetic of unrefinement changed into one of refinement, and explores the ethical dimensions of both consumption and non-consumption, just as vegetarianism itself does.

Carter begins 'The New Vegetarians' by introducing her neighbourhood wholefood shop as a recognized example of what Nicholas Saunders, in *Alternative England and Wales* (1975) calls a 'genre masterpiece'.[5] As Carter describes the furniture and the food commodities, these seem to irradiate health in an attempt to eradicate unwholesome contamination:

> There are baskets of splendid cabbages of many different kinds, of leeks, of kale, of ruddy-cheeked apples blotched and wenned as if on purpose so you can see at a glance no chemical spray has been near them . . . and all manner of cookies and flapjacks and goodies made with honey and dates and raisins, all the natural sweetenings – never a trace of the killer white sugar. (Carter 1998a: 79)

This concern about sugar seems to come from the shop's origins as a 'regular macrobiotic food shop'. According to Carter, the first sign of the decline of the shop came with selling tomatoes, a fruit she ironically labels as 'poison' for being outside of that theory or practice of promoting well-being and longevity, above all by means of a diet consisting chiefly of whole grains and beans.

Carter also mentions the shop's concern with recycling and the curious discount of a penny or two if customers weigh their own beans and grains. Since one cannot be part of the production of their 'peasant comestibles', one may at least participate in the process before the consuming part. Carter lists some of the 'peasant comestibles' on offer and an attentive reader recognizes how international food had become – moong beans originally from India, buckwheat domesticated first in southeast Asia, aduki beans from China and Korea, whole yellow millets (from China, Korea and India), pot barley from Syria and Egypt, lentils originally from Near East/South Asia, black-eyed beans from China, India and the Middle East, and brown rice from Asia. The globalization of food production has increased greatly since Carter was writing in the 1970s; nevertheless, in the case of pulses, fruit, nuts and cereals specified by Carter the globalization process was already well underway.[6] According to Carter, the health food shop and the vegetarian movement that underpins it represents 'a positive aesthetic of unrefinement transformed into refinement' (Carter 1998a: 79); the index of such an improvement or elaboration is the carrots' roots that 'retain a substantial coating of the earth that bore them', quite different from the supermarkets scrubbed ones in their 'condom-like plastic sheath' (ibid., 79–80). The former sometimes even come from Paradise Farm and so Carter concludes that these must be the *real* carrots, that is, having verifiable existence, not artificial or spurious. Carter discerns an underlying food ideology at work in which 'wholefood makes you a whole person' and diet becomes a matter of morality; identifying the shop's religious overtones, she comments, 'there's something of the air of a Non-conformist chapel about this shop' (ibid., 80).

To put Carter's observations about vegetarianism in context, meat is, in fact, across all cultures 'by far the most common focus of taboo, regulation and avoidance' (Twigg 1983: 18) since there are profoundly implanted associations between religion and the complete avoidance of meat or compulsory banning of particular types of meat. However, it is also a fact that such religious taboos have, to some extent, survived beyond the downfall of religion as the most important set of values by which the majority of westerners live; even though, as Bob Ashley states, the shift from pre-modernity to modernity marks a break from other positions towards meat-eating (Ashley *et al.*, 2004: 189). What is more, meat avoidance may relate to broad social and cultural changes, such as the growth of bourgeois culture or even the rise of the urban middle-classes (Mennell 1996: 307), and to a sentimentalization of animals along with a general faith in human progress towards a stronger bond with nature.[7] It is noteworthy that the Vegetarian Society was founded in the UK as early as 1847. On the other hand, notwithstanding a growing loss of confidence in the teleological view of the world in the post-war period, the Vegetarian Society claims to have witnessed a major growth in vegetarianism since the 1970s, which suggests a complex relationship between food and social change.

Food consumption is, moreover, related to economic and cultural capital and it can be used to demonstrate and generate social capital. For Pierre Bourdieu the rise of the new middle classes is based in new service industries and white-collar jobs rather than more traditional professions, which transforms the social space of class relations. The new bourgeoisie rejects the moderation of the old bourgeoisie in favour of a self-indulgent moral of consumption. These new classes seek to achieve a sense of distinction through what is often called the 'aestheticization of everyday life'. Accordingly, the means to make the dispositions of these classes visible, as they practice distinction, can be done through food (Bourdieu 1984: 190). A similar point about taste and distinction is made by Carter in these two short texts, and seems to be implicitly present in some of her fiction work. A year after writing the two articles considered here, Carter's fifth novel *The Passion of New Eve* (1977) portrays the misogynistic tyrant Zero whose relation to his female followers can be read from the beginning in terms of a social and economic perspective on food. Whereas, his female followers 'did not think they were fit to pick up the crumbs from his [Zero's] table, at which he always ate in solitary splendour' (Carter 1982: 85), we learn how they were the ones financially keeping parasitic Zero well-fed throughout the winter by buying him and his dog 'good red meat' (ibid., 98). In addition, Zero's female counterpart, Mother, bets on the social capital in her community generated, in part, by a diet which embodies her system of moral determinations.

Furthermore, one of the main ways through which food politics and food ethics became more and more visible springs from the political radicalism associated with the counter-cultures of the late 1960s and 1970s (Ashley *et al.*, 2004: 190). Stephen Mennell stresses historical change as the main trigger for ongoing changes in human food systems, minimizing the significance of the idea that class differences in food consumption are still relevant differences in the economic, social and cultural area. Nevertheless, there has been a great concern with the 'persistence of social differentiation' (Warde 1997: 39) for sociologists. For example, Michael Nelson's review of historical changes in the British diet from 1860 to 1980 suggests a persisting class difference in terms of food consumption, while Mark Tomlinson demonstrates such persistence in food tastes in the late 1980s and early 1990s. In her journalism, Carter emphasizes a similar moral and class distinction, which is still evident in her last novel, *Wise Children* (1991), through a variety of references to the food choices of both the Chance and Hazard families.[8]

Emphasizing food as 'moral right', 'The New Vegetarians' describes a scene in which a vegetarian declares a plate filled with potatoes to be *really* good and nice and chants 'Dead Pig!' at the sausage sitting on his neighbour's plate. Such a 'display of moral superiority' accepts no substitutes – 'this is the real stuff. *Really* real' – but it is not enough to convert Carter who finds the pork delicious (Carter 1998a: 80)! Barbara Ellen, another fierce social critic, identifies a breed of 'New Veggies' who, she argues, are 'gate-crashing' the feast. She blames vegetarians for giving people 'permission' to eat sushi and organic chicken sandwiches in the name of vegetarianism, and considers modern vegetarians to have diluted their ethical criteria; stripped of its once exacting morality, vegetarianism therefore becomes increasingly meaningless (Ellen 2000). Although by no means so bitterly denunciatory, Carter endorses the idea of a morally based time-honoured vegetarianism even as she cannot concur with it.

Carter views the New Vegetarianism as an 'alternative growth industry, a dietary sign system indicating spiritual awareness, expanded consciousness and ecological concern' which sets it apart from the old vegetarianism portrayed by her as 'part of a lifestyle embracing socialism, pacifism and shorts, a simple asceticism expressing a healthy contempt for the pleasure of the flesh' (Carter 1998a: 81). The quoting of the Old London music hall song 'Boiled beef and carrots' by Charles Collins and Fred Murray cheekily encourages the reader to question a vegetarian diet, consisting of food they give to parrots. What Carter is at pains to suggest is that diet goes beyond the usual food and drink of a person or animal and becomes a way of living.[9] To provide evidence for the view that eating has become a quasi-religious experience, Carter cites *Super Natural Cookery*, which contains a quotation from the epigraph of the ancient Sanskrit text *Bhagavad Gita*. Carter accuses the cookbook of using a 'curiously flabby language' and 'a tone of sneering patronage' to approach what is considered to be a sacramental food experience (ibid.). Other manuals which appear to Carter to aim at a hearty joyousness are decorated with drawings that turn out to be embarrassing: 'I mean *really*' (ibid.). The *East West Journal* is also cited by Carter and she emphasizes immediately the contrast between the big and 'fat' size of this American magazine and its content; although geared towards healthy food, it was itself far from slender. Highlighting the movement's moralistic and spiritual overtones, Carter cites the first macrobiotic experience of a young man, which demonstrates the New Vegetarian belief that one can chew one's way 'back to a lost harmony with nature' (ibid.).

It is the choice of words, 'Food that was *alive*', in the *East West Journal* that Carter finds so curious since its author embraces the mythology of a benign nature by making himself a 'healing' farm. She sardonically compares this version of benign nature to the one that Voltaire felt had been shaken by the Lisbon Earthquake on All Saints' Day, 1755, which killed 30,000 people in six minutes. How, Carter asks, has that elusive harmony with nature been lost? It is apparently through the 'ritual consumption of sufficient quantities of wholefood' (ibid., 82) that man will theoretically be able to restore such lost harmony, according to the New Vegetarianism. As Carter poses the question, she refers to the fact that it was a shortage of elements in the original ape's diet (eggs, nestlings and fruits) that sent it down from the trees, exterminating other species and learning to kill other larger species (ibid.). She thus disputes the lost harmony ideology associated with a vegetarian way of living by suggesting how easy it is to turn into carnivores instead of omnivores. By using the term 'extermination', Carter stresses the non-adherence to conventionally accepted standards of conduct. Furthermore, the notion of carnivores covers predators and scavengers, who are either secondary or tertiary consumers in a food chain.

For Carter it comes as no surprise that 'the Aquarians and the New Age Seekers and the Natural Lifers turn against this unedifying scenario' (ibid.) of carnivorousness, which ostensibly turns humanity away from what is primary and original. In fact, one knows the Aquarians are called Hydroparastatae, because they offer water instead of wine in the Eucharist and they are also known as Encratites because they neither drink wine nor eat animal food (from which they abstain because they abhor it and see it as something evil); as for the New Age Seekers, they believe we are now on the threshold of 'the Aquarian Age' where universal love and harmony will come. Carter does not procrastinate on these groups' beliefs, but she summarizes their perspective through the reference to *Seed*, the Forum of Natural Living, and its brisk refutation of Darwin's evolutionary theory. The reader of 'The New Vegetarians' may include here the consumption of 'good' food as physically and morally nutritious since it is presented most often as a duty. There are those chefs, for example, for whom 'cooking is contextualized as a practical and social skill' (Strange 1998: 310) and thus is used as a key motif of lifestyle – the promise of having and taking the opportunity we all have of improving ourselves through making over our lives. Furthermore, the concept of 'good' food practices no longer simply refers to nutritional value, but carries with it moral and aesthetic values (Ashley *et al.*, 2004: 62,182). Such assumptions are embodied in the French gastronomer Auguste Escoffier's idea that good cooking is the basis of good living (cited by Rhodes and Blake 1996: 10).

The notion of 'grain, the foundation of civilization' (*East West Journal*) and the ability to see the universe in a grain of wheat 'and heaven in a wholewheat loaf' (according to a Harmony Foods advert in *Seed*) justify Carter's conclusion that indeed the New Vegetarianism conceives man as a microcosm, whose system has been poisoned with 'meat, white sugar, refined flour, chemical additives' (Carter 1998a: 82). The self-sufficient farming unit becomes for those whom Carter scathingly refers to as 'freaks' a dream of a model of environment over which the maximum control may be exerted. This process of production, nonetheless, ensues as regulation, since these macrobiotic/natural diets are control systems in themselves – 'Dietary self-policing will keep the demons of physic disorder away' (ibid.). This amounts to a matter of absolute control of man himself, the microcosm, and of life, the macrocosm. Carter ends the article depicting the process as another example of consumption. In the form of religious communion, the elected people consume 'casseroles of chickpeas and wheat grains, or lentil and sesame paste pasties, or mixed bean stews' (ibid.). Both casseroles and the cooking method, stewing, are closely related to British cuisine. Evidently Carter does not ignore the ritual aspect of this gathering scene, as they would mutter 'It's really good' and 'This is really nice' (ibid., 80). Hence, the reference to Edward Gibbon's thought about how the primitive Christians' similar ritual was the last little burden or problem that caused everything to collapse in the Roman Empire.

The meaning of the individual and collective consumption of goods, more precisely food in this case, has been increasingly understood as central to any successful comprehension of the modern world. Roland Barthes highlights the centrality of food to other forms of social behaviour, when he speaks of the need for a 'veritable grammar of food' (Barthes 1997: 22) to clarify the variety of modern social activities. As he believes, a certain food behaviour replaces, sums up and signals other behaviours, like 'activity, work, sports, effort, leisure, celebration' and, accordingly, 'we might almost say that this polysemia' of food characterizes modernity (ibid., 25). One such example of food as social behaviour is discussed in Carter's article 'Saucerer's Apprentice', also published in *New Society*. It focuses on Elizabeth David's 'Gospel of Good Food' as the end of an era 'in which middle-class, educated Englishwomen took a positive pride in an inability even to boil an egg' (Carter 1998b: 83). The title of the article is made clear by the example Carter gives of 'mint sauce', which English women, before David, made by just adding a 'scant spoonful of dried mint in a cup of malt vinegar' (ibid.). This example sets the tone for the article, which compares the 'darkness' of the period when food was simply the necessary fuel for the English cuisine – 'in which the sensuous appreciation of food and drink had no place' – and what she terms 'Elizabeth Davidisation' (ibid.). The culinary result is as follows:

> [All this] newly lovingly prepared food is a curious, hybrid cuisine, based on a vividly eclectic compilations of elements from other cultures and derived from the printed word rather than, as in countries with a vigorous traditional cuisine, one mother's example. (ibid.)

Carter identifies the emergence of a new class of 'foodie', coming from a post-war generation whose meals derived from the scarce pickings of the depression – 'the marge and spam and dried eggs of the 1940s'. The striking feature about David's writing in the 1950s was that it offered the kind of food of which dreams are made at the end of a period of austerity when the 'standardized, government-regulated, plain but adequate diet' (ibid., 84) was the norm.

The importance of the Education Act of 1944 to this change makes sense, according to Carter, if we consider that one of its effects was to educate and mobilize women and the working class, and increase their awareness of their disadvantaged social position. Carter recognizes that equal opportunities and an educational system do not necessarily guarantee social equality. In terms of Bourdieu, moral reproduction (i.e. the transmission of values, virtues and competences) serves as a base to the legitimate filiation of distinct habitus, considering that habitus is grounded on the principle of the immediate affinities which coordinate the social relations and choices. Carter views such experiences as playing an important part in one's life, which David's work takes advantage of, as Carter acknowledges in a 1982 article about *English and Yeast Cookery*, also by David.

Moreover, food can embody a sense of place as well as status. David's description of place allows her readers to travel vicariously, as Carter quotes from *French Provincial Cooking*:

> Here in London, it is an effort of will to believe in the existence of such a place at all. But now and again the vision of golden tiles on a round southern roof or of some warm, stony, herb-scented hillside will rise out of my kitchen pots with

the smell of a piece of orange peel scenting a beef stew. (Carter 1998b: 84; David 1970: 23)

David's verbal magic permits the process of cooking and consumption to transcend time and place in what Carter sees as 'pure witchcraft'. Her sardonic tone is evident as she underlines how precious it is for the reader of David's books to get the knowledge without going through the 'inevitable disillusionment of actual travel' (Carter 1998b: 84). Accordingly, Carter ponders on the 'exquisite alienation' of such a cuisine which involves the imaginative reconstruction of another country, and depends on a service industry to provide the ingredients and utensils to back up this magic – notice the clever choice of adjectives in 'esoteric vinegars, obscure cheeses' (ibid.). Still, even David perceives the changes brought about by the Industrial Revolution as it simplified things and put an end to whatever native British peasant cookery might have existed.

On the other hand, as Carter reminds us, it is extreme poverty that brings the drastic simplification of a cuisine – 'Nothing destroys the palate like poverty; food as a sensuous experience is not the same thing as food which serves merely to alleviate hunger' (ibid., 85). David's *French Country Cooking* was first published when food rationing was still in force, in 1951, and although it necessarily 'contained suggestions as to what ingredients might be substituted for quantities of bacon, cream, eggs, meat stock, and so on' ('Preface to Second Edition'), the whole book heralds the rebirth of abundance. Its success lay in the way David focused on the nature of food, as much as it did on recipes – 'books for a generation that had forgotten what food was like. And also forgotten what Abroad was like' (ibid.). The current Penguin edition of *French Country Cooking* has a colour photograph on the cover, suggesting Mediterranean cuisine and health, but the former decorations by John Minton's etchings remain inside, still giving the book a certain period charm. Carter discusses the evolution of the covers, up until 1976, suggesting that the first edition of the book must have been an object of fantasy, one which had apparently become real. In her usual witty way, Carter concludes that over the time it has been in print

> [*French Country Cooking*] has accomplished the change from a dream guide to food as an aspect of the Good Life to a handbook of actual techniques for reconstructing the elements of the Good Life in your own kitchen. The fantasy of the age of austerity has become actualized on the scrubbed pine work surfaces of the age of affluence. And we are all cooks now.
> *Après* Elizabeth David *le deluge*. (ibid. 86)

Indeed, David's mission was to resuscitate fading and amnesiac palates with the prospect of dishes which would have been inconceivable at the time. Food had no need to be rich; it simply had to taste of something, to bear recognizable links to natural produce, and, most important, to be non-grey. Whether it ever saw light of day, or the candlelight of evening, was beside the point; the mere promise of it, David herself confessed, was a form of nourishment. Even if people could not very often make the dishes described in her books, she pointed out, 'it was stimulating to think about them' (David 1965: 12). That was why, on the first page of *A Book of Mediterranean Food*, David started with the Provencal dish *soupe au pistou* (a minestrone like summer soup that includes white beans, green beans, tomatoes, summer squash, potatoes and vermicelli) and its accompanying spoonful of aïllade (a very thick sauce based on a purée of garlic). The garlicky reek of Nice hit England full in the face, and the nation – or, at any rate, the middle classes – came back to life, according to Anthony Lane, who also states two decades later that the 'situation is reversed. We know too much about food (Lane 1995: 54).

Carter's two articles, 'The New Vegetarians' and 'Saucerer's Apprentice', may be read and studied as important commentaries on the evolving character of personal identity in relation to social and cultural changes within postmodern societies. For Carter, the new-wave Vegetarianism becomes visible as a way to regenerate man, by exulting food as a generous gift from nature. Like numerous cultural theorists before and after her, Carter is alive to the ways in which any food phenomenon involves the production of meanings and identities. In the story 'The Kitchen Child' (1985), for instance, Carter manages to create a whole world entangled in kitchen culture, from religion, to society, education and expertise. Believing that we use food as a way of establishing relationships and social positions, Carter chooses to demythologize what some believe to be the *real* real by questioning its supposed transcendence. A similar idea is implied in *The Passion of New Eve*, through the figure of the Count, a latent consumer who having 'willed his completion and destruction' (Sceats 2000: 109) turns out to be the food itself. As food, the Count attains a momentary consummation before dying. He represents one of many of Carter's characters who acknowledge their own identity while sharing moments of food consumption. During the 1970s, Carter's general demythologizing project is echoed in her journalism; in the two articles discussed here, 'The New Vegetarians' and 'Saucerer's Apprentice', her politically astute and very funny satire of the quasi-religious attitudes and principles of the various movements around food illustrate her ongoing critique of established and new circuits of culture.

Notes

1 'Food Fetishes' refers to the title of a section in *Shaking a Leg: Collected Journalism and Writings* (1998) which contains examples of Carter's food journalism including the two articles discussed here – 'The New Vegetarians' and 'Saucerer's Apprentice'.
2 The saying is based on the philosopher Ludwig Feuerbach's dictum that 'man is what he eats'.
3 The term 'foodways' is used by scholars to describe the study of what and why we eat and its meanings. See, for example, the refereed journal *Food and Foodways*, published by Taylor & Francis.
4 In British culture, for example, 'chips' are associated with what is seen as morally and aesthetically impoverished taste of the working class.
5 Nicholas Saunders was considered a free-thinking British figure of the 'alternative' movement from the 1970s and *Alternative London and Wales* includes chapters on homemaking, herbalism, community action, ecology, women and crafts, among others.
6 As Anthony Giddens states, the invention of new modes of refrigeration along with the use of container transportation have increasingly allowed food to be stored

for longer periods and to be delivered from across the world (Giddens 2006: 255). Furthermore, this consequent increase in the variety of food habits and tastes results in what Stephen Mennell terms a new 'culinary pluralism' where there is not one dominant culinary style (Mennell 1996: 329–31).

7 This idea is based on Adrian Franklin's work *Animals and Modern Cultures: A Sociology of Human-animal Relations in Modernity* (1999).

8 Although Bourdieu dismisses the notion that economic explanations by themselves account for class differences and credibly demonstrates this (through detailed statistical and epidemiological analysis), Carter's last novel, *Wise Children* shows how income may be a formative factor in what people eat.

9 This idea comes from the Greek (diaita) and Latin (diaeta) roots of the word 'diet'.

Works Cited

Almansi, G. (1994), 'In the Alchemist's Cave: Radio Plays', in Lorna Sage (ed.), *Flesh and the Mirror: Essays on the Art of Angela Carter*, London: Virago, 216–29.

Ashley, B., Hollows, J., Jones, S. and Taylor, B. (2004), *Food and Cultural Studies*, London and New York: Routledge.

Barthes, R. (1997), 'Toward a Psychosociology of Contemporary Food Consumption', in Carole Counihan and Penny Van Esterik (eds), *Food and Culture: A Reader*, London: Routledge, 20–7.

Bourdieu, P. (1984), *Distinction*, London: Routledge.

Brecht, B. (1993 [1928]), The Threepenny Opera, Baal, and the Mother, New York: Arcade Publishing.

Carter, A. (1982) [1977], *The Passion of New Eve*, London: Virago Press.

—(1996) [1985], 'The Kitchen Child', *Black Venus*, London: Vintage, 62–9.

—(1998a), 'The New Vegetarians', *Shaking a Leg: Collected Journalism and Writings*, London: Vintage, 79–83.

—(1998b), 'Saucerer's Apprentice', *Shaking a Leg: Collected Journalism and Writings*, London: Vintage, 83–6.

David, E. (1965), *A Book of Mediterranean Food* (1950), London: Penguin Books.

—(1970), *French Country Cooking* (1951), London: Penguin Books.

Ellen, B. (2000), 'There's a Moral Dimension to Being a Vegetarian – so Stuff the Chicken and let's get Radical', *Observer*, February 13, http://www.vegsoc.org.au/forum_messages.asp?Thread_ID=395&Topic_ID=10. Accessed 14 July 2008.

Franklin, A. (1999), *Animals and Modern Cultures: A Sociology of Human-Animal Relations in Modernity*, London: Sage Publications.

Gibbon, E. (2005) [1776], *The History of the Decline and Fall of the Roman Empire*, vol. 1, unabridged facsimile of the 1787 edition, Boston: Adamant Media Corporation.

Giddens, A. (2006), *Sociology*, 5th edition, Cambridge: Polity Press.

Lane, A. (1995), 'Look Back in Hunger', *The New Yorker* (18 December), vol. 71, editions 39–48, 53–4.

Mennell, S. (1996) [1985], *All Manners of Food: Eating and Taste in England and France from the Middle Ages to the Present*, Chicago: University of Illinois Press.

Nelson, M. (1993), 'Social-class Trends in British Diet, 1860–1980', in Catherine Geissler and Derek J. Oddy (eds), *Food, Diet and Economic Change: Past and Present*, Leicester: Leicester University Press, 101–20.

Parker, E. (2000), 'The Consumption of Angela Carter: Women, Food, and Power', *Ariel: A Review of International English Literature*, vol. 31 (3), Calgary: University of Calgary, 141–69.

Rhodes, G. and Blake, A. (1996), *Open Rhodes Around Britain*, London: BBC Books.

Saunders, N. (1975), *Alternative England and Wales*, Manchester: Philips Park.

Sceats, S. (2000), 'Food and Manners: Roberts and Ellis', *Food, Consumption and the Body in Contemporary Women's Fiction*, Cambridge: Cambridge University Press, 125–54.

Strange, N. (1998), 'Perform, Educate, Entertain: Ingredients of the Cookery Programme Genre', in Christine Geraghty and David Lusted (eds), *The Television Studies Book*, London: Hodder Arnold, 301–12.

Tomlinson, M. (1998), 'Changes in Tastes in Britain, 1985–92', *British Food Journal*, vol. 100 (6), 295–301.

Twigg, S. (1983), 'Vegetarianism and the Meanings of Meat', in Anne Murcott (ed.), *The Sociology of Food and Eating: Essays on the Sociological Significance of Food*, Gower International Library of Research & Practice, Aldershot: Ashgate, 18–30.

Warde, A. (1997), Consumption, Food and Taste: Culinary Antinomies and Commodity Culture, London: Sage Publications.

7

The Alchemy of Reading in Angela Carter's 'Alice in Prague *or* The Curious Room'

Michelle Ryan-Sautour

The Czechoslovakian cinema director Jan Svankmajer, also known as the 'alchemist of film' says: 'alchemy is about trying to connect things that you cannot connect, that are "un-connectable." Poetry is a parallel for alchemy, and alchemy is a parallel for poetry' (Svankmajer 1997). This analogy between literature and alchemy overflows into Angela Carter's short story aesthetics, as Svankmajer appears in a paratextual dedication for 'Alice in Prague *or* The Curious Room' (Carter 1990). The figure of the director, as well as his film *Alice* (1987) appear as the framing devices for a story that sets forth a flurry of alchemical references and baffling games with genre and the temporality of the intertextual utterance. Since the initial publication of this story, the term 'curious room' has frequently been cited in relation to Carter's work, and her ongoing questioning about origins and textual identity is underlined by a metafictional fragment set apart in the text:

> There's a theory, one I find persuasive, that the quest for knowledge is, at bottom, the search for the answer to the question: 'Where was I before I was born?'
>
> In the beginning was . . . what?
>
> Perhaps, in the beginning, there was a curious room, a room like this one, crammed with wonders; and now the room and all it contains are forbidden you, although it was made just for you, had been prepared for you since time began, and you will spend all your life trying to remember it. (Carter 1993a: 127)

A parallel is often drawn between the baroque medley of person, tense, register and intertext in Carter's fiction, and the obscure and often incongruent articles found in cabinets of curiosities, these 'curious rooms' of which the narrator speaks in this passage. The concept of the 'curious room' indeed seems to resonate with Carter's recurrent foregrounding of the thorny question of identity. Kim Evans' *Omnibus* 1992 video documentary, 'Angela Carter's Curious Room,' uses the metaphor through which to explore Carter's life and works. Susannah Clapp also borrows the title for Carter's posthumously collected dramatic works, *The Curious Room* (1997b).

Clapp has observed how: 'Angela Carter had a gift for making her ideas dance, for making a spectacle out of strenuous thought' (Clapp 1997: x), and Lorna Sage has commented on the inscription of Carter's intellectual vagrancy into her metafictional structures, and the resulting frustration of attempts to make connections: 'She is just not the kind of writer whose fiction abides interpretation with docility . . . she was an intellectual, of the vagrant self-appointed kind less common in Britain than in France or Italy; as a result, there's a generous amount of "metafictional" critical reflection built in' (Sage 1994: 19). 'The Curious Room'[1] is particularly daunting in its obscurity, and the relative absence of critical reflection about the piece, as compared to Carter's other writing, speaks strikingly of the story's tendency to challenge the reader's speculative grasp. Because of this 'vagrancy', the reader's cultural and literary repertory, or encyclopedia as Umberto Eco calls it,[2] is rarely adequate to decipher Carter's allusions. Even informed critics are compelled to furtively consult Google or Wikipedia resources, thus adopting a reading pattern of the hypertextual sort, continually going beyond the story to find meaning. Marina Warner has commented on this effect: 'I used to look up words all the time when reading her; but I also had to look up things she would mention, needing an illustrated encyclopaedia to understand the references to items and cuts of dress, to technical tools, to flora and fauna' (Warner 2001: 252–3).

It is the predominance of such reading effects that fosters an image of Carter in 'Alice in Prague *or* The Curious Room' as a figure that haunts the text, seemingly echoing the author's provocation: 'I like creeping up on people from behind and sandbagging them with an idea that maybe they hadn't thought of for themselves' (Carter 1992). This effect is heightened by narrative strategies that play upon degrees and types of reader involvement. It is in such pragmatic structures that power manifests itself in Carter's fiction, through the reader's interpellation by the alchemical transmutations staged in her texts. The performative dimension of Carter's fiction has been underlined on numerous occasions. However, I would like to shift the emphasis from theme and textual identity to refocus it on the forces of interpellation at work in reading, on what Carter's fiction *does*. As Sage has observed: 'this is performative and political writing, writing that means to *work*' (Sage 1994: 16). Carter has commented on the importance of curiosity as a 'moral function' in relation to literature, the 'moral compunction to explicate and to find out about things' (Carter 1985: 96). In this chapter I will take a closer look at how 'Alice in Prague *or* The Curious Room' stages this 'moral function', this will to explore, as a part of the political alchemy at work in Carter's writing.

The framing of the story has shifted from its initial publication in a 1990 volume of essays about 'Strangeness',[3] edited by Margaret Bridges, in which Carter first introduces 'The Curious Room'[4] as a 'piece of speculation in the form of a short story' (Carter 1990: 215). The text echoes the initial statement in Svankmajer's *Alice*, which begins with the words of Alice, broken up with pauses 'Alice thought to herself . . . now you will see a film . . . made for children . . . perhaps . . . but I nearly forgot . . . you must . . . close your eyes . . . otherwise . . . you won't see anything'. Carter's paratext reads: 'Alice said: "now you are going to read a story"' (ibid.).[5] A metafictional, critical dominant is thus highlighted from the start, and foreshadows the interweaving of fictional and historical intertexts that will follow. Carter's short texts blur the edges of fiction and critical, historical thought, playing with the realms of creative non-fiction, historiographic metafiction, and even the literary essay. Richard E. Lee, although sceptical about the label 'postmodern', observes how the short story form inherently embraces the postmodern ethic of favouring the fragment over the whole: 'Short fiction is always and already "new historical" in its celebration of the ort. And what more appropriate structure to evaluate than the idea of the title of a work of short fiction: an interesting version of synecdoche – of the part standing for the whole?' (Lee 2003: 109–10). By extending this observation to the title, he also points to paratext as a form of 'simulacra' that speaks to a 'dehistoricized history' (ibid., 110). Carter's work plays upon this effect with the choice of two titles which reflect different layers of historical and artistic fragments. The 'Alice in Prague' part was indeed added to the 1993 version. The reference to Svankmajer through the connection of 'Alice' and 'Prague' reveals a spiral of intertextual layering in search of the Alice hypotext, as Svankmajer's work is already a revision of Carroll's *Alice* series. The 'curious room' in addition to the speculation and intrigue it announces, and its play with Carroll's repetition of the word, also alludes to the tradition of *Kunskammer*, that is cabinets of curiosities, eclectic collections of objects from different parts of the world, and the period of the Renaissance. It is also worth noting the shift in the subtitle in the 1993 version from the aforementioned 'now you are going to read a story' to the conflicting modes of: 'In the city of Prague, once, it was winter' which raises the question: will the story deal with historical Prague, or will it tend towards the fairy tale in accordance with the atemporal resonance of 'once'? The first subtitle highlights a reflection about the fictional dimension of the story, and the second tends towards ambivalence about its generic status. In addition, Carter's introduction to the 1990 publication provides explanations and background information that fill in gaps and orient the reader's attention. This introduction does not appear in subsequent publications of the story. In fact the 1993 version includes the postscript, 'Alice was invented by a logician and therefore she comes from the world of nonsense, that is, from the world of *non-sense* – the opposite of common sense; this world is constructed by logical deduction and is created by language, although language shivers into abstractions within it' (Carter 1993a: 139), a statement that appears in the introduction of the 1990 version. Such shifts and tensions in paratextual framing highlight generic play as dominant, and are obvious suggestions of an underlying will to inform and involve the reader. In the 'floating effect' that occurs as the text resists generic appropriation a space can be found for potential transformations or transmutations in ideas. Generic play can in turn be transferred to the image of a slippery authorial figure, one who fosters ambiguity through textual instability.

The body of the text is stitched together from historical and intertextual fragments, in a story that as Milada Frankova notes 'has little plot and even less movement' (Frankova 1999: 129). Similarly Jeff Vandermeer comments on how the story 'breaks every rule of the conventional short story – zero dialogue; didactic lecturing; no plot – and yet it is a beautiful and self-contained fiction about the conflict and crosshatching between science/logic and non-sense' (Vandermeer 2001). The arrangement of blank spaces and text on the page emphasizes a discontinuity that requires the reader to draw connections between the seemingly 'un-connectable' temporal levels of Rudolf II (1552–1612), a Renaissance monarch known under various titles in the area historically known as 'Bohemia'; the world of Lewis Carroll's Alice (openly referred to in Carter's footnotes as well as in the obvious presence of the Alice character in the text); and the surrealist aesthetics of Svankmajer's film 'Alice.' Carter thus places different modes of knowing (Renaissance art and philosophy, alchemy, nonsense, surrealism) in tension with each other within a vertiginous space reminiscent of Carroll's *Alice in Wonderland*, inviting echoes of bewilderment: ' "Curiouser and curiouser!" Cried Alice' (Carroll 2000: 20). Rudolf II with his cabinet of curiosities emphasized wonder in the pursuit of a quasi-transcendental knowledge. Carter's piece explores the historical convergence of Rudolf II, Dr. Dee (the English Renaissance Magus who seeks out the apparition of angels), his assistant Edward Kelly (known as an alchemist charlatan), Johannes Kepler (the German astronomer) and the Renaissance artist Giuseppe Arcimboldo, known for his 'mannerist' fruit paintings, human likenesses composed of various fruits and vegetables.

The ideas associated with these diverse figures are suggestive of connections, a process further accentuated by Carter's playful superposition of the figures of Renaissance 'confidence man'[6] Kelly and his historical counterpart, the Australian 'Billy the Kid', Edward (Ned) Kelly (1854–80), an Australian outlaw known for wearing an iron mask, pictured in numerous photographs, and also, for example, in Australian artist Sidney Nolan's series of paintings about the 'Ironoutlaw.' Carter's descriptions of Kelly's mask conflates the historical details about Renaissance Kelly's ears being clipped off with the mask of Outlaw Kelly, thus openly playing with character identity:

> But his ears were cropped for him in the pillory at Walton-le-Dale, after he dug up a corpse from a churchyard for purposes of necromancy, or possibly of grave-robbing, and this is why, in order to conceal this amputation, he always wore the iron mask modelled after that which will be worn by a namesake three hundred years hence in a country that does not yet exist, an iron mask like an upturned bucket with a slit cut for his eyes. (Carter 1993a: 126)

With the phrase 'modelled after that which will be' Carter's games with temporality are highlighted, reversing the cause and effect of historical linearity so as to experiment with the confluence of different historical levels and modes of thinking. This playfulness is underlined metafictionally in the story as Alice bursts 'out of "time will be" into "time was" ' (ibid., 132), bringing historical time to bear upon the speculative, nonsense time of Carroll's 'Alice' texts. Such is the converging and overlapping of zones of speculation, as time limits shift and slip.

With provocative conceptual and historical resonances, Carter's fiction is indeed the paradise of literary critics. The critic is often faced with the difficult task of moving beyond the reflection inscribed in Carter's metafictional mixing of forms and modes to propose ideas that are not already embedded in her texts. There is indeed great pleasure, a sort of intellectual *jouissance* that can be procured through her fictional matrices. I, myself, can admit to a sense of giddiness as I delve deeper into the intricate intertextual genealogy of 'Alice in Prague *or* The Curious Room.' Indeed, the story typifies this process; its inscribed hermeneutics providing an echo of the 'titillation' Jean-Jacques Lecercle sees as being characteristic to nonsense: 'As commentators of texts, we live in the midst of proliferating and conflicting interpretations. An extreme but representative example of this is provided by interpretations of *Alice's Adventures in Wonderland*, as the text, claiming to be nothing but nonsense, titillates the reader's need for meaning, thereby multiplying interpretations' (Lecercle 1999: 22–3). The expression 'conflicting interpretations' indeed sums up 'Alice in Prague *or* The Curious Room' where the reader is led to establish connections in the ontologically unstable fictional frame of the story. As a result, speculative tensions are often resolved by placing special emphasis on certain conceptual fields. Frankova, for example, in her article, 'Angela Carter's Mannerism in Rudolf II's Curious Room' draws links between Carter's aesthetics and Rudolf II's world, weaving intricate parallels between the story's form and metafictional commentary and the aesthetics of mannerism inscribed in the historical field represented in the text. She engages with what she calls 'Carter's artful jigsaw puzzle' (Frankova 1999: 133), and Renaissance Mannerism is accentuated as a speculative dominant in the text. Karima Thomas similarly enters into a dialogue with the story's concepts, but rather focuses on Surrealism in its articulation with the 'Alice' dimension of the piece. She offers a particular focus on Carter's 'indebtedness' to the work of philosopher Gilles Deleuze, and his use of Carroll's *Alice's Adventures in Wonderland* to develop his ideas in *The Logic of Sense* (1969), the English translation of which was published around the time the story was written (Thomas 2009: 35). According to Thomas, the piece displays 'artistic creation as a true pleasure of confluence' (ibid., 36). The aforementioned reference to time, for example, provides the occasion for a relevant crossing of surrealism with Deleuze's discussion of Carroll's time:

> Actually in the light of the Stoic's logic, Alice's time is not Chronos but Aion. 'In accordance with the Aion, states Deleuze, only the past and the future inhere or subsist in time. Instead of a present which absorbs the past and future, a future and past divide the present at every instant and subdivide it ad infinitum into past and future, in both directions at once.' (Deleuze 1990: 164)
>
> This vision of time threatens the common sense perception of the unity of the present and comes closer to the surrealist celebration of the fragmented and desultory time of dreams. (Thomas 2009: 38)

These nuanced studies by Frankova and Thomas bear witness to the speculative complexity of Carter's story, while also revealing, in their silences and elision of certain ideas, recognition of the irreconcilable tensions inherent to the story's dominant mode: paradox. According to David Meakin, this is characteristic of alchemical practice: 'alchemy plunges us into the realm of paradox which, it might be argued, is its characteristic mode and one that will not be without fascination for modern writers. It deals, as we shall see, with the drive to marry irreconcilable opposites, to mediate contradictions, and is itself in turn the product and producer of different but intersecting and merging traditions, audacious syncretisms' (Meakin 1995: 11).

The story indeed functions as an invitation to syncretic thinking. Its multi-tiered labyrinthine workings reflect, in fact, the quest mechanism of alchemical writing: 'We shall see that twentieth-century fiction testifies to the persistence of this convergence of motifs, alchemical quest and labyrinth' (ibid., 23). To extend this literary analogy further, the reader, like the alchemist is led to engage in the pursuit of origins as his/her reflex for textual exegesis is aroused by Carter's speculation. Meakin observes how nostalgia for origins characterizes the alchemical quest, and in its link to reading and language, functions analogically with literary quests for truth:

> The adept is always a late-comer, a devout reader, a 'mental archeologist' in Butor's term, whose whole study is one long nostalgia. . . . One of the most frequent and abiding myths in the alchemical canon is that of the mysterious and obscurely written Book, discovered usually by chance, which provokes a life-long quest to unravel its hidden, encoded secrets. (ibid., 28–9)

The question of origins and unrevealed 'secrets' is foregrounded in much of Carter's fiction, thematized, for example, in the various configurations of the cave motif in *The Passion of New Eve* (1977) and, as mentioned previously, the comment, 'Perhaps, in the beginning, there was a curious room' (Carter 1993a: 127), is often set forth as being emblematic of Carter's writing, where the core of ideas and ideological forces are shown to be relative, part of the ongoing performance of identity in language.[7] Deleuze's observation concerning laterality in Carroll's *Alice in Wonderland* can easily be applied to the fictional universe of 'The Curious Room,' which is not one of depths, of penetration to origins, but rather one of lateral shifts and slides in reflection:

> In all his works, Carroll examines the difference between events, things, and states of affairs. But the entire first half of *Alice* still seeks the secret of events and of the becoming unlimited which they imply, in the depths of the earth, in dug out shafts and holes which plunge beneath, and in the mixture of bodies which interpenetrate and coexist. As one advances in the story, however, the digging and hiding gives way to a lateral sliding from right to left and left to right. The animals below ground become secondary, giving way to *card figures* which have no thickness. . . . It is not therefore a question of *the adventures* of Alice, but of Alice's *adventure*: her climb to the surface, her disavowal of false depth and her discovery that everything happens at the border. This is why Carroll abandons the original title of the book: *Alice's Adventures Underground*. (Deleuze 1990: 9)

On the structural level of intertext Carter's work is laterally based, not reaching back to the original *Alice in Wonderland* text but rather engaging in its textual genealogy, implicitly through the work of Deleuze and the surrealists, and explicitly through her reference to Jan Svankmajer. However, a nostalgia for textual origins, a search for an original intertext, for a core of truth, fuels the reader's quest for palimpsestic and conceptual resonances, a quest that is continually undermined by paradox and temporal relativity: 'All transformations move both backwards and forwards, every discovery – and this is truly alchemical – is part of an endlessly repeated search for origins' (Meakin 1995: 75). Meakin, in reference to Eliphas Lévi, characterizes this process as a 'dance of seven veils . . . subject to the dynamics of frustration and desire' in a dialectic of 'offering and withholding' (ibid., 30).

Carter's story is indeed a conglomeration of speculative strands that provoke thought but withhold clear answers. As Thomas observes, the text thus functions as an homage to surrealism, as a dream in its series of dislocations and sense of discontinuity (Thomas 2009: 38). This is evident in the numerous temporal manipulations inscribed in the text.

Like the crystal sphere, the reader is confronted with a story that 'contains everything that is, or was, or ever shall be' (Carter 1993a: 121) as Carter guides the reader through 'The hinge of the sixteenth-century, where it joins with the seventeenth-century' (ibid., 123). The piece also engages in a structural complexity through shifting narrative tenses which flicker between the past, a present that fosters a sense of temporal immediacy, and even anachronistic past futures such as in the case of Ned Kelly mentioned above. Such echoes of surrealist manoeuvres are fraught with the temporal spirit of alchemy. Meakin observes how André Breton, 'the high priest of surrealism', emphasized the analogical link between surrealist and alchemical research (Meakin 1995: 76), and underlines how Breton's texts reproduce the functioning of a metaphorical ancient text attributed to Hermes, in that they 'move not by conventional logic, nor the metonymy associated with narrative, but by the metaphorical process of association of ideas' (ibid., 77), a perception that can certainly be applied to 'The Curious Room.'

Carter gradually detached herself from strict surrealist modes of enquiry because of the representation of women: 'When I realised that surrealist art did not recognise I had my own rights to liberty and love and vision as an autonomous being, not as a projected image, I got bored with it and wandered away' (Carter 1997a: 512). Nonetheless a consciousness of surrealist aesthetics as related to politics and knowledge frequently emerges in her writing: 'Surrealism was not an artistic movement but a theory of knowledge that developed a political ideology of its own accord' (ibid., 508). Carter has also commented on the artistic quality of surrealist thought: 'Like most philosophical systems put together by artists – like neo-Platonism itself – surrealism was intellectually shaky, but artistically speaking, the shakier the intellectual structure, the better art it produces' (ibid.). The aforementioned lack of 'docility' that Carter's texts display in regards to her intellectual vagrancy is here translated as surrealist conceptual activity; as strands of reflection that tend towards the status of art, they defy intellectual appropriation. The resulting effect is a complex sense of vertigo that borders on the visceral:

> Surrealist beauty is convulsive. That is, you *feel* it, you don't see it – it exists as an excitation of the nerves. The experience of the beautiful is, like the experience of desire, an abandonment to vertigo, yet the beautiful does not exist *as such*. What do exist are images or objects that are enigmatic, marvellous, erotic – or juxtapositions of objects, or people, or ideas, that arbitrarily extend our notion of the connections it is possible to make. In this way, the beautiful is put to the service of liberty. (ibid., 512)

Vertigo is an integral part of what Carter has identified as a surrealist preoccupation with the power of words and images: 'A poem is a wound; a poem is a weapon' (ibid., 508–9). In 'Alice in Prague *or* The Curious Room' such forces are evident from the first obligation to make connections upon entering the 'door' to the 'curious room' via the incipit of the story: 'Outside the curious room, there is a sign on the door which says "Forbidden." Inside, inside, *oh, come and see!*[8] The celebrated DR DEE' (Carter 1993a: 121).

At first glance, it seems highly uncharacteristic of Carter to dabble in alchemy, a realm where spirituality coexists with speculation, at the borders of the occult and reason, a tradition that 'was essentially a continuation of the Renaissance dream of bringing man to perfection through a new kind of knowledge blending natural science, non-denominational Christianity and the hermetic tradition' (Meakin 1995: 17). However, in harnessing the vertigo of surrealist modes of enquiry, Carter is actually following the shift from religion to dream, or rather, religious experience giving way to aesthetic experience (ibid., 30). Part of this aesthetic experience can be found in the syncretic urgings of a speculative narrative, but another part may be perceived in her harnessing of the processes of suspension of disbelief, the poetic 'faith' with which readers, through the force of convention, approach the reading of fictional narrative. Vincent Jouve in *L'Effet personnage* (The Character Effect) provides a number of helpful hypotheses to address such forms of 'faith.' In reference to French theorist Michel Picard's (*La Lecture comme jeu* (Reading as a game), 1986), he conflates processes of reading and game-playing, with a strong emphasis upon psychoanalysis. Jouve identifies three different levels of reading in relation to the fictional narrative, that of the *lectant* (the intellectually aware reader who reads from the perspective of outside fiction and sees the characters as pawns in a game), the *lisant* (the reader who is drawn into the illusion proposed by the text, who believes and plays the fictional game in the spirit of Coleridge's oft cited 'suspension of disbelief') and the *lu* (the passively 'read' reader who interacts on a more visceral level with the text via pornographic or violent scenes, for example) (Jouve 1992: 82). Jouve's model provides a practical basis to address the varying levels at which the reader is led to engage in Carter's quasi-fictional texts. In 'Alice in Prague' as seen above, the intellectual dominant of her intertwined reflections appeals to the *lectant*, or even the excessively acute *lectant* present in the literary critic as we work to construct intricate connections in Carter's speculative laboratory. However the *lisant* (the reader engaged in the fictional illusion) and the *lu* (the instinctive reader) continue to play an essential role, contributing an essential, affective aspect to the alchemy of ideas apparent in Carter's story. As she comments in relation to her novel *Nights at the Circus* (1993b): 'it does seem a bit of an imposition to say to readers that if you read this book you have got to be thinking all the time; so it's there only if you want it. From *The Magic Toyshop* onwards I've tried to keep an entertaining surface to the novels, so that you don't have to read them as a system of signification if you don't want to' (Carter 1985: 87). The result of such 'entertaining' 'systems of signification' is a confluence of conflicting modes of reading[9] where the aforementioned intellectual vertigo is heightened by textual aspects that play upon the visceral, upon the dreamlike state inherent to reading fiction.

A perfect example in 'The Curious Room' is that of Rudolf's copulation with Arcimboldo's 'Summer' figure: 'Meanwhile, the Archduke, in the curtained privacy of his bed, embraces something, God knows what. Whatever it is, he does it with such energy that the bell hanging over the bed becomes agitated due to the jolting and rhythmic lurching of the bed, and the clapper jangles against the sides' (Carter 1993a: 128). The reader later learns the identity of the 'what' which is qualified as a 'thing' that 'is not, was not and never will be alive, has been animate and will be animate again, but, at the moment, not, for now, after one final shove, it stuck stock still, wheels halted, wound down, uttering one last, gross, mechanical sigh' (ibid., 136). This is a fruit composition of the form of a woman upon a wicker frame. The reference to the temporal ontology of the figure as a work of art by 'Arcimboldo the Milanese,' in relation to the act of copulation, simultaneously appeals to the reader on a more primitive level (the *lu*) and stimulates the *lectant* to interpret the ephemeral nature of this piece of art in its animate 'thingness' as it 'subsided, slithered, slopped off her frame into her fruit bowl, while shed fruit, some almost whole, bounced to the rushes around her. The Milanese, with a pang, watched his design disintegrate' (ibid., 137). The *lectant* reads the intertextual resonances with the figure of Arcimboldo; the *lisant* invests in the characterization of Rudolf as an eccentric and wildly speculative character and empathizes with Arcimboldo over the disintegration of his art; and the *lu* is affected on a visceral level by the pornographic, abject nature of the scene, whether the reaction be one of repulsion, pleasure or fascination This is accentuated by the constant, overt solicitation of the reader by the narrator. An explicit example lies in the narrator's invitation to the reader, 'you,' to 'taste' the juice yielded by Rudolf's act of copulation:

> But before you accuse the Archduke of the unspeakable, dip your finger in the puddle and lick it.
> Delicious!
> For these are sticky puddles of freshly squeezed grape juice, and apple juice, and peach juice, juice of plum, pear or raspberry, strawberry, cherry ripe. (ibid., 130)

The imagined sensuousness of licking one's finger indeed appeals to the 'lu' in its tension between disgust and enthralment, and lends a strong tactile, even gustatory, impression to the segment.

Such narrative imperatives are recurrent throughout the story, and the complex fluidity of the narrative tone between gothic darkness and jubilatory irony amplifies the range of appeals to the different levels of reading. The narrator's irreverent scatological description, 'Dr Dee, ever the seeker after knowledge, has calculated the velocity of a flying turd' (ibid., 126), resonates playfully with the concept of base materials in alchemy: 'faeces can happily coexist with gold and other precious materials. Edward Kelly writes that the stone is "buried not only in the earth, but in a dung heap . . . This, says the Sage, is the thing which all have, and yet there is no greater secret under heaven"' (Meakin 1995: 28). One cannot help but see further speculative potential in the various holes through which 'your excreta' (Carter 1993a: 126) must pass before reaching the cesspit below in the story. Similarly, the narrator's joke about the 'Archduke . . . effecting intercourse with a fruit salad' (ibid., 129) or with 'Carmen Miranda's hat' (ibid.) in combination with the speech of the toothless lion, '"Why can't he make do with meat, like other people," whined the hungry lion' (ibid.), lends a playful aura to the various 'forking paths' of reflection which split even further when the *lectant* realizes the implications of the Carmen Miranda reference, as Carter comments in her 1990 introduction to the piece: 'Carmen Miranda was the favourite film actress of the linguistic philosopher Ludwig Wittgenstein' (Carter 1990: 215–16). The paratextual reference to Wittgenstein and his language games discussed in *Philosophical Investigations* (1953) frames the story so as to reinforce intertextual links to Carroll's nonsense and Carter's own play with language. Such frolic with ideas recalls Mikhail Bakthin's work. Bakhtin, whose theory of carnival pervades much previous criticism of Carter's work, has also explored the concept of 'images of ideas' in Dostoevsky's writing: 'As an artist, Dostoevsky did not create his ideas in the same way philosophers and scholars create theirs – he created images of ideas found, heard, sometimes divined by him *in reality itself*, that is ideas already living or entering life as idea-forces' (Bakhtin 1984: 90). In the jostling and fluctuation between the different levels of reading, Carter's fiction echoes this process, as the reader's dreamlike investment in the illusory images of the story converges with the emergence of ideas, and the appeal of alchemical connections. The result in the ongoing process of reading Carter's fiction is a sense of a flickering movement of ideas.

Such play with ideas in conjunction with a strongly didactic narrator, who appears to manipulate pronouns and narrative tense, leaves the reader with the impression of an authorial spectre, a figure easily transformed into that of Angela Carter as irreverent jokester. This is how Salmon Rushdie describes her: 'Angela Carter was a thumber of noses, a defiler of sacred cows. She loved nothing so much as cussed – but also blithe – nonconformity' (Rushdie 1997: 5). French theorist Jean-Jacques Lecercle has explored the forces intertwined with such 'ghosts,' moving beyond the implied author to explore how the 'fantasy' of the author (Lecercle 1999: 150) functions within a pragmatic structure: 'The [ALTER][10] structure is a structure not of communication, but of ascription. Interpellation is what circulates in the structure; and imposture is the action through which interpellated subjects segment or invert the flow of interpellation' (ibid., 151). Basing his study of interpellation on the theory of Louis Althusser, Lecercle emphasizes the respective posturing of the author and reader that is the positions they adopt in relation to the flow of ideology in the textual communication situation. As the reader seeks out the author, and as the author seeks out the reader, their imagined relationship to the other figure affects his/her interaction with the performative forces of the reading process released through the text. Carter's work, because of the metafictional dominant, and the constant appeal to the *lectant* in the reader, exaggerates and stages this process. The reader is tempted to ascribe a position to the authorial figure (Carter) as the writer of the speculative maze of a story; he/she is drawn to seek out the figure of authority as a central pivot to the interrogations set forth. As I have argued elsewhere[11] Carter's fiction exercises a didactic pull on the reader, a relevant perlocutionary effect that in turn becomes a part of the 'work' her fiction does. When this didactic pull is counterbalanced by a series of multi-layered, intertextually saturated language games, the reader's subsequent vertigo becomes the laboratory in which the alchemical processes of Carter's aesthetic occur, where the ideological forces of language momentarily surface and interpellate the reader.

This is perhaps where the 'alchemy of the word' becomes political, but not political in the sense of a specific agenda. This, according to Carter, was never voiced as an intent (tricky concept as this is): 'I believe myself to be a quite deeply political person – and therefore everything comes out. But, obviously I don't write fiction about specific social injustices' (Carter 1987). Yet the seeking out of this political intent, a quest we've shown to be analogical to that of the alchemist, is fed by the general spirit of questioning that characterizes Carter's writing. As Joan Smith comments in her introduction to Carter's non-fiction collection, *Shaking a Leg*: 'it's a kind of writing which invites the reader to think, to argue back, to accost its creator with sentences beginning: "yes, but what about"?' (Smith 1997: i). Carter's writing, hovering at the boundaries of fiction and non-fiction, incites the reader to 'accost' her authorial figure with questions, thus setting the forces that work through language into play. Herein lies, perhaps, the impact of Carter's political aesthetics. In her recuperation of the titillating character of nonsense, Carter's work harnesses what Lecercle sees as the anticipatory potential of the genre:

> Like history, linguistic consciousness progresses the wrong side up. So the function of this type of literature is not only to read philosophy . . . thus reversing the usual relationship of exploitation, but to read it *in advance*. Nonsense is anachronistic because it blurs the question of the origin of the philosophical theses it anticipates: it is the anoriginal illustration of theoretical theses, the 'truth' of which was still dormant at the time. There lies the profound 'originality' of such texts. (Lecercle 1994: 167)

It is possible to entertain the conjecture that 'Alice in Prague *or* The Curious Room' proposes such philosophical and conceptual potentialities. Carter's story, like the Mad Hatter's puzzles in *Alice in Wonderland* ('Why is a raven like a writing-desk?' (Carter 1993a: 70)), indeed functions much like a riddle in that it sends readers and critics scrambling, only to discover, like Alice, there is no single solution:

> 'Have you guessed the riddle yet?' the Hatter said, turning to Alice again.
> 'No, I give it up,' Alice replied. 'What's the answer?'
> 'I haven't the slightest idea,' said the Hatter.
> 'Nor I,' said the March Hare.
> Alice sighed wearily. 'I think you might do something better with the time,' she said, 'than wasting it in asking riddles that have no answers.' (Carroll 2000: 72)

The editor of *The Annotated Alice* comments on the 'parlor speculation' provoked by the Mad Hatter's riddle, and includes a quotation from Carroll which inadvertently points to the reader's persistent need for answers, a drive for certainty that prevails in even the most sophisticated reader:

> Enquiries have been so often addressed to me, as to whether any answer to the Hatter's Riddle can be imagined, that I may as well put on record here what seems to me to be a fairly appropriate answer, viz: 'Because it can it can produce a few notes, tho they are *very* flat; and it is never put with the wrong end in front!' This, however, is merely an afterthought; the Riddle, as originally invented, had no answer at all. (ibid., 71)

Carter explicitly embeds riddles from Carroll's *A Tangled Tale* (1885) in the 1993 version of her story, and conundrums from *What is the Name of this Book: The Riddle of Dracula and Other Logical Puzzles* (1986) by Raymond Smullyan in her 1990 publication, to which clear answers are provided in a note at the end of the story. Such playful forms of interrogation effectively add a layer of reflection to the nonsense strands in the story. However the conundrums ultimately speak more of the overwhelming spirit of enigma that reigns in 'The Curious Room' as a story that proposes a mesh of insoluble riddles, opening, in its anticipatory gesture, possibilities for future reflection, and eliding, as always, final answers. Even in the Kim Evans documentary filmed shortly before Carter's death, *Angela Carter's Curious Room*, in which Carter reflects on her own origins, evasion can be seen in the foregrounding of images of cyclical patterns (cherry blossoms), and an emphasis on the slippery quality of knowledge, particularly knowledge of the self. Typically, as did the readers of Carroll, we return to the figure of Carter for answers, conscious of how language betrays her and us, yet persistent in our quest for a sense of a coherent message, or 'book' contained within her writing. Such is the nature of alchemical exegesis that her fiction successfully puts to the service of perpetuating thought. It feeds our impulse for syncretic thinking yet also exploits the tension inherent to alchemical unions to destabilize certainties and propose endless threads of reflection. In this sense, Carter's writing truly acts, as does Carroll's writing, as an 'anoriginal illustration of philosophy treatises' (Lecercle 1994: p. 167) which perhaps still lie 'dormant' in the text, in the reader, in our time.

Notes

1　For practical purposes, the text will be referred to as 'The Curious Room' throughout the article.

2　According to Umberto Eco in his *Lector in Fabula* (French edition), the encyclopedia consists of the general linguistic and cultural (in relation to tradition) competencies which a text solicits. The encyclopedia is, of course, a process that involves a complex coordination of linguistic and cultural skills throughout the reading process. Carter's texts, with their dense layering of intertexts, amplify this complexity as the reader must peel back the layers of each word and put these into relation with the context. The possible combinations are seemingly infinite.

3　This information is omitted from the Virago 1993 edition of *American Ghosts and Old World Wonders*, but appears in *Burning Your Boats: The Collected Short Stories* (1995a: 462).

4　Note the original title of the 1990 piece is simply 'The Curious Room.'

5　The conundrums used by Carter at the end of the story are also different in the two versions: She uses conundrums borrowed from Raymond Smullyan in the 1990 version ('The three conundrums posed by Alice come from Raymond Smullyan's *What is the Name of This Book: The Riddle of Dracula and other Logical Puzzles*, New York, 1986.' Carter 1990: 231–2) and conundrums from Lewis Carroll in the 1993 version ('Problems and answers from *A Tangled Tale*, Lewis Carroll, London, 1885' (Carter 1993a: 139)). The framing and the conundrums are the only significant differences between the two stories.

6　Carter comments on Kelly's questionable status in her 1990 introduction to the story: 'Dr. Dee visited the court of Rudolph II accompanied by his assistant, Edward Kelly, who really was a confidence man, in 1584' (Carter 1990: 216).

7　I am referring here to the well-known research of Judith Butler on performance and identity in *Gender Trouble* (1999).

8　My italics.

9　It might also be interesting to consider how Carter, through the generic ambiguity that characterizes her stories, also plays upon the *lisant*, as the reader is led to fluctuate between playing the 'game' as fiction and playing the game as non-fiction, conceptual thought.

10　[Author – Language – Text – Encyclopedia – Reader].
　　I have also used Lecercle's reading model to study the authorial figure in three of Carter's autobiographical texts, 'Autobiographical Estrangement in Angela Carter's

"A Souvenir of Japan", "The Smile of Winter" and "Flesh and the Mirror"', *Etudes britanniques contemporaines*, 32, 2007.

11 See my PhD. dissertation, *Le jeu didactique et l'effet sur le lecteur dans* The Passion of New Eve *(1977) et* Nights at the Circus *(1984) d'Angela Carte*, ANRT Thèses à la Carte 2001.

Works Cited

Bakhtin, M. (1984) [1963], *Problems of Dostoevsky's Poetics*, Minneapolis: University of Minnesota Press.

Butler, J. (1999) [1990], *Gender Trouble*, New York: Routledge.

Carroll, L. (2000), *The Annotated Alice: The Definitive Edition*, Martin Gardner (ed.), New York: Norton.

Carter, A. (1985), Interview by John Haffenden, in *Novelists in Interview*, London: Methuen, 76–96.

—(1987), Interview by Lisa Appegnanesi, 'Angela Carter in Conversation', London: ICA Video.

—(1990), Introduction, 'The Curious Room', *On Strangeness*, Tübingen: G. Narr Verlad, *SPELL, Swiss papers in English language and literature v. 5*, 215–232, Google Books, http://books.google.fr/books?id+VZKNBCBNlD0C&pg+PA242&dq+SPELL, +Swiss+papers+in+English+language+and+literature+angela+carter&hl=en& ei=XRJmTq7aNorAtAbW15y9Cg&sa=X&oi=book_result&ct=result&resnum=3& ved=0CDAQ6AEwAg#v=onepage&q=SPELL%2C%20Swiss%20papers%20in%20 English%20language%20and%20literature%20angela%20carter&f=false, Accessed March 2008.

—(1992), Interview, *Angela Carter's Curious Room*, Dir. Kim Evans, BBC 2, BFI Film archives, London.

—(1993a) [1990], 'Alice in Prague *or* The Curious Room', *American Ghosts and Old World Wonders*, London: Vintage, 121–39.

—(1993b) [1994], *Nights at the Circus*, New York: Penguin.

—(1995a), *Burning Your Boats: The Collected Short Stories*, London: Penguin.

—(1995b) [1977], *The Passion of New Eve*, London: Virago.

—(1997a) [1978], 'The Alchemy of the Word', in *Shaking a Leg* (ed.) Jenny Uglow, London: Chatto & Windus, 506–11.

—(1997b), *The Curious Room*, London: Vintage.

Clapp, S. (1997), Introduction, Angela Carter, *The Curious Room* (ed.) Mark Bell, 1996, London: Vintage, vii–x.

Deleuze, G. (1990), *The Logic of Sense*, New York: Columbia University Press.

Eco, U. (1985) [1979], *Lector in Fabula*, Paris: Grasset, Trans. Myriem Bouzaher.

Frankova, M. (1999), 'Angela Carter's Mannerism in Rudolf II's Curious Room' *Brno Studies in English: Sborník Prací Filozofické Fakulty Brnenské Univerzity*, Anglistická/ Series Anglica (BSE); 25 (5), 127–33.

Jouve, V. (1992), *L'effet personnage dans le roman*, Paris: Presses Universitaires de France.

Lecercle, J. (1994), *Philosophy of Nonsense: The Intuitions of Victorian Nonsense Literature*, London: Routledge.

—(1999), *Interpretation as Pragmatics*, New York: St Martin's Press.

Lee, R. (2003), 'Crippled by the Truth: Oracular Pronouncements, Titillating Titles, and the Postmodern Ethic', in (eds) Farhat Iftekharrudin, Joseph Boyden, Mary Rohrberger, and Jaie Claudet, *The Postmodern Short Story: Forms and Issues*, Westport CT: Praeger Publishers, 109–22.

Meakin, D. (1995), *Hermetic Fictions: Alchemy and Irony in the Modern Novel*, Keele: Keele University Press.

Picard, M. (1986), *La lecture comme jeu*, Paris: Minuit.

Rushdie, S. (1997) [1995], Introduction, Angela Carter, *Burning Your Boats*, New York, Penguin, ix–xiv.

Ryan-Sautour, M. (2001), *Le jeu didactique et l'effet sur le lecteur dans* The Passion of New Eve *et* Nights at the Circus *d'Angela Carter,* Lille: ANRT Thèses.

—(2007), 'Autobiographical Estrangement in Angela Carter's "A Souvenir of Japan", "The Smile of Winter" and "Flesh and the Mirror" ', *Etudes britanniques contemporaines*, 32, 57–76.

Sage, L. (1994), Introduction, in (ed.) Lorna Sage, *Flesh and the Mirror*, London: Virago, 1–23.

Smith, J. (1997), Introduction, Angela Carter, *Shaking a Leg*, London: Chatto & Windus, xii–xiv.

Svankmajer, J. (1997), Interview by Wendy Jackson, 'The Surrealist Conspirator: An Interview With Jan Svankmajer', *Animation World Magazine*, 2.3. June, http://www. awn.com/mag/issue2.3/issue2.3pages/2.3jacksonsvankmajer.html Accessed 5 May 2009.

Thomas, K. (2009), 'Angela Carter's Adventures in the Wonderland of Nonsense,' in (eds) Maisonnat, Claude, Josiane Paccaud-Huguet and Annie Ramel, *Rewriting/Reprising in Literature: The Paradoxes of Intertextuality*, Newcastle upon Tyne: Cambridge Scholars Publishing, 35–42.

Vandermeer, J. (2001), 'Angela Carter', *The Modern Word: Scriptorium,* 26 October, http://www.themodernword.com/scriptorium/carter.html. Accessed 10 May 2009.

Warner, M. (2001), Introduction ('Angela Carter'), 'Ballerina: The Belled Girl Sends a Tape to an Impresario,' *Angela Carter and the Fairy Tale* (1998) (ed.) Danielle M. Roemer and Cristina Bacchilega, Detroit, Michigan: Wayne State University Press, 250–3.

8

'Cradling an Axe Like a Baby':
Angela Carter's *Lulu*

Mine Özyurt Kılıç

Adrienne Rich's essay 'When We Dead Awaken: Writing as Re-vision' (1996) ruminates on the experience of a young girl or woman 'go[ing] to fiction', 'looking for her way of being in the world' and there 'meeting the image of Woman in books written by men' (Rich 1979: 39). Angela Carter's 1988 stage adaptation of Frank Wedekind's Lulu plays, *Erdgeist* (*Earth Spirit*, 1895), originally commissioned for the National Theatre by Richard Eyre, is an example of such a 'meeting' reconstructed to restore 'the image of Woman written by men' as much as possible. Although it was meant to be an adaptation of an existing work, Carter does her best to inscribe her 'demythologising' potential on it; her *Lulu* becomes a manifestation of the psychic energy of a woman who is, in Rich's idiom, 'in touch with her anger' (Rich 1979: 39). Carter's re-vision exposes how Lulu's femininity is a social fiction and palmed off on her as the real thing. Of course, Lulu's voice echoes Carter's well-known account of the self-realization she experienced in the summer of 1968, her 'Year One'. As she writes in her 1983 essay 'Notes from the Front Line', that summer she was probing 'the nature of her reality as a woman' and asking: 'How that social fiction of [her] "femininity" was created, by means outside [her] control, and palmed off on [her] as the real thing' (Carter 1997a: 26).

Frank Wedekind wrote *Lulu: A Monster Tragedy* around 1894 and was subsequently published in 1898. It seems Wedekind's depiction of Lulu as a monster is directly related to the social fiction that Carter aims to deconstruct. In *Lou: Histoire d'une femme libre* (2007), a biography of Lou Andreas-Salomé, an intellectual who inspired Nietzsche and Rilke, Françoise Giroud recounts an anecdote about Wedekind. Wedekind met Andreas-Salomé, 'one of the most intriguing women of all' at a party in 1894 and found her very attractive.[1] This love at first sight made him propose, which she typically refused. Andreas-Salomé's response did not only earn her the undeserved title, *femme fatale* as a way of avenging this rejection, Wedekind decided to write a play called *Lulu* with a very unpleasant portrayal of Lou as a *femme fatale*. When the play was produced in Berlin at the turn of the century it was 'detested, condemned, and banned' and declared to be 'immoral and inartistic' (Brooks 2000: 94).

This was ideal material for Carter to put 'new wine in old bottles' (Cater 1997a: 26), so when the National Theatre approached her to rewrite the play she accepted intending to refashion Lulu as 'the Life Force incarnate, Wedekind's earth spirit, the Dionysiacally unrepressed Lulu, who must die because she is free' (Carter 1997c: 276). Carter's 1978 review of G. W. Pabst's *Pandora's Box* (1929), an early screen version of the Lulu plays, reveals her ongoing interest in the figure; for her Lulu is 'one of the great expositions of the cultural myth of the *femme fatale*' (Carter 1997b: 249). Upon seeing the same film Wedekind had observed: 'Lulu is not a real character, but the personification of primitive sexuality who inspires evil unaware. She plays a purely passive role' (Brooks 2000: 94). While he found Pabst's version 'sweetly innocent', Carter saw in this sweetness subversive potential to be exposed. Her Lulu is a sweet, sharp and active protagonist who is meant to engage the audience as a 'case' to be investigated.

The play's formal divisions might partly explain why it was not performed: 'It is a long evening's entertainment of at least five hours in seven acts' (Christensen 1998: 325). Susannah Clapp's remark about its diction adds another reason observing that it was 'the capaciousness and dense verbal quality' that made her plays 'in the view of some directors, difficult to stage' (Clapp 1996: ix). In 'Production Notes' to Carter's version, Mark Bell quotes Richard Eyre's comment on the adaptation, which also cites the play's textual richness as an obstacle to its production: 'Maybe it was a wrong marriage – if you take on somebody else's piece, you have to submerge your own personality in the original. I wanted Wedekind with the colour and graphic edge of Angela, which may have been an impossible combination' (Bell 1996: 510). Ultimately, Carter would not see her Lulu on stage, a fact about which she remained embittered.[2] Clapp's notes record her frustration: 'Angela was not forgiving about this: I remember her white and narrow-eyed with fury at a party explaining: "The National Theatre has just flushed my *Lulu* down the toilet" ' (Clapp 1996: ix).

It does not come as a surprise that Carter's plays resonate with the ideas she proposes in her stories, novels and non-fictional works, a style which Haffenden describes as 'argument stated in fictional terms' (Haffenden 1985: 79). Peter G. Christensen rightly sees Carter's adaptation 'as an extension of her project of reworking fairy tales in a feminist manner' (Christensen 1998: 320). In her brief introduction to *The Curious Room: Plays, Film Scripts and an Opera*, Clapp also identifies the recurrent themes in Carter's works and argues that: 'The voice in these pieces is the voice of her fiction and journalism. Sometimes it almost takes the words from their mouths' (Clapp 1996: ix). Like many of Carter's works, *Lulu* makes known the mechanisms that victimize women and showcases Lulu newly aware of her power to challenge those mechanisms. So, recast in the light of her Sadeian woman, Carter's *Lulu* represents a version of a *femme fatale* that is featured in her other works. As a 'charming child', an attractive woman who has 'a certain child-like vulnerability' (Carter 1996: 393), she clearly resembles Fevvers of *Night at the Circus*: 'the pure child of the century that now is waiting in the wings, the New Age in which no women will be bound down to the ground' (Carter 1985: 25).

Like Fevvers, whose wings evoke the question 'Is she fiction or is she fact?' (ibid., 147), Lulu is meant to stimulate discussion: is she an innocent girl gone awry or a villain doomed to be wayward? Carter leaves the question unanswered to suggest how impossible it is to decide on her 'true nature'. Set in *fin de siécle* London like *Nights at the Circus*, *Lulu* is influenced by the public debate over the Woman Question and the New

Woman in the 1880s. Unsure how to deal with the changing image of the Victorian angel-in-the-house, the New Woman is 'an unpleasant thing, an anomaly, or at best, as an object of gaze' (Özyurt Kılıç 2006: 7). Indeed, the anonymous poet of 'What is a (New) Woman Like?' that appeared in *Punch* on 3 October 1896 asserts that with her 'male manners', evident in the way she spends her time by writing, biking and chatting, she is like a 'queer dish' (Anon. 1896: 110). After listing all the disagreeable beings to which the New Woman might be compared, the poem calls on the reader to share his diagnosis that 'She's like most things on earth – but a woman!' (ibid.). Described as dubious in nature, 'Neither flesh, fowl, nor fish', she is impossible to grasp:

> But she'll shock you and vex you,
> Disgust and perplex you.
> Immodestly ranging,
> Continually changing (ibid.)

It is this riddle-like nature of the New Woman that makes it almost impossible to arrive at a single definition for Lulu. Noting that Wedekind continually rewrote the play as a consequence of censorship until 1913, Karin Littau in her 'Refractions of the Feminine: The Monstrous Transformations of Lulu' observes that in all the versions Lulu acts as a 'screen onto which her rewriters, censors, translators, adapters, dramaturgs and critics project their Lulus' (Littau 1995: 888).[3] Her observation that the 'monstrously different reworkings' trace the origins of Lulu in mythical figures such as Pandora, Eve and Lilith underscores ambiguity as the central quality of Lulu:

> As an actress then, she deceives, and perhaps her greatest deception is precisely that she plays with the roles that are projected onto her. Sometimes she is Mignon, then she is Nelli, then Eve, then a devil, an angel, a beast, a snake and a sweet little animal (these being names and designations given her by her lovers). (ibid., 900)

Carter signals Lulu's obscure nature by following Wedekind in having each of her lovers name her differently. Nobody calls her Lulu except Schigolch, her so-called father and first seducer, who claims to have saved Lulu from the gutter. Dr. Goll calls her Nell, Schwartz Eva, and Schoen Mignon. Trying to confine her within the limits of their definition of femininity, they avoid seeing Lulu as she is. In her study *Femmes Fatales*, Doane argues that Lulu's riddle-like quality is derived from the *femme fatale*:

> The *femme fatale* is the figure of a certain discursive unease, a potential epistemological trauma. For her most striking characteristic, perhaps, is the fact that she never really is what she seems to be. She harbours a threat which is not entirely legible, predictable, or manageable. (Doane 1991: 1)

As the reader is left to ask whether there can be such a woman, a naïve friend, a confident woman, a murderess, a sweet lover, a loving wife and a seductress all in one, *Lulu* recalls *Nights at the Circus* in which Walser, the American journalist, is unable to decide whether Fevvers is a fact or fiction. In the play it is Schwartz posing a series of questions, which Lulu senses are not 'about her paternity or her origins' but about her very nature (Carter 1996: 407). While investigating what she is, Schwartz becomes the mouthpiece of all the men who are perplexed by the autonomous women labelled *femmes fatales*. He bombards Lulu with his vulgar questions: 'Who are you? What are you?', 'Do you believe in God?', 'Is there anything that you'd swear by, swear to tell the truth by? Like your mother's grave', 'Do you believe in anything?', 'Have you got a soul?', 'Have you ever been in love?' (ibid.). Trying to remain calm, Lulu defends herself against these bullet-like questions and repeats 'in a normal voice': 'I don't know'. But she gets 'coldly furious' and shows she is no fool when she asks: 'I don't know. Just what is it, exactly, that you want to know?' (ibid.).

These questions echo the frustration Lulu's men feel at the sight of such an elusive figure. By reducing her to a name they find it easier to deal with the complexity of her identity. Thence she is a sex machine for Alva, a prostitute for Schoen and a mere object of desire for Prince Escerny. For him, Lulu is an automaton, happily dancing, 'just for him', to offer relaxation after a hard day's work (ibid., 432). Carter has the Prince ask: 'What is the question of the age? I'll tell you – it's 'What does a woman want?' (ibid., 433). The sarcastic answer hidden in his rhetorical question reveals the male fear of losing control; it also exposes the distorted view that catalogues powerful women as *femmes fatales*. He continues: 'Can a woman imagine more happiness than to have a man utterly in her power?' (ibid.). This skewed vision corresponds to the diagnosis Carter makes in *The Sadeian Woman*: 'A free woman in an unfree society will be a monster' (Carter 2001: 27).

Presenting Lulu as a wayward girl violating the norms of this repressive society, Carter obscures her origins. As with Fevvers mysterious origins, this symbolizes Lulu's transgression of the traditional norms. In other words, Carter seems to employ Lulu's vague origins as a device more explicitly than Wedekind to emphasize that a woman like Lulu, an orphan brought up by Schigolch, a surrogate father recalling Dickens' Fagin, is a product of her circumstances. Cast as unchained to any set paradigm, Carter suggests that evil is not intrinsic to her nature. To the same end, characters are introduced who recall Lulu's childhood. For instance, shocked to see his little 'Eva' turned into a *femme fatale*, Schoen recounts that when she was twelve 'she used to sell flowers outside the Alhambra Café. Barefoot, in rags. Every night, from midnight on, she'd pick her way among the tables, offering little bunches of violets to the gentlemen. Violets' (Carter 1996: 418). He says he is only recounting this so that Schwartz understands that 'it's not a question of innate depravity. Far from it' (ibid.). Sorry because his 'Mignon', Lulu, is now 'in a state of utter degradation', Schoen reveals Carter's critique of the moral standards that denounce Lulu. By ironically presenting Schwartz as a man who 'lives on a higher moral plane', Carter's stage directions indicate that he should be 'consoled' that 'corruption is both normal and inevitable' (ibid., 420). At this point his consolation becomes an indirect address to the middle-class audience; he warns Schwartz not to judge Lulu: 'Don't apply middle-class standards to a person of her background' (ibid.).

Defining her neither as completely evil nor as a mere innocent victim, Lulu's doubleness is a textual strategy which figures her as a woman not to be easily grasped in established terms. Both an archetypal woman and an emblem of change, Lulu is a typical Carter character who refuses to be pinned down. Her response to the forces at work to victimize her illustrates Lulu's dexterity in resisting these agents of oppression. In this way Carter's *Lulu* offers a version of the *femme fatale* inculcating a 'demythologising' attitude. As Carter argues in 'Notes from the Front Line' she is interested in myths since 'they are extraordinary lies designed to make people unfree' (Carter 1997a: 27). By rewriting *Lulu*, Carter explodes another myth and the doubleness in Lulu's nature exposes the lies making her unfree. In his essay 'Farewell to the *Femme Fatale*: Angela Carter's Rewriting of Frank Wedekind's Lulu Plays', Christensen offers an insightful comparison between Carter's and Wedekind's *Lulu* by defining this doubleness in terms of a conflict: 'The tragedy and doom surrounding Lulu stem from her having to play a role for which she is not cut out' (Christensen 1998: 328). As Sarah Gamble concludes in her comparison of the narrative strategies of Carter's *Shadow Dance* and *Love* and Godard's film *Vivre sa vie*, Carter often employs the 'risky tactic of exhibiting exploitation for the very purpose of its deconstruction' (Gamble 2006: 61). Following a similar demythologizing tactic in *Lulu*, the Lulu she envisages speaks so much like her creator that Carter even declared: 'Should I ever have a daughter, I would call her not Simone, nor even Rosa, but Lulu' (Clapp 1996: x).

In her 1978 review of Pabst's 1929 film *Pandora's Box* and Marlene Dietrich's performance in *The Blue Angel* (1930), Carter makes a significant remark about what renders women *femmes fatales*: 'Because [Pabst's Lulu] is perceived not as herself but as the projection of those libidinous cravings which, since they are forbidden, must always prove fatal. So Lulu gets off with the countess and obligingly sets up an Oedipal situation for her stepson when she shoots his father' (Carter 1997b: 249). With her discussion of the term *femme fatale*, Carter poses a challenge to the patriarchal definition of what it is to be a sexually active and self-autonomous woman. Thus, in her enjoyably bold diction, she draws attention to the misunderstanding of the female characters in *The Blue Angel*. In her summary of the plot, she describes the *femme fatale* of the film Lola-Lola, a cabaret singer 'who marries a boring old fart in a fit of weakness, lives to regret it but is too soft-hearted to throw him out until his sulks, tantrums and idleness become intolerable' (Carter 1997b: 352). Celebrating Lola-Lola's free spirit, which recalls Lulu in every way, Carter sardonically observes that: 'If that is the story of a *femme fatale*, then some of my best friends are femmes fatales and anybody who feels ill-used by them has only himself to blame' (ibid.). Accordingly, Carter's Lulu is a 'complex phenomenon' (Carter 1997c: 277). She might appear to be a monster, but still has the eyes of a shy and silent little girl. Even Alva, who knows her for years, has difficulty seeing what she really is observing: 'If I didn't know you by your eyes, I'd think you were a real *femme fatale*' (Carter 1996: 462; original emphasis).

To understand the *femme fatale* Carter locates the figure in a cultural continuum. Different from Wedekind's portrayal of Lulu as a crude product of nature and 'unlimited sexuality' (Bond 1993: 65), Carter presents her as the product of social and cultural conditions. This is resonant in the interrogating tone of Hugenbach, one of Lulu's lovers. When she is condemned as a murderer, a literal *femme fatale*, and treated as a fallen woman at the court, he stands up for Lulu and challenges the judge by asking if he would be any better under such conditions: 'How do you think you might have turned out yourself if you'd had to sell flowers barefoot round the cafes when you were only ten?' (Carter 1996: 458). As in *The Sadeian Woman* Carter argues that it is not only femininity but also sex that is a cultural construct and that cultural values are inseparable from sexual myths. Making explicit the strong link between the nature of sexual relations and the social relations in which they take place, the 'Polemical Preface' contends:

> But our flesh arrives to us out of history, like everything else does . . . We do not go to bed in simple pairs; even if we choose not to refer to them, we still drag there with us the cultural impedimenta of our social class, our parents' lives, our bank balances, our sexual and emotional expectations, our whole biographies – all the bits and pieces of our unique existences. (Carter 2001: 9)

Similarly the play contends that in this patriarchal order, sex can only be discussed in terms of power relations so when Lulu attempts to communicate her desire freely, she is catalogued as evil. As a result, Alva who repeats the accepted norm, 'High summer for a woman is when she's ripe to destroy a man', considers Lulu to be a threat asserting that, 'There's danger oozing out of every pore of her. She's like a pirate ship; she's come to wreck the bourgeoisie with the terrible weapon of her sex' (Carter 1996: 486–7).

In an attempt to discuss and go beyond the Sadeian models of women symbolized by Justine, the victim, and Juliette, the *femme fatale*, Carter places a necessary emphasis on the cultural continuum in which this woman acts. As in her analysis of Sadeian women, she offers her reader practice in creative and critical thinking to imagine this woman who is neither prey nor a monster. Although as an adaptation she can only stretch the limits of Wedekind's play so far, she still offers a fascinating glimpse of a free being who can act on equal terms with men, which would also allow her to enjoy her sex. Presented as a figure that allows for thinking in comparative terms, Carter's Lulu challenges the established norms. As soon as she appears on stage to sit for a painting, she is set as an antagonist to Schoen's 'respectable' fiancée. Unlike this controllable and well-mannered young woman who attended a convent school, Lulu is trouble (Carter 1996: 394). Enjoying every moment of the sitting, Lulu extravagantly poses in her Pierrot costume, symbolic of her sex as performance. As Lilith to Eve, Lulu is the other to the decent fiancée; she wets her lips freely, opens her mouth, finds the bra-straps 'terribly constricting' and gets rid of them (Carter 1996: 394). Fighting free of the costume and throwing it on the floor, she shows that the sky is her limit: 'I'm climbing right up to the sky and I'm going to pick off all the stars in my hair . . .' (ibid., 400).

What best describes this sweet and sour Lulu is Carter's stage direction in Act Two: 'Lulu comes back, cradling an axe in her arms as if it were a baby' (ibid., 423). She has capacity for love and affection, but she also knows how to use evil means to defend herself. When blamed, she is ready to spot at a glance the one who attacks her. For instance, Schwartz calls her 'disgusting' as she lustfully kisses him just after her husband, Dr. Goll, dies, but Lulu is quick to respond and wittily reminds him: 'It takes two to be disgusting' (ibid., 406). Following in the footsteps of Marquis de Sade's Juliette, Lulu figures as a model who knows how to survive in a hostile world. Carter's analysis of Juliette fully applies in a character she created almost a decade after *The Sadeian Woman*:

> She is rationally personified and leaves no single cell of her brain unused. She will never obey the fallacious promptings of her heart. Her mind functions like a computer programmed to produce two results for herself – financial profit and

libidinal gratification. By the use of her reason, an intellectual apparatus women themselves are still inclined to undervalue, she rids herself of the more crippling aspects of femininity. (Carter 2001: 79)

In self-defence, Lulu plays tricks on those who want to take advantage of her. She deceives Rodrigo, Schigolch and Casti-Piani when they try to make money out of her. Lulu can also enjoy life to the full despite all the calamities visited upon her because she can put things behind her and move on – as she dances, she forgets all (Carter 1996: 429). In line with Doane's description of *femmes fatales*, Lulu is so confident that 'her self-admiration, narcissism annihilates men as the subjects of desire' (Doane 1991: 161). Celebrating herself, she never needs approval from men. On the contrary, she boldly 'worships her body'. Her pride is manifest in the self-image she communicates to Alva: 'When I looked in the mirror, I envied your father' (Carter 1996: 446). She never falters even in the face of danger; not once does she play the helpless girl who begs 'Not yet, not yet! I am still so young/Why should I leave the world so soon?' (Wedekind 1993: 148).

Carter adds to this self-confidence an awareness about her place in this order. It is evident that Carter wanted to create a class-conscious and mature Lulu. When Schoen explodes at her 'I hate you, I hate you, I hate you', she promptly gives a perceptive response: 'That's because of my working-class origins' (Carter 1996: 437). Through Alva who comments on his play about Lulu, Carter reminds the audience that Lulu is a product of her circumstances; in so doing, she also satirizes both the middle-class moralizers and censorship that artists, includingWedekind, have had to satisfy. Interestingly, Alva's voice not only echoes Carter's iconoclastic views, but it also reads as an ironic foreshadowing of the fate of the very play he speaks in:

> But that's the curse that's crippling writers today! Literariness! When what we need to make an art that speaks to the masses is sheer, stark, brutal realism! Christ, I'm through with Art. I'm going to throw in my lot with real people, not desiccated intellectuals, but with people who live vital, real, instinctual lives . . . I did that in the last play. She's the realest woman I know. She's been in prison for a year now, and I put her in my pay. And isn't it ironic, I couldn't find a producer anywhere. (Carter 1996: 450)

Painted by artists, explored by playwrights and examined by scientists, the *femme fatale* is 'not the subject of feminism but a symptom of male fears about feminism' (Doane 1991: 3). As if to justify this definition, Carter makes Rodrigo, an acrobat who is in love with Lulu, articulate those male fears about this bold, 'realest' woman:

> She's still only twenty years old. Buried three husbands, already. God knows how many lovers. High time she settled down. The snag is, a man needs the seven deadly sins tattooed on his forehead before she'll give him a second look. Pure evil, that's what gets her juices working, know what I mean. (Carter 1996: 459)

Carter lifts the veil of this monstrous woman and shows that this myth is another 'consolatory nonsense' freeing men from the burden of controlling their desire (Carter 2001: 5). Failing to come to terms with their desire, they repress or deny it and thus idealize or demonize her.[4] In other words, what these men have in common is a pathetic inability to relate to this powerful woman as an equal. Thus Lulu wants to liberate herself from the codes labelling her either an angel or a monster and complains: 'I feel such a fool, stuck up on my bloody pedestal' (Carter 1996: 415).

To defend her *femme fatale*, Carter portrays all of the male characters as unpleasant figures. Alva, for instance, is educated enough to talk about the mechanism of 'repression' and 'idealisation' but he cannot speak his mind as freely as Lulu (ibid., 447). Carter also exposes his moral hypocrisy. When they become very poor, what Alva first gives up is not whisky but his so-called principles. He wants Lulu to find a 'customer' to make some money but Lulu who sells her body for no reason responds sharply: 'You've never brought home so much one single penny in all your pampered and over-privileged life, you idle sod. Why don't you go out and peddle your arsehole, give me a rest' (ibid., 481). Similarly, his father Schoen is portrayed as a timid and soulless man behind the mask of a patriarch; when he discovers that his wife has had an affair with Alva, he speaks only as a master disillusioned by his servant: 'I gave you everything and asked for nothing in return except the respect any decent servant gives his master' (ibid., 450). Carter displays both his foolishness and hypocrisy since Schoen quickly forgets that Lulu is the very girl with whom he had an affair when she was married to another man. As he applies his moral criteria only to Lulu, Schoen calls her 'a sickness' of his soul that he wants 'so badly to be cured of' (ibid.).

To satirize the undeserved title, deathly woman, with which independent women are labelled, Carter ironically sends Lulu's husbands to the grave, one after the other. The way the absurdly sudden deaths are designed serves to undermine the myth that such charming and autonomous women bring death to men. The first of these *deus ex machina* endings is cast for Dr. Goll; he has a stroke when he discovers his 'Nell' in a compromising position with the painter, Schwartz. The second husband, Schwartz, who gains wealth and fame via Lulu's connection to Dr. Goll, cuts his throat with a razor when he understands at last, rather belatedly, that Lulu was not a virgin when he married her. Schoen, who breaks his engagement to a 'respectable' woman as a result of Lulu's whims, is presented as another casualty; as he sees Alva, his son, falling prey to Lulu, he gives a revolver to her and orders her to kill herself. Foolishly thinking she would obey, he is instantly killed by her. And Alva's death which looks like a punishment for his moral hypocrisy makes Carter's satire even more visible. Tongue-in-cheek, Carter seems to even the score by letting Alva die at the hands of Jack the Ripper. It is not always *femmes fatales* who are punished and killed.

Following Wedekind's plot, Carter kills Lulu too; like other Lulus, she is killed by Jack the Ripper. Carter's reflection on this conclusion can be found in her essay, 'Femmes Fatales', in which she considers Lulu's end as the 'price' she pays for being an independent woman in a repressive society: 'This is the true source of the fatality of the *femme fatale*; that she lives her life in such a way her freedom reveals to others their lack of liberty. So her sexuality is indeed destructive, not in itself but in its effects' (Carter 1997b: 251). In Carter's version, the finale that introduces Jack the Ripper ends the play with typically dark Carteresque humour. It is bitter because Lulu dies as she offers her love to Jack, but it is also light-hearted thanks to the last-minute joke about Lulu's lesbian lover. Just a second before she is stabbed, the Countess feels resentful as she fails to get a response from her 'angel'.[5] Thus, she rapidly resolves: 'I will go back to Germany. My mother will pay for the ticket. I'll go to the university. I'll study law. I'll fight for women's rights' (Carter 1996: 495). Her final words softens Wedekind's hair-raising finale with Jack confidently uttering as he rips up Lulu's uterus, Pandora's box: 'When I'm dead and my collection is put up for auction, the Medical Society will pay three hundred pounds for the prodigy I have conquered tonight. The professors and students will say "That is astonishing!" ' (Wedekind 1993: 209).

Carter finds the prevailing notion of *femme fatale* rather one-dimensional and criticizes Wedekind for making Lulu 'the passive instrument of vice' (Carter 1997b: 249) and for failing to see beyond the stereotype:

> Her loyalty to her old friends; her fidelity to her first seducer, the repulsive Schoen; her willingness to support her adoptive father and effete stepson by the prostitution she loathes – Wedekind records all this but cannot see it as any evidence of human feeling at all. (ibid.)

Recalling the argument in *The Sadeian Woman* that 'Justine and Juliette do not cancel one another out; rather, they mutually reflect and complement one another, like a pair of mirrors.' (Carter 2001: 78), Lulu is 'a synthesis of their modes of behaviour, neither submissive nor aggressive, capable of both thought and feeling' (Carter 2001: 120). In one of the rare tender moments in the play, Lulu reveals the truth about herself: 'I only wish I was a real *femme fatale*. I've made a bit of a botch of it so far' (Carter 1996: 462). She says farewell neither to Juliette nor to Justine; she inhabits the wilderness in between. Almost a decade before she refashioned Wedekind's Lulu, Carter was well-aware of the fact that:

> Repressive desublimation – i.e. permissiveness – is giving the whole idea of the *femme fatale* a rather period air. But this is only because the expression of autonomous female sexuality is no longer taboo. To clarify the point, a remake of 'Pandora's Box', or even 'The Blue Angel', ought, perhaps, to star a beautiful boy in the *femme fatale* role. Fassbinder could direct it. The significance of the *femme fatale* lies not in her gender but in her freedom. (Carter 1997b: 251)

Carter's Lulu is challenging enough, but one wonders what it would be like if Carter and Fassbinder were alive today to shoot a 'Lulu' together; maybe, like the Princess and Mignon in *Nights at the Circus*, the Countess and Lulu would walk hand in hand to help Jack come to terms with his infernal desire. Perhaps, Carter could go far beyond Wedekind's limits and show that the significance of the *femme fatale* lies not in her gender but in her freedom.

Notes

1 From the translation in progress, *Lou: The Story of a Free Woman*, Robin Mackay. http://www.docstoc.com/docs/49829974/Lou-The-Story-of-a-Free-Woman-Fran%C3%A7oise-Giroud. Accessed on 14 December 2011.

2 Christensen notes that the play was performed at Leeds in the mid-1990s (Christensen 1998: 319). It must have been after Carter's death in 1992.

3   Littau's careful analysis does not include Carter's text because it was written a year before its publication, but she cites her adaptation as 'Angela Carter's feminist rewrite of Lulu' (Littau 1995: 888).

4   Lulu's reduction to a prostitute recalls Simone de Beauvoir's philosophizing (1997) over Brigitte Bardot in *And God Created Woman'* (1957), which some feminists wittily renamed as 'And Man Created a Tart (Tidd 2004: 46). Like de Beauvoir, Carter sees reciprocity as the *sine qua non* of a sexual relationship. This is a clue for anti-pornography feminists like Dworkin and McKinnon who condemned Carter for supporting Sadism; what Carter does in fact is to study Sade's work in its historical context and see its liberatory potential. Like her Lulu, who is reluctant to sell her body, her characters in many of her works like *The Bloody Chamber* (1986) and *Nights at the Circus* also exemplify that without love and reciprocity sex is just a boring, mechanical act.

5   The Countess is the only figure to save Lulu from danger when all the other lovers try to make money out of her. Imprisoned after killing Schoen in self-defence, Lulu is liberated when the Countess swaps clothes in return for Lulu's love. But although the Countess promises a safe haven for Lulu, she rejects this as decidedly as she denies selling her body in the absence of love.

Works Cited

Anon. (1896), 'What is a (New) Woman Like?', *Punch*, 3 October.

Bell, M. (1996), 'Production Notes', in *The Curious Room: Plays, Film Scripts and an Opera* (ed.) Mark Bell, London: Chatto and Windus, 500–10.

Bond, E. (1993), 'Using Lulu', in Frank Wedekind, *Plays: One*, trans. Edward Bond and Elizabeth Bond-Pable, London: Methuen, 63–8.

Brooks, L. (2000), *Lulu in Hollywood*, Minnesota: University of Minnesota Press.

Carter, A. (1985), *Nights at the Circus*, New York: Viking.

—(1986) [1979], *The Bloody Chamber and Other Stories*, Harmondsworth: Penguin.

—(1996) [1988], 'Lulu', in *The Curious Room: Plays, Film Scripts and an Opera*, London: Chatto & Windus, 391–497.

—(1997a) [1983], 'Notes from the Front Line', in *Shaking a Leg: Collected Writings* (ed.) Jenny Uglow, New York and London: Penguin, 36–43.

—(1997b) [1978], 'Femmes Fatales', in *Shaking a Leg: Collected Writings* (ed.) Jenny Uglow, New York and London: Penguin, 248–51.

—(1997c) [1990], 'Barry Paris: Louise Brooks', in *Shaking a Leg: Collected Writings* (ed.) Jenny Uglow, New York and London: Penguin, 275–9.

—(2001) [1979], *The Sadeian Woman: An Exercise in Cultural History*, New York: Penguin Books.

Christensen, P. G. (1998), 'Farewell to the Femme Fatale: Angela Carter's Rewriting of Frank Wedekind's Lulu Plays', *Marvels and Tales: Journal of Fairy Tale Studies*, Vol. 12, No 2, 319–36.

Clapp, S. (1996), 'Introduction', in Angela Carter, *The Curious Room: Plays, Film Scripts and an Opera* (ed.) Mark Bell. London: Chatto and Windus, vii–x.

de Beauvoir, S. (1997), *Sade'i Yakmalı mı?* trans. Cemal Süreya, İstanbul: Yapı Kredi.

Doane, M. (1991), *Femmes Fatales: Feminism, Film Theory, Psychoanalysis*, New York: Routledge.

Gamble, S. (2006), 'Something Sacred: Angela Carter, Jean-Luc Godard and the Sixties', in *Re-Visiting Angela Carter: Texts, Contexts, Intertexts* (ed.) Rebecca Munford. New York: Palgrave Macmillan, 42–64.

Giroud, F. (2007) [2002], *Lou: Özgür Bir Kadının Öyküsü*, trans. Saime Bircan, Ankara: İmge.

Haffenden, J. (1985), *Novelists in Interview*, London: Methuen.

Littau, K. (1995), 'Refractions of the Feminine: The Monstrous Transformations of Lulu', *MLN*, Volume 110, Number 4, September, 888–912.

Özyurt Kılıç, M. (2006), 'A Mirror-Like Pool of Ink: The New Woman in Angela Carter's *Nights at the Circus*', *Nineteenth-Century Gender Studies*, 2. 2 Summer, 1–12.

Rich, A. (1979), 'When we dead awaken: writing as re-vision', in *On Lies, Secrets and Silence* (ed.) A. Rich, New York: W.W. Norton, 33–49.

Sage, L. (2001), 'Angela Carter: The Fairy Tale', in *Angela Carter and the Fairy Tale* (eds) Danielle M. Roemer and Cristina Bacchilega, Michigan: Wayne State University Press, 65–81.

Tidd, U. (2004), *Simone de Beauvoir: Routledge Critical Thinkers*, New York: Routledge.

Wedekind, F. (1993), *Plays: One*, trans. Edward Bond and Elisabeth Bond-Pable, London: Methuen Drama, 73–209.

Part Two

Philosophies

9

Sex, Violence and Ethics – Reassessing Carter's 'Moral' Relativism

Lawrence Phillips

In *The Introduction to Metaphysics* Heidegger observed:

> The violent one, the creative one who sets forth the unsaid, who breaks into the unthought, who compels what has never happened and makes appear what is unseen – this violent one stands at all times in daring. (Heidegger 2000: 115)

To begin an essay that proposes to discuss violence in an author's work with a quotation from Heidegger carries with it a number of risks, not least because of Heidegger's early associations with National Socialism, which in turn invites popular association with a number of politically extreme positions. Indeed, to argue that an author uses violence philosophically and figuratively with an ethical and moral purpose that should be explored critically is still, perhaps, as much at risk of misinterpretation as it was for the author in the first place. Certainly for Angela Carter this has attracted extensive condemnation, as Paulina Palmer argued in response to *The Sadeian Woman* (1979): 'the attitude she adopts to the atrocities which he [de Sade] depicts in his fiction raises problems for the feminist reader. It is one of detached interest and intellectual curiosity, not indignation' (Palmer 1987: 194–5). To reflect 'intellectual curiosity' rather than 'indignation' defines the problem of discussing violence in anything other than condemnatory terms. Yet like most human actions, the fact of violence itself can be rather equivocal; its motivation as ideological as the many strategies that might discuss it. This is not to represent violence as a 'good thing' by any means. Indeed, that Merja Makinen feels compelled to point out in her perceptive essay on sexuality and violence in Carter's work, 'textual violence is very different from actual violence, both in terms of the delineation of violence and the often aggressive assaults on the readers' expectations' (Makinen 1997: 151), is itself representative of the problems of approaching the issue directly. Rather than restrict this question to that of a textual effect, this chapter will argue that Carter's discursive and aesthetic use of violence enters into a much broader debate about Western ethics and morals than just the representation of sexuality, significant as this is in her work. Indeed, Carter pointed to such wider concerns in her important 1983 essay, 'Notes from the Front Line':

It seems obvious, to an impartial observer, that Western European civilisation as we know it has just about run its course and the emergence of the women's movement, and all that implies, is both symptom and production of the unravelling of the culture based on Judeo-Christianity, a bit of Greek transcendentalism via the father of lies, Plato, and other bits and pieces' (Carter 1997: 39)

The violence of her work has much to do with this unravelling which, from an early twenty-first century perspective, has proven rather protracted. Yet this is not some simple postmodern nihilism tilting at a series of *grand récit*: to return to the epigraph from Heidegger, the violence in Carter's work is a striving for creative change and represents great daring although at a cost of doing some uncomfortable violence to the *status quo* and, indeed, the reader. This is not so easily contained as textual play as Makinen would have it, for as Carter also argues in the same essay: 'This is also the product of an absolute and *committed materialism* – i.e., that *this* world is all that there is' (ibid., 38; italics original). It is clear that Carter expected to contribute to a process of material change and, again echoing Heidegger, the first victim of this violence is the creator: 'This erasure can take different forms. The first is physical destruction – from Moses and Julius Caesar onwards, we know that a founding figure has to be killed' (Žižek 2009: 59). This brings us to Carter's third significant statement in 'Notes from the Front Line':

> . . . in order to question the nature of reality one must move from a strongly grounded base in what constitutes material reality. Therefore I become mildly irritated (I'm sorry!) when people, as they sometimes do, ask me about the 'mythic quality' of work I've written lately. Because I believe that all myths are products of the human mind and reflect only aspects of material human practice. I'm in the demythologising business.
>
> I'm interested in myths – though I'm much more interested in folklore – just because they *are* extraordinary lies designed to make people unfree. (Whereas, in fact, folklore is a much more straightforward set of devices for making real life more exciting and is much easier to infiltrate with different kinds of consciousness). (Carter 1997: 38)

It is tempting to read here a mythic edifice that has to be battered down and unravelled versus folklore as some form of cheeky Bakhtinian narrative strategy that facilitates subversiveness. Carter's practice is, however, more profound and equivocal. The aesthetic battleground informing this chapter is her novel *The Passion of New Eve* (1977) and the title story from the collection of interconnected folktale retellings *The Bloody Chamber* (1979). However, the opposition is not quite as simple as it first appears; while the folktale form might be more congenial to Carter as a writer (and certainly more fun for the sympathetic reader), the iconoclasm founded on violence is more complex and disturbing in both texts.

The place to begin is power. Eve/Evelyn's figurative, mythic and literal journey in *The Passion of New Eve* across the Atlantic from Britain to the United States and then from the East to the West Coasts and from man, to woman, to mother is the exploration and unravelling of a number of ancient myths and their more recent manifestations in popular culture. The principal framework contrasts religious myth – given pride of place in the title 'New Eve' – and the popular mythmaking of the quintessential twentieth-century cultural technology, Hollywood film in the form of the femme fatale actress Tristessa. Perhaps unsurprisingly the novel follows the schematic form typical of myth. Eve/Evelyn's experience as a man is a state largely bounded by two cities, London and New York, both in a state of advanced social and material collapse. The forced translation between genders occurs during self-exile in the desert. The physiological change is provided courtesy of Mother and her underground desert city of Beulah and is consummated by the rape of the anarchist-poet Zero. The transition to mother is accomplished by enforced sex between Eve and Tristessa who has retired to the desert and is revealed to be a man in drag. Approaching the West Coast city of Los Angeles the trajectory of the novel veers away from an urban coda to a figurative rebirth and encounter with a diminished and broken-down Mother, the novel concludes – or rather deliberately evades a conclusion – with the pregnant Eve sailing out into the Pacific. Alongside the obvious reworked biblical structure that evokes Jesus as much as Eve (thence Old and New Testaments; life, death and resurrection), there is a persistent sprinkling of Greco-Roman mythology which is particularly evident in the desert where Eve/Evelyn's transformation is accomplished, including Cybele (Carter 1982: 46, 54, 67), Oedipus, of course (ibid., 50–2, 64), Ariadne (ibid., 53), the Minotaur (ibid., 55), Danae and Demeter (ibid., 58), Aphrodite (ibid., 59), Jocasta (ibid., 59–60), Tiresias (ibid., 68) – this is not intended to be an exhaustive list and by no means encompasses the range of mythological and literary reference. However, the particular concentration of Greco-Roman and Judeo-Christian myth dominates and points to the cultural 'unravelling' – Žižek's 'destruction' – Carter describes in 'Notes from the Front Line'. Moreover, it is difficult to ignore the echo of Ovid's *Metamorphoses* through this mythological melange. Yet is this quite as iconoclastic as it might seem? Both the Christ myth and the theme of transformation teased out of the Greco-Roman mythological pantheon via Ovid are inherently about transition and change following violence. The half-human Christ is crucified and resurrects while in Ovid the gods do (often sexual) violence to unsuspecting mortals who are transformed/translated for better or worse – both arguably forms of Carter's Greek transcendentalism. Violence provides the energy for change to take place, albeit potentially unpredictably. Ethically, however, it is rather hard to accept violence as a positive agent of change and brings the discussion back to the double jeopardy of the quotation from Heidegger and the connection to fascism, if not a particular view of Darwinian 'red in tooth and claw' that leads us into eugenics. If violence is the change agent then it is arguably only humanity of all animals that uses violence for any other use beyond securing dinner and determining who breeds; as Girard argues in *Violence and the Sacred* (2005): 'Violence is not to be denied, but it can be diverted to another object, something it can sink its teeth into' (Girard 2005: 4). Striping aside the sexual politics and satire for the moment, it is hard not to read Eve/Evelyn as a sacrificial victim thence Jesus rather than Eve: a necessary diversion to at least initiate a process leading to change. The problem is that is not what the novel ultimately delivers. Carter pushes and pushes but ultimately can offer no more than an indeterminate conclusion. Much like most myths the conclusion is transcendent: 'Ocean, ocean. Mother of mysteries, bear me to the place of birth' (Carter

1982: 187). No wonder that Carter found the more flexible narrative structure of the folktale more congenial since it seems she tries and fails to escape the form of myth that leads inexorably towards the determinism of the metaphysical. What is surprising, given the influence of Ovid on the text, is the refusal to emulate his subversiveness. Ovid invalidates the metaphysical by explicitly giving his gods human motivations and capriciousness. It is his mortals who are trapped between states by their encounter with the gods thence elevating them to a feature of the realm of the gods while pulling the gods towards the human which is a sly comment on the immobility of myth where the principal aim is to continue, to persist. Eve's recession into the sea ensures that the metaphysical framework of myth persists unchallenged. There is life after death; a rebirth.

Yet if this reveals the persistence of the Christ myth as Girard's sacrificial victim elevated to the godhead, what of the biblical Eve's status as victim? Surely it is her sacrifice and that of her gender that allows linear time to enter the timeless space of the Garden and supplant the cyclical time associated with 'mother' nature thence foreshadowing man's domination and the construction of cities. What then of the very carefully constructed spatial arrangement of this novel. The rejection of masculine linear time and the reassertion of cyclical time is certainly the preoccupation of Mother and the inhabitants of her city where 'time is a man, space is a woman':

> Oedipus wanted to live backwards. He had a sensible desire to murder his father, who dragged him from the womb in complicity with historicity. His father wanted to send little Oedipus forward on that phallic projector (onwards and upwards!); his father taught him to live in the future, which isn't living at all, and to turn his back on the timeless eternality of interiority.
>
> But Oedipus botched the job. In complicity with phallocentricity, he concludes his trajectory a blind old man, wandering by the seashore in a search for reconciliation.
>
> But Mother won't botch the job.
>
> Man lives in historicity; his phallic projector takes him onwards and upwards – but to where? Where but to the barren sea of infertility, the craters of the moon! Journey back, backwards to the source! (Carter 1982: 50)

This loudspeaker announcement to the incarcerated Evelyn is a subtle narrative prolepsis. Like Oedipus, by the conclusion of the novel Mother is found to be 'wandering by the seashore' befuddled, while the pregnant Eve, contradictorily perhaps, sails off into the 'barren sea'. Yet are things quite as neat as that? The novel has three carefully demarcated spatial sections: an urban realm that is associated with Evelyn's masculinity and where he is the perpetrator of a certain violence towards women; the desert where violence is done to his/her body to transform it into a women which is then violated by the barren Zero and fertilized by the cross-dressing Tristessa and finally the transcendental landscape of the West Coast and the Pacific. All three of these symbolic landscapes are deeply embedded in Western culture. The urban evokes both the 'city on the hill' tradition of American Christianity as well as the utopian city of Plato – 'the father of lies' – through Thomas Moore and beyond; the desert may be biologically barren but it is the locale of Christ's visions (forty days and forty nights) and, indeed,

Evelyn 'went from nightmare to nightmare' (ibid., 41); while the indeterminate detail of the West Coast and the sea suggest a fully symbolic landscape for a diminished Mother to gaze upon in confusion and for Eve to be reborn and then to recede into the sea.

Indeed, these landscapes might be further redefined into the material (the city, the monument of human artifice); the visionary (a barren, fever-inducing trial of tears) and finally the fully symbolic, transcendent landscape of coast and sea which suggests a further intertext for the novel, Bunyan's *Pilgrim's Progress* (1678) originally billed as a 'dream' with the full title *The Pilgrim's Progress from this World to that which is to Come* which is rather suggestive in relation to *The Passion*. Yet while these distinct spaces may be thus categorized by environment and to a certain degree by narrative function, what do they signify? What is the purpose of this careful emplotment (pun intended)? Henri Lefebvre argues that 'It is not the work of a moment for a society to generate (produce) an appropriated social space in which it can achieve a form by which of self-presentation and self-representation – a social space to which that is not identical and which is indeed is its tomb as well as its cradle. This act of creation is, in fact, a *process*' (Lefebvre 1991: 34). The mention of creation echoes Heidegger's notion of creative destructiveness, yet as a linear, historical process, the city in the novel appears to operate in reverse – to regress not progress. It is certainly a social space of self-presentation and self-representation, but the urban spaces of the novel are in advanced stages of decomposition and fragmentation questioning the power of Western society to sustain itself, particularly that direct product of the Western Enlightenment, the grid city of North America. As Evelyn reflects:

> It was, then, an alchemical city. It was chaos, dissolution, nigredo, night. Built on a grid like the harmonious cities of the Chinese empire, planned like those cities, in a strict accord with the dictates of a doctrine of reason, the streets had been given numbers and not names out of respect for pure function, had been designed in clean, abstract lines, discrete blocks, geometric intersections, to avoid just those vile repositories of the past, sewers of history, that poison the lives of European cities. A city of visible reason – that had been the intention. And this city, built to a specification that precluded the notion of Old Adam, had hence become uniquely vulnerable to that which the streamlined spires conspired to ignore, for the darkness had lain, unacknowledged, within the builders. (Carter 1982: 12)

The grid city, supposedly the product of the *Western* Enlightenment is subtly defamiliarized. As much as its embodiment of reason as the cure for the European canker of unreason, it is not Western at all being of 'nigredo night' and reminiscent of the 'Chinese empire' such that reason itself is an appropriation and thence the city space generated on a false foundation, a facade bound to crumble. The term 'nigredo' is quite slippery here. While meaning literally 'black', in alchemy it signifies putrefaction or decomposition. In Jungian psychology it refers to the process of individuation as a moment of acute despair presaging the development of the self. And then of course its near homophone status with 'negro' hinting at the unreason that Western racism and sexism has pinned on blacks and women, points to the various communities that are in a state of becoming as the white, male dominated Western city unravels. When unreason – the 'nigredo', 'the darkness' – is denied an outlet, the edifice begins to collapse and fragment into micro-communities defined by ethnicity, gender, religion, class etc. The city is a spatial model deeply embedded in the Western psyche and it is no surprise that Freud should cast the mould of his theory along the same pattern. This city has denied the unconscious in the name of reason and it returns with all the violence of psychosis. Reason does not have the power of myth to hold both the conscious and unconscious mind. The city built on reason denies the process between the two. As Lefebvre continues:

> such sites are needed for symbolic sexual unions and murders, as places where the principle of fertility (the Mother) may undergo renewal and where fathers, chiefs, kings, priests and sometimes gods may be put to death. Thus space emerges consecrated – yet at the same time protected from the forces of good and evil: it retains the aspect of those forces which facilitates social continuity, but bears no trace of their other, dangerous side (Lefebvre 1991: 34)

Reason may embody linear time, historicity, but precludes the cyclical time of renewal.

Ironically, Mother's city, Beulah, built under the desert extols cyclical time but fails on much the same ground – a failure to grasp the irrational. Mother may cast herself as an 'incarnated deity' having undergone a 'painful metamorphosis', but Beulah remains a scientific romance and thence based on the same Enlightenment foundation as the grid city; an 'abstraction of natural principle' that exudes an artificial quality (Carter 1982: 46). The rational city of man no less than the rational city of woman is doomed to failure. In this light, at a spatial level, the novel gains some traction against the inevitable transcendentalism of myth, lending the apparent acquiescence to the form at the conclusion greater critical and discursive weight. Rather than transcendence, might the vague landscape and the featureless sea actually represent something of a blank canvas, a *tabula rasa* that anticipates the birth of Eve's child? Of course Locke's formulation itself has a problematic provenance originating with the same Greeks (Aristotle rather than Plato this time) and influencing Freud, but it lies at the foundation of twentieth-century arguments that 'blood', or, rather, gender, or ethnicity, or class does not determine character – behaviour is learnt. Eve's child can be born to become something else and the relatively featureless natural landscape of the conclusion of the novel will militate against behaviour being imposed by a particular experience of social space. But this still leaves little room for the irrational, for if the mind is initially blank, the irrational counterpoint to culture which one might, following Heidegger, dub a creative violence, is absent unless learnt. Indeed, this might be further linked to how culture is transmitted via language. While Eve's child remains unborn at the end of the novel, will it be introduced to language which then recreates the tension that the novel explores: that between 'nature' and 'culture'. The conclusion of the novel suggests a stripping away of the latter leaving Eve as a rather paradoxical 'Mother Nature' a creation, as she is, of the violence of Western science and culture. As Žižek notes: 'Reality in itself, in its stupid existence, is never intolerable: it is language, its symbolisation, which makes it such' (Žižek 2009: 57). While the novel strips away much of the stifling incrustation of myth revealing the raw oppressiveness it exists to maintain, it is still unable to offer much beyond the implication that the cycle will begin again. While Lefebvre posits this as a positive process with its roots in nature myths, given the elaboration of the various manipulations of mythic structures that the novel explores, it is difficult to be quite so sanguine. Thence no doubt Carter's dissatisfaction with her attempt at demythologizing through *The Passion* which she discusses in 'Notes from the Front Line'. But does the shift to the folktale, the relative ease by which she can deal with 'the shifting structures of reality' through that form, prove to be the discursive breakthrough to which she aspires (Carter 1997: 38)?

On one level, then, Carter's preference for the folktale is a leaning towards the popular, or rather an intervention into another contentious debate contingent on the rise of cultural studies in the late 1970s. Raymond Williams argued in 1976 that

> the unevenness and complexity of origin of various folk elements have been increasingly demonstrated, and within modern cultural studies, where there is an unwillingness either to isolate the pre-industrial and pre-literate folk or to make categorical distinctions between different phases of internal and autonomous, sometimes communal, cultural production (Williams 1976: 137)

The re-worked folktales of *The Bloody Chamber* are certainly informed by a similar intellectual ethos. In Carter's hands they can be transplanted from a traditional quasi-medieval pre-modern setting to a twentieth-century of guns, cars and modern warfare creating a rich sense of historical anachronism as the pre-modern atmosphere of the tales contrasts with – and defamiliarizes – various signs of modernity. Thence the opening story, a reworking of the folktale form known as the wife murdering Bluebeard, has an early twentieth-century setting with trains, cars, the telephone and a Debussy soundtrack provided by the heroine-victim, contrasting with the Marquis's remote castle by the sea and his feudal domination of his new wife, servants and the surrounding countryside. The violence of the tale preserves the anachronism: the archaic torture devices in the castle's dungeon include an Iron Maiden, a wheel and a rack with the added frisson of the bodies of two previous brides. When he comes to kill his latest bride, his preferred form and instrument is decapitation by sword. It is modern violence that ultimately wins out as the White Knight of the tale turns out to be no less than the bride's mother who crashes into the castle to put a clinical bullet between the eyes of the Marquis in just the nick of time. Yet the resonance of this final image exceeds the import of the original tale. While the scene ostensibly offers up on the one hand a positive feminist image of the mother having gained control of the phallic gun and thence power, her dexterity with the weapon is the consequence of 'an adventurous girlhood in Indo-China, daughter of a rich tea planter' (Carter 1981: 7). So these two newly powerful political discourses, feminism and a nascent postcolonialism, are in apparent conflict: the violent assertion of the mother seems to be possible only as a consequence of the violent oppression of the colonized. Indo-China also brings to mind the Vietnam War which had only concluded in 1975 with the fall of Saigon. This is further reinforced by the French setting of the tale since Vietnam was a French colony and anti-colonial resistance predated the involvement of the Americans.

These discursive, cultural and social fragments create a tension that strains against the narrative resolution of the tale. Placing the mother in place of the father as the arbiter of violence does not represent progressive change as the hierarchy and violence remain, just in different hands. But this is necessary to justify the violence – the Marquis's violence is excessive, perverse and criminal whereas the violence of the Mother is measured, natural and legitimate. Clearly, in one sense the fate of the Marquis represents a rejection of de Sade in that there has to be a hierarchy representing control for the tale to reach this resolution, and yet as a consequence of the need for a hierarchy to justify violence there is a multiplication of predators which was Carter's conclusion to her discussion of de Sade's *Justine* and *Juliette*, the Mother nurtured by colonialism countering the Marquis nurtured by patriarchal perversity; and it is not even that clear cut given the patriarchal nature of colonial discourse. Either way, might is right. As in *The Passion* the role of violence is both energizing and hugely problematic. As Jean Marie Muller argues: 'It is essential to define violence in a way that it cannot be qualified as "good" . . . as soon as we claim to be developing criteria by which we to define a supposedly "good" violence, each of us will find it easy to make use of these in order to justify our own acts of violence' (Žižek 2009: 53). Žižek argues that 'there is something inherently mystifying in a direct confrontation with [violence]: the overpowering horror of violent acts and empathy with the victims inexorably function as a lure that prevents us from thinking' (ibid., 3). There is something of Žižek's observation in the violence of this scene in that there is a degree of mystification, of mythologizing, around the violence. The horror of the Marquis's perverse, archaic and specular violence and sympathy with the fate of the heroine initially blinds reflective thought to cheer on the resolution brought by the Mother and her deftly targeted bullet. Yet the matter does not rest there. The problematic colonial background provided for the Mother refuses to give us this satisfaction; the violence may save here but it is has been learnt through the illegitimate oppression of others via colonial culture. This in turn forces attention onto how this resolution maintains existing hierarchies regardless of who exercises violence. The coda to the tale sees mother, daughter and the blind piano tuner happily installed as the proprietors of a music school hinting figuratively at the resolution of *Jane Eyre* and the blinding and taming of Rochester as a consequence of the self-immolation of another colonized individual. In both this tale and in *Jane Eyre* the sense of justice that accompanies the violence and our sympathy for the victim can obscure the problematic resolution. Greco-Roman myth also lurks here in the resemblance of the blind piano tuner and Rochester to Oedipus and Tiresias. As much as Brontë, Carter leaves us with only the masquerade of a resolution, but with the full means to question where that leaves us by the many mythological, literary and ideological echoes that fizzle through the text. Narrative resolution is unable to settle by virtue of this supplementarity and the restlessness (if not violence) of language.

While folktales might have originated in an oral form and Carter points to the 'shifting structures derived from orally transmitted traditional tales' as 'easier to deal with' compared with myth, this is a structural preference that in her hands leads to a greater free play of language, particularly as the oral is translated into the written (Carter 1997: 38). As Derrida argues: 'if supplementarity is a necessarily indefinite process, writing is the supplement par excellence since it proposes itself as the supplement of the supplement, sign of a sign, taking the place of a speech already significant' (Derrida 1976: 281). But where does this leave Carter's 'committed materialism'? Lefebvre argues that 'any "social existence" aspiring or claiming to be "real", but failing to produce its own space, would be a strange entity, a very peculiar kind of abstraction unable to escape from the ideological or even the "cultural" realm. It would fall to the level of folklore and sooner or later disappear' (Lefebvre 1991: 53). The historical anachronism Carter features in 'The Bloody Chamber' and other tales from the collection can be read as an attempt to counter the problem of abstraction. By translating the traditional setting of the tales into a more modern one they approach our 'social existence' and thence offer the possibility of influencing our social space and thence material 'reality'. This revives the debate opened up in *The Passion* over the tension between linear and cyclical time in space. In 'The Bloody Chamber', the Marquis's existence is clearly built on the cyclical; his association with the feudal and also the repeated cycle of marriage then murder – the promise of new life cut short by death (which is rather suggestive given his sword) – versus the intervention of the Mother and metropolitan linear history represented by her colonial background and both mother and daughter's previous home in the city. This reverses the gendered time of *The Passion*, but only to reinforce the notion that all that has happened is that the wielder of authorized violence has been replaced while the system and hierarchy remain unchanged. To return to Williams' observation mentioned previously, Carter does manage to resist the relegation of the folktale to an anachronistic survival of the past, an irrelevant fragment destined to the abstraction that Lefebvre posits. She detaches the form from its roots in cyclical time tied to natural cycles and maturation, a position very much associated with Edward Burnett Tylor through his influential *Primitive Culture* (1871), where the folktale survives 'by force of habit into a new state of society' (Tylor 2010: 137). In response, Carter sets the folktale loose in historical time where force is met by force.

The violence is then potentially liberatory but hardly unproblematic, as the limitations of the Mother simply replacing the father principle in 'The Bloody Chamber' indicates recalling Girard's contention that violence can be diverted but not contained. Even more disruptive is the implication of language. Its excess through all the stories of the collection most readily suggests the Gothic and the connection is there through de Sade. As Foucault writes 'Sade and the novels of terror introduce an essential imbalance within works of language: they force them of necessity to be always excessive and deficient' (Foucault 1977: 65). Yet while utilizing the language of terror and excess, many of the tales curiously do not evoke terror despite their cast of Bluebeards, werewolves and vampires, but rather replace it with the anticipation of violence – an exercise of creation through violence to recall Heidegger again. The productivity of Carter's language is the agent of supplementarity, of ongoing change even when the story appears to end (which is always present even if re-written). This is a conundrum. Myth might be 'extraordinary lies' in the service of oppressiveness, but Carter's new folktales are spectacular lies that refuse to cloak themselves in metaphysics. Their linguistic and specular preposterousness refuses to be concealed. In this respect the tales of *The Bloody Chamber* are Carter's *Metamorphoses* revelling in crimes, violence, sexuality and perversion which enable her to approach the subversiveness she was unable to grasp discursively in *The Passion*. Whatever the constraints of the original tale which reasserts or maintains the *status quo*, the cat has been let out of the bag. Indeed, as Peter Sloterdijk puts it: 'More communication means at first above all more conflict' (Sloterdijk 2006: 84). The excess of language encourages conflict between ideas, hierarchies, culture, time and space; nothing is taken seriously, everything is subject to question. Perhaps this is where reality finally lies for Carter as a practice, a need to question, to rip up, to reassemble and above all not to respect the organizing, hierarchical, symbol. It cannot be done away with, but it can be perpetually toppled and supplemented. As Girard argues, 'the sacrificial act assumes two opposing aspects, appearing at times as a sacred obligation to be neglected at grave peril, at other times as a sort of criminal activity entailing perils of equal gravity' (Girard 2005: 1). The passage between *The Passion* and 'The Bloody Chamber' mediated by Carter's engagement with de Sade, is the realization of the necessary obligation of repetition and the crime of contradiction towards the many symbols that govern the consciousness of our existence. Perhaps, even, the acute pain of transformation represented by the 'nigredo'.

Works Cited

Carter, A. (1979), *The Sadeian Woman: An Exercise in Cultural History*, London: Virago.
—(1981) [1979], *The Bloody Chamber*, London: Penguin.
—(1982) [1977], *The Passion of New Eve*, London: Virago.
—(1997), *Shaking a Leg: Collected Writings*, London: Penguin.
Derrida, J. (1976), *Of Grammatology*, trans. Gayatri Chakravorty Spivak, Baltimore: John Hopkins University Press.
Foucault, M. (1977), *Language, Counter-Memory, Practice*, trans. Donald F. Bouchard and Sherry Simon, Oxford: Blackwell.
Girard, R. (2005) [1972], *Violence and the Sacred*, trans. Patrick Gregory, London and New York: Continuum.
Heidegger, M. (2000) [1935], *Introduction to Metaphysics*, New Haven: Yale University Press.
Lefebvre, Henri (1991) [1974], *The Production of Space*, trans. Donald Nicholson-Smith, Oxford and Cambridge, Mass: Blackwell.
Makinen, M. (1997), 'Sexual and textual aggression in *The Sadeian Woman* and *The Passion of New Eve*', in Joseph Bristow and Trev Lynn Broughton (eds), *The Infernal Desires of Angela Carter: Fiction, Femininity, Feminism*, London and New York: Longman, 149–65.
Palmer, P. (1987), 'From "coded mannequin" to bird woman: Angela Carter's magic flight' in Sue Roe (ed.), *Eomen Reading Women's Writing*, Brighton: Harvester Press, 194–5.
Sloterdijk, P. (2006), 'Warten auf den Islam, *Focus* (October), 84.
Tylor, E. B. (2010) [1871], *Primitive Culture*, Cambridge: Cambridge University Press.
Williams, R. (1976), *Keywords: A Vocabulary of Culture and Society*, London: Fontana.
Žižek, S. (2009), *Violence: Six Sideways Reflections*, London: Profile Books.

10

Angela Carter, Naturalist

Anja Müller-Wood

The suggestion that Angela Carter's work may be naturalistic, whether thematically or stylistically appears to violate the constructionist focus of much of the existing criticism of her work. Yet Carter inspires such a naturalist perspective herself, confessing 'to a minor but passionate interest in natural history' in a 1985 interview and added: 'I suppose I am a Darwinian in that way' (Cagney Watts 1974: 164). This intriguing self-assessment points to an as yet unconsidered facet of Carter's work: her interest not only in 'nature', but also in 'human nature' and her repeated reminders that humans are animals – albeit 'with particularly complex social institutions' (Carter 1997: 301) – which I take as a hint at a naturalist bent that deserves to be investigated.

To argue that Carter's work may express naturalist concerns is not to deny her astute awareness of the cultural codes that shape (feminine) identity and determine sexual relations, her interest in 'how that social fiction of my "femininity" was created, by means outside my control, and palmed off on me as the real thing' (Carter 1983: 70; cf. also Carter 1979: 9). Especially in her early novels such as *Shadow Dance* and *The Magic Toyshop*, Carter explores the destructive implications of this cultural ballast on individual identity and intimate relationships, against which some of her characters struggle in vain.

Nevertheless, her work also reveals that the shaping influences of individual identity are not exclusively cultural, and the deconstruction of social codes is up against powerful material realities. Carter subscribed to an 'absolute and committed materialism' and saw it as the basis of our 'question[ing] the nature of reality' (Carter 1983: 70); however, in her work this material reality is not limited to the socio-economic conditions of human existence, but extends into its physiological and psychological dimensions. Sexuality is one of its most powerful manifestations, and in Carter's own words 'sexual conflict makes-the-world-go-round, is what produces the tensions that any society needs to continue forward' (Sage 1977: 55). Her concern with the material quality of human existence inevitably undermines the metafictional solipsism often ascribed to her writing, dovetailing neatly with her numerous savvy aphorisms about the relationship between literature and life: 'books about books is fun but frivolous' (Haffenden 1985: 79); 'the Ur-book is really Life, or The Real World' (Goldsworthy

1985: 5; capitalization in original); and, 'living and reading are the real training for writing fiction' (Cagney Watts 1974: 166).

Contrary to the enduring critical assumption that Carter was an out-and-out postmodern culturalist (cf. Pollock 2001: 35; Dennis 2008: 117), then, her work reveals a more complex awareness of the integral relatedness of culture and nature, and one that is entirely germane to her materialist stance. As a result, her understanding of human nature is as complex and differentiated as her view of human culture; 'the demythologising business' (Carter 1983: 71) in which she famously saw herself also extended to the mythical functionalization of nature, although she never doubted the reality of that nature *per se*. For Carter, against all her subversive speculations about the malleability of human identity, there is no escaping our animal nature, which presents the inexorable material limit with which all culture and ideologies fend. In fact, as I hope to show, this nature manifests itself in our most cultured activities – such as the writing and reading of literature.

The naturalist concerns that I have laid out above manifest themselves in three main ways in Carter's work: first, in the numerous cameo appearances of 'ordinary animals' in her work – prowling cats, curious piglets and the ubiquitous urinating dog (featured in several texts); secondly, in the many hybrids in her writing, from fantastic creatures (the werewolves and several quasi-vampires in her fairy tales) to freaks like the Ape-Man in *Nights at the Circus* (1984) and the winged protagonist Fevvers of the same novel; and, finally, in the many animal analogies and comparisons she uses to foreground specific human character traits. Critics have seen such instances as tokens of Carter's 'searching curiosity about the barriers which separate human animals from all others' (Pollock 2001: 39) – what she called the 'arbitrary division between man and beast' (Carter 1997: 301) – and as evidence that she transcends the anthropocentrism that typically characterizes representations of animals.[1]

Given that this anthropocentrism has a crucial function in Carter's particular brand of 'Ideologiekritik', however, it is doubtful whether transcending it would have been her prime intention. For Carter's writing, while full of animals, is also full of naturalists studying them, and it would appear that understanding the terms of human inquiry into the naturalist world was of far greater interest to her than a purportedly authentic representation of the animals themselves. In several novels, characters own stuffed animals – for example, the group of pigeons bought by Morris in *Shadow Dance* (Carter 1994: 27), the fox Lee in *Love* keeps in his bedroom (Carter 1988: 83), Melanie's teddy bear in *The Magic Toyshop* –which allow Carter to make a number of related points about the human relationship with the natural world. As objects of observation, taxonomy and imagination, these animals affirm humans' presumed distance from and power over nature, as well as their inability to represent it adequately; as slowly disintegrating *memento mori*, they point up the limits of this power by evoking the mortal materiality that all animals share.

The ideological investments of the human observation of animals are unmasked in a passage at the end of *The Passion of New Eve*, in which the narrator–protagonist Eve, during the ritual rebirth that concludes her protracted physical and mental transformation from ruthless Lothario to suffering Barbie-doll, progresses towards her own origins until she finally meets her maker, the gargantuan 'Mother'. In the process of retracing her development alongside that of evolution at large, Eve invokes a fossilized archaeopteryx:

> At that time, there was a bird called 'archaeopteryx' whose fossil will be found in the schist in Solenhofen [sic]; bird and lizard both at once, a being composed of the contradictory elements of air and earth. From its angelic aspect spring the whole family tree of feathered, flying things and from its reptilian or satanic side the saurians, creepy crawlers, crocs, the scaled leaper and the lovely little salamander. The archaeopteryx has feathers on its back but bones in its tail, as well; claws on the tips of its wings; and a fine set of teeth. One of those miraculous, seminal, intermediate beings brushed against a pendant tear of rosin in the odorous and primeval amber forests and left behind a feather. (Carter 1982: 185)

Critics reading this passage have singled out the 'intermediate' nature that the narrator ascribes to the prehistoric bird. Hence for Ricarda Schmidt the archaeopteryx is 'a combination of contrarieties' that 'symbolizes a wholeness before the separation into two different strands of evolution' and serves as 'a model for a future symbol of femininity' unifying 'what had been split into feminine and masculine in the course of evolution' (Schmidt 1989: 65). Yet this interpretation, apart from its underlying, slightly off-kilter notion of evolution, is that it misinterprets the passage in question. The protagonist's reflection upon the archaic proto-bird does not refer to *Homo sapiens'* sexual dimorphism, as Schmidt suggests: for Eve, the archaeopteryx heals a *spiritual* Manichaeism – the contrast between the angelic and the satanic – rather than the biological difference between male and female.

By extension, this flawed interpretation squarely ignores that Eve's depiction of the archaeopteryx, however naturalistic or pseudo-scientific it may appear, is itself an idealizing misinterpretation functionalizing the animal for Eve's ideology of hybridity. This ideology is in itself only superficially subversive of gender binaries and ultimately safeguards the negative characteristics that Evelyn's enforced sex-change and female conditioning were meant to cull. The curious reference to 'the lovely little salamander' – an animal that mythology describes as being so cold it can extinguish fire – recalls Evelyn's cruel abandonment of his lover after her botched abortion, for which he is punished by Mother's militant feminists, while the reference to the bird's angelic qualities recalls Tristessa de Saint-Ange, the faux feminine Hollywood icon that Evelyn had idolized from afar. Both can be seen to symbolize his ideal of transcendence and therefore, by association, come to bear on Eve's take on the prehistoric bird. Rather than illustrating the protagonist's differentiated understanding of evolutionary history, the archaeopteryx serves to assert her/his superior position within this process. Thus casting doubt over the positive effects of Eve's reverse evolution, symbolized by a piece of amber given to her at the outset of her final journey that is slowly turning back to resin as she approaches her own point of origin, the archaeopteryx is crucial to the novel's 'anti-mythic' strategy (Carter 1993: 71). Rather affirming the protagonist's transformative self-construction, it suggests that Evelyn's old identity will persist in 'New Eve'.[2]

A similar ideological misreading characterizes the Pythonesque taxonomy of marine invertebrate listed in *Heroes and Villains*:

Before them and around them were all the wonders of the seashore, to which Marianne could scarcely put a single name, though everything had once been scrupulously named. The fans, fronds, ribbons, wreaths, garlands and lashes of weed had once been divided into their separate families, wracks, tangles, dulses, etc. Purse sponge, slime sponge, breadcrumb sponge, blood red sponge; tube sea squirt, rough sea squirt, gooseberry sea squirt, star sea squirt (or golden star). Rag worms, lug worms, tube worms. The soft corals and sea anemones, known as dead men's fingers, snake locks, wartlet or gem anemone, the globehorn, the daisy anemone, cup coral, sea firs, sea oaks. The spiny skinned family of echinoderms, which include the brittle stars, feather stars, the sea cucumbers with their mouth fringe of whispy gills and the sea lilies which have ten feathery arms waving in the water. The jellyfish. And innumerable other names. (Carter 1981b: 136)

Although this curious inventory seeks to do justice to the immensely diverse, mysterious and potentially unknowable marine fauna, it also illustrates the human proclivity to categorize and 'scrupulously' label the natural world; as such, it seemingly subscribes to the rationalism of the Professors, one of the two clans whose conflict provides the backdrop to the plot. The list can be taken as illustrative of the discursive power of the symbolic order – which, as the final sentence suggests, is ultimately unconnected to the reality that it names.

Nevertheless, at the same time as illustrating the triumph of this order, the list undermines it, exemplifying what Carter in another context calls 'taxonomy run riot' (Carter 1997: 143) and drawing attention to the absurdity of the familiar and homely analogies that serve to describe the alien otherness of nature (gooseberry sea squirt, sea cucumbers, sea oaks, dead men's fingers etc.). For Marianne, these names are also no longer all available and/or effective, leaving her confronted with nature's pure visceral otherness. Her wordlessness indicates the limits of the Professors' scientific optimism and language, and identifies the dilemma in which human beings find themselves *vis-à-vis* the natural world: a part of nature and yet the only species able to reflect upon their position within it; their efforts to investigate and name nature only affirm their distance from it.[3]

In *Heroes and Villains*, Carter contemplates a dilemma that appears to have been of particular significance in her work from the late 1970s onwards. In a 1979 *New Society* review of David Attenborough's *Life on Earth* documentaries, she discusses how this popular introduction to evolution is marred by a tendency to slip into a grand narrative that has little to do with the actual process of evolution. 'Dedicated to pure wonder and the dissemination of fact', the programme documents how scientific objectivity falls prey to its own mythmaking; it is a 'romance about evolution', with presenter Attenborough unwittingly attaining the quasi-magical status of a 'guardian angel of terrestrial creation' (ibid., 310), able to give words to animal experience: 'The beasts can't speak for themselves so he has to do it for them and he knows more about them than they do themselves' (ibid.). In the event (and however unintentionally), the programme turns evolution's blind process of natural selection into a functional development steered by foresight, anticipation and will, and Carter comments with characteristic acuity: 'It is curious to see how the realisation there is no Grand Designer after all has not affected the notion of the Grand Design' (ibid., 313).

Carter here shrewdly identifies a crucial problem of natural history, namely that, in the words of Richard Dawkins: 'the living results of natural selection overwhelmingly impress us with the appearance of design as if by a master watchmaker, impress us with the illusion of design and planning' (Dawkins 1991: 21; see also Williams 1996, esp. 5–19.). Although the human propensity for teleology may itself be an evolved predisposition (Tooby and Cosmides 1990: 379), the confusion of the processes and 'goals' of evolution with the interests and concerns of individual organisms (ibid., 379–80) – which informs fallacious sociobiological formulae like the vulgar 'my genes made me do it' – is a misunderstanding of how evolution works. This is not to argue that a critique of the misapplication and misinterpretation of evolutionary theory was a central concern of Carter's writing; however, this critique is implicit in her guiding interest in human beings' animal nature.

This interest is expressed on the one hand when Carter compares animals and humans, usually to a negative or at least unsettling end. In *Love*, Lee has a leonine profile (Carter 1988: 30) (which recalls the name Leon that he had chosen as a first pseudonym), his brother Buzz is compared to 'a giant, hairy toad squatting upon his life and choking him' (ibid., 66), and Annabel, the mysterious ingénue who moves in with Lee, is presented initially as an undefined stray animal, fed and caressed by her new owner (ibid., 15). In *The Magic Toyshop*, the prim protagonist Melanie is taken aback by the 'ferocious, unwashed, animal reek' (Carter 1981a: 36) of her cousins by marriage, Finn and Francie, and dismisses the whole family for 'liv[ing] like pigs' (ibid., 77). These animal references overshadow Melanie's nascent emotional involvement with Finn, whose 'closeness, rank and foxy' (ibid., 68) she experiences as a physical infringement; earlier, in order to express pitiful distance, she had compared Finn to 'the petrol-soaked wreck of a swan come to grief in a polluted river' (ibid., 46). Lady Atalanta Hazard in *Wise Children* is likened to a sheep, which emphasizes her apparent ovine stupidity and passivity *vis-à-vis* her philandering husband, although the image collapses in the end (thus affirming the novel's motto that appearances are deceptive). In these and other instances, animals serve to make sense of humans.

But the full implications of such comparisons are revealed when the relationship between humans and animals is reversed, as for instance in Carter's 1976 *New Society* essay 'At the Zoo'. Superficially seen 'an exercise in comparative zoo-keeping' (Pollock 2001: 42), the essay is actually a study of the human condition, with human life as its firm point of reference. In the essay, the behaviour of the gorillas in London Zoo is viewed through the frame of popular soap operas, the ape enclosure in Turin Zoo is described as a Kafkaesque 'penal colony' (Carter 1997: 296), and the apes in the zoo at Verona – 'designed by people who saw the beasts' side of things completely' (ibid., 297) – are imagined as exchanging cocktail party commonplaces about the advantages of their situation: 'Well, taking all things into consideration, how much better off we are here than in the wild! Nice food, regular meals, no predators, no snakes, free medical care, roofs over our heads . . . and, after all this time, we couldn't really cope with the wild, again, could we' (ibid., 298). When the animals are not translated into human terms they remain alien, a puzzle, leading the narrator to ask repeatedly what the apes might be thinking. In thus asserting the distinction between humans and animals, Carter would seem to undermine her own belief that humans are separated by a mere 'whimsical quirk' from their animal relatives (ibid., 294, 307), and one might therefore accuse Carter of naïvely recreating a dilemma that she treated more critically in other contexts. Conversely, Carter's presumably naïve use of the anthropocentric perspective in 'At the Zoo' might be considered a strategic means to critically ventriloquize this viewpoint.

But the essay can also be read in another way. Carter's persistent assertions that humans are animals not only emphasize that even human behaviour that seems entirely cultural must result from our animal nature. They also invite another inference: namely, that to study human behaviour actually means to study the behaviour of a particular animal species, and that to understand other animals we only need to look at ourselves. By extension, to criticize this perspective as anthropocentric would mean to reinstate a division that for Carter did not exist. I will now turn to instances in Carter's writing in which the animal nature of humans is addressed in yet another way. In her work, I argue, Carter reveals that we come to literature with animal minds, that indeed literature is geared to the emotional and cognitive predispositions of these minds and that the most striking pointers towards our animal natures can therefore be found in the interaction between literary text and reader.

In a deliberately disconcerting passage in 'At the Zoo' Carter describes 'the chimp patriarch patrol[ling] the chimpanzee enclosure, round and round and round, on all fours, his flaming rump jutting well out and his tongue, also, stuck out at full length; on his tongue, he balances a great lump of the bright yellow shit produced by a fructarian [sic] diet' (ibid., 295). Despite the casual tone of this unflinching piece of ethology, the apparent superiority of its human observer creates a visceral sense of incomprehension which I believe is central to Carter's understanding of human nature and its reflection in literature. What are actually being described in the scene are two types of behaviour: first, the alien and incomprehensible actions of the chimp; second, the far more familiar response marked by the question of a child among the visitors: 'What's he doing that for, mummy?' (ibid., 296). The child's question, in which curiosity is tinged with disgust, gives voice to what a reader of the scene might have thought or felt her- or himself. Readerly responses to such stimuli are also triggered when Carter describes the baboons living in Turin Zoo who 'pickover the piles of straw-coloured shit on the floor of the arena, extract from it undigested husks, and eat them' (ibid., 297). The fact that the second scene goes uncommented only emphasizes its ability to achieve the specific physical reaction of disgust.

'At the Zoo' therefore is only superficially about the behaviour of non-human animals in an animal enclosure. What Carter addresses and uses in such scenes are the kind of human emotions that her critics, more interested in higher-level concepts like desire, pleasure or abjection, have been neglecting: the simple – 'garden-variety' (cf. Kivy 1989: 153; Carroll 1997: 191) – emotions like fear, awe, pity, admiration, anger, disgust and empathy, all of which are habitually exploited in literature and other art forms. Such emotions are not cultural constructs (although they may be culturally coded), but rather an evolved 'part of our biological makeup' (ibid., 198; cf. also Damasio 2000: 53–6). They are, in short, universal, an emotional architecture developed in the course of *Homo sapiens*' evolution as 'best-bet responses' to recurring situations of adaptive significance in the ancestral past of our species; as such they motivate behaviour, prepare the organism for action – for example, fight, flee or pretend that you are not there – and thereby potentially improve the prospect of survival. Seen from this perspective, to experience an emotion means that a specific emotion programme is initiated by a particular stimulus (or several particular stimuli) and in turn triggers a variety of sub-mechanisms – from physical reactions to cognitive evaluations and readjustments – in response (cf. Tooby and Cosmides 2000: 93–4).

Although 'natural', emotions are far more complex than the animal instincts with which they are related since, unlike animals, human beings do not inevitably act upon an emotional stimulus. Stimulus and response in humans are decoupled, creating a latency phase (in the psychological, not the psychoanalytical sense of the term), during which the situation that had triggered the emotion programme in the first place is reassessed and the body primed accordingly. For instance, certain stimuli in a horror movie might trigger an initial physical readiness and indeed initial physical reactions in the viewer. As her or his body reassesses the situation, the initial, instinctive responses might be arrested and retracted. Fiction, literature and film can therefore be seen as providing emotional 'dummies' similar to those used in animal experiments (cf. Mellmann 2006: 42–3): they are fictional triggers that incite real emotions within a framework that prevents these emotions from leading to actions. It is this structural specificity of the human emotional apparatus that explains the famous 'paradox of fiction' – the question why we can react vehemently and physically to literary artefacts even though we are aware of their fictionality (cf. Radford 1975).

'At the Zoo' reflects on literature's ability to act as such a dummy by exploiting the evolved emotion of disgust. It thereby returns to a topic central to Carter's first novel *Shadow Dance*, in which Honeybuzzard's (Honey's) manipulative nature is expressed by the novelty articles that he peddles in his junk shop: artificial snot, fake turds and deceptively realistic plastic insects, all of which illustrate his tendency to 'arrang[e] the world in terms of brutal slapstick' (Carter 1994: 76). Juvenile though these toys may seem they express his very serious desire to wield power over others, which is illustrated by his fantasy of a life-size chess game in which he would be directing real human beings from the sidelines through a megaphone. These fantasies also sum up Honey's manipulative relationship with his friend Morris, symbolized by the jumping Jack with Morris's face that Honey designs to remind his friend of who pulls the strings (thereby foreshadowing Uncle Philip in *The Magic Toyshop*).

The emotional impact of Honey's toys is explored in a scene in which he and Morris are suddenly surprised in an abandoned house they are searching for loot to sell in their shop:

> As Morris moved towards the bare boards of the door that had a great iron latch, the 'lift-up-the-latch-and-walk-in' latch of nursery tales, they heard slithering footsteps on the area steps outside and a voice raised uncertainly in indecipherable song. He froze in his tracks with fear and apprehension, eyes and mouth open like a Greek mask of horror. There were wheezings and bangings at the door and the jutting latch jiggled; the sound of a push, breath, effortfully expressed, wood grating on stone.
>
> Suddenly the door, out of control, swung open and banged against the frame. A gust of sweet night air blew into the room and was immediately extinguished by the

> black breath indoors. Their candles blew out. A finger of light from a street lamp
> outside widened into a cone and was then blotted out by a large, dark, lumbering
> shape, sighing and moaning and rancid.
>
>   It brushed past them but by some miracle did not touch them. Morris wanted
> to run for the door and escape but as he stirred, he felt a cold hand on his wrist.
> He nearly cried out; but he felt the familiar ridge of Honey's poison ring against his
> palm. Honey was stopping him. Honey wanted to stay. (ibid., 135)

The scene contains unambiguous signals to incite physical emotional responses in
the reader: the jiggling latch, the panting of an unidentified creature, the candle
extinguished by a breeze, the cold hand touching the protagonist. Carter's references
in the passage to nursery rhymes and Greek tragedy link these signals to other
cultural applications and deployments of the emotions and, by self-referentially
pointing to the novel itself, place it within a long tradition of literary horror. But
the situation is more complicated since on the level of the plot Morris and Honey's
encounter is of course 'real' and would require them to act appropriately. That
Honey holds Morris back once again illustrates their power relationship, in which
an emotion like fear is an easily manipulated resource for those who, like Honey,
can hide their responses behind a 'mask like nothing' (ibid., 59). Morris's problem,
by contrast, is that his relations with the world are overshadowed by his emotions,
which hinder his wish to transcend the material reality of life. These emotions
manifest themselves not only in his feelings of guilt, regret and compassion, but
also in his dependence on Honey, which makes him easy prey. Like a fish, he rises
to Honey's bait (ibid., 73) until he is finally 'hooked' (ibid., 74) by his manipulative
friend and partner.

     In Carter's later novels, the lack of emotionality that is Honey's mark of superiority
is depicted as the female characters' main strategy of resistance (cf. Sage 1994: 14). In
The Magic Toyshop, the protagonist Melanie distances herself from the erotic encounter
with Finn by imagining herself in a movie watched by someone else (Carter 1981a:
106), while Marianne in *Heroes and Villains* – who had already witnessed the violent
murder of her brother from the distance of her turret room – manages to mentally
detach herself from her own rape. In the speculative fictions of Carter's middle period
this distance is also echoed on the level of the narrative and style, which address the
readers' analytical faculties without engaging their emotions.

     In Carter's later work, however, the emotions that are persistently perceived
as dangerous and threatening by many of her characters acquire a somewhat more
productive function. Emotions are the basic material through which any art form
involves an audience: in Noël Carroll's words, they 'are the cement that keeps audiences
connected to the artworks, especially to the narrative fictions, that they consume'
(Carroll 1997: 191). As Carter's treatment of emotions in *Shadow Dance* reveals, she
was aware of their power. In that regard, Honey – whose obscene novelties are concrete
manifestations of the imaginary horrors of literature – can be seen as a fictional version
of herself. Carter's awareness that as an author she might have echoed one of her
disconcerting (male) characters is suggested by her dismissive comments on her early
style, in which she noted her manipulativeness and called herself a 'female impersonator'
(Carter 1983: 70–1). But if emotions do indeed function as the material that connects

author/text with the audience/reader, then how could Carter have detached herself from this essential prerequisite of her work? While achieving this detachment was central to Carter's earlier writing, her final novels suggest reconciliation with the emotions she had previously dismissed, precisely because she envisaged modes of resistance to productively put them to use.

Carter's increasingly functionalist take on literature, possibly encouraged by her mature acknowledgement that as a writer she was herself 'in the entertainment business' (Haffenden 1985: 82), explain why the celebration of emotional distance in her early and middle period transformed into a more active engagement with the emotional dimension of literature in her later work, much of which was influenced by her research into fairy tales. A gloss in Perrault's manuscript of 'Little Red Riding Hood' leads Carter to conclude 'that acting out the story has always been part of the story, traditionally' and that the telling of fairy tales must be seen as 'a rough kind of game' (ibid., 83). This idea seems to have influenced her last two novels. With *Nights at the Circus*, parts of which are told from the perspective of the winged woman Fevvers, Carter turns to a style that more overtly engages the readers' emotions. She also, interestingly enough, turns to comedy. The comic-conversational style launched with her character Fevvers comes into its own with the voice of Dora Chance, the narrator of *Wise Children*. Dora's confessional first-person narrative is unreliable, persistently warning us of the deceptions of memory, foregrounding human forgetfulness and confusing us with the intricacies of the byzantine Hazard dynasty. Yet while on the one hand, family history thus becomes subject to speculation and interpretation, the novel also suggests that there is a world beyond the stories. The motif of kinship that runs through the novel, Nora and Dora Chance's desire to be acknowledged by their biological father Melchior and the focus on inheritance (both genetic and pecuniary) all confirm Carter's critique of an all-too constructionist reading of the human identity. And it is precisely Dora's manipulations of the reader that tell us something about what lies beyond the text.

Dora does not so much narrate as perform her story, engaging the reader in an immediate, seductive and interactive way in her confessional first-person account. Seemingly addressing an unidentified conversational partner whose responses provide cues for her narration, she echoes the comic routine of Gorgeous George, the vaudeville comedian that Nora and Dora had accidentally watched on Brighton Pier when they were little:

> '. . . and this boy's thoughts turned lightly to' – big poke in the air with the gold club – 'so he says to his dad, "I want to get married to the girl next door, Dad"'.
>
> '"Ho, hum", says his dad. "I've got news for you, son. When I was your age, I used to get me leg over –"'
>
> Roars, shrieks, hoots; but all so much titillation without any substance, I tell you, because he gave them a shocked look, pursed his lips together, shook his golf club in reproof.
>
> '*Filthy* minds, some of you have', he grieved in parenthesis. Renewed hoots and shrieks.
>
> 'What I was about to say before I was so rudely interrupted . . .'
>
> That was his other catch phrase. (Carter 1991: 64)

George's smutty skit about the perils of paternity relies on his exploiting the audience's grasp of double entendre and linguistic ambiguity. But the audience is not merely passively exposed to this routine, as George's cheeky reminder of the audience's 'filthy minds' suggests. The point is, of course that they do indeed have these filthy minds (at least potentially) and not only that, it is crucial to the comedian's salacious routine. In other words, George's joke does not create the emotions at which his stimuli are directed; the fact that his audience is capable of responding to them makes it possible for him to trigger them in the first place.

Granted, the imperious George is far from a positive character. A direct descendant of Honey in Carter's first book – whose theatrical qualities are noted by a marginal figure of the novel (ibid., 111) – and the later puppet master Uncle Philip in *The Magic Toyshop*, George lords it over his audience just as the once dominant British Empire whose map he has tattooed all over his body did over its colonies. Yet like the Empire that he literally attempts to embody, the comedian comes to a sorry end on the streets of London where Dora encounters him on the eve of her father's birthday, begging for 'a bob' (ibid., 196).

The former vaudeville star's fall might be put down to the transformation of the entertainment business that Dora bemoans throughout her narrative. From that perspective, George (no longer gorgeous) is simply a victim of changing fashions. Yet however much we might read his demise as evidence that humour (and the emotions to which it appeals) are culturally coded and hence culturally specific, Carter also emphasizes the continuing relevance of humour across generations. After all, Dora Chance – whose genealogic yarn keeps Carter's readers in thrall without reducing them to passive consumers – had learnt her lesson from none other than Gorgeous George. Transforming this tradition into an engagingly oral account, Dora gives voice to Carter's perceptive, performative naturalism, according to which emotions are to be taken seriously and the reader for real.

Notes

1   For Elaine Jordan, 'Carter's use of wolves and other beasts in her stories reminds us that we are animals, and, in the tradition of the fable, says that animals may have more sense than us, when we think ourselves most sophisticated' (Jordan 1990: 25). Pollock rightly criticizes Jordan's 'conflation of the human with the animal' (Pollock 2001: 38), claiming that in her short story 'The Quiltmaker' Carter avoids this anthropocentrism by depicting a cat as 'a thoroughly feline character . . . rather than a projection of human nature onto a feline form' (ibid., 43). Pollock's idealism reveals her to be immune to the obvious irony of Carter's cat portrait while being at the same time entangled in the very structures that she disavows. Her claim that 'it is clear that the cat loves Letty for the comfort she provides' (ibid., 44) is anthropocentric itself, imposing a human concept of love upon the animal.

2   I here beg to differ with Lorna Sage, who interprets the passage in question by drawing on paleontologist Stephen Jay Gould's argument in his book *Wonderful Life* (1989), that the process of evolution could potentially have led to entirely different outcomes – that our natural world is no inevitable development. 'Going back', Sage glosses, 'you encounter a world of possibilities' (Sage 1994: 37). It is striking

that Sage singles out the work of a particularly contentious evolutionary biologist for her argument, especially as this choice is clearly anachronistic: Gould's book was published over a decade after *Passion*. Most importantly, however, Gould's speculations ultimately apply neither to the novel nor to our lives: we cannot go back. Whatever alternative evolutions we may imagine, we and our lives are the results (and bear the consequences) of one specific, irreversible evolutionary process.

3   For Pollock nature can only 'be understood darkly when we manage to minimize our own investments in the symbolic order' (Pollock 2001: 39). Carter, she argues, manages to abandon the symbolic order by using an 'antic language' (ibid.) that remains true to nature's complexity. This division between nature and humans is fundamentally at odds with Carter's belief in human beings' animal nature.

Works Cited

Cagney Watts, H. (1974), 'An Interview with *Angela Carter*', *Bête Noir* 8, 161–76.

Carroll, N. (1997), 'Art, Narrative, and Emotion', in Mette Hjort & Sue Laver (eds), *Emotions and the Arts*, Oxford: Oxford University Press, 190–211.

Carter, A. (1979), *The Sadeian Woman*. London: Virago.

—(1981a) [1967], *The Magic Toyshop*, London: Virago.

—(1981b) [1969], *Heroes and Villains*, London: Penguin.

—(1982) [1977], *The Passion of New Eve*, London: Virago.

—(1983), 'Notes from the Front Line', in Michelene Wandor (ed.), *On Gender and Writing*, London: Pandora Press, 69–77.

—(1984), *Nights at the Circus*, London: Picador.

—(1988) [1971], *Love*, London: Picador.

—(1991), *Wise Children*, London: Virgin.

—(1994) [1966], *Shadow Dance*, London: Virago.

—(1997), *Shaking a Leg: Collected Writings*, London: Penguin.

Damasio, A. (2000), *The Feeling of What Happens: Body, Emotion and the Making of Consciousness*, London: Vintage.

Dawkins, R. (1991), *The Blind Watchmaker*. London: Penguin.

Dennis, A. (2008), ' "The Spectacle of her Gluttony": The Performance of Female Appetite and the Bakhtinian Grotesque in Angela Carter's *Nights at the Circus*', *Journal of Modern Literature*, 31 (4), 116–30.

Goldsworthy, K. (1985), 'Angela Carter (Interview)', *Meanjin* 44, 4–13.

Haffenden, J. (1985), *Novelists in Interview*, London: Routledge, 76–96.

Jordan, E. (1990), 'Enthralment: Angela Carter's Speculative Fictions', in Linda Anderson (ed.), *Plotting Change: Contemporary Women's Fiction*, London: Routledge, 19–40.

Kivy, P. (1989), *Sound Sentiment: An Essay on the Musical Emotions*, Philadelphia, Temple University Press.

Mellmann, K. (2006), *Emotionalisierung – Von der Nebenstundenpoesie zum Buch als Freund: Eine emotionspsychologische Analyse der Literatur der Aufklärung*, Paderborn: Mentis.

Pollock, M. S. (2001), 'Angela Carter's Animal Tales: Constructing the Non-Human', *Literature – Interpretation – Theory* 11, 35–57.

Radford, C. C. (1975), 'How Can We be Moved by the Fate of Anna Karenina?' *Proceedings of the Aristotelian Society*, Supplementary Volume 49, 67–80.

Sage, L. (1977), 'The Savage Sideshow: A Profile of Angela Carter', *New Review* 39/40, 51–7.

—(1994), *Angela Carter*, Plymouth: Northcote House.

Schmidt, R. (1989), 'The Journey of the Subject in Angela Carter's Fiction', *Textual Practice* 3, 56–75.

Tooby, J. and Cosmides, L. (1990), 'The Past Explains the Present: Emotional Adaptations and the Structure of Ancestral Environments', *Ethology and Sociobiology* 11, 375–424.

—(2000), 'Evolutionary Psychology and the Emotions', in Michael Lewis and Jeannette M. Haviland-Jones (eds), *Handbook of Emotions*, New York: Guilford Press, 91–115.

Williams, G. C. (1996), *Plan and Purpose in Nature*, London: Trafalgar Square.

11

The Surrealist Uncanny in *Shadow Dance*

Anna Watz

'Surrealism', stated Angela Carter in a 1984 interview, 'didn't involve inventing extraordinary things to look at, it involved looking at the world as though it were strange' (Haffenden 1985: 92). This comment is an apt definition of surrealism's project of defamiliarizing everyday reality; of rendering the familiar strange, uncanny or dreamlike in order to reveal the marvellous within. It also captures the essence of Carter's own surrealist practice in her début novel *Shadow Dance* (1994). This novel, profoundly surrealist in both style and imagery, portrays a dreamlike reality that has been infiltrated by unconscious fears and desires. Focalized mainly through the perspective of its neurotic protagonist Morris, *Shadow Dance* depicts a world in which the unconscious and the imagination are as material as reality itself. The two pioneering tracts on surrealism – Louis Aragon's 'A Wave of Dreams' (2003) and André Breton's first *Manifesto of Surrealism* (2004), both originally published in 1924 – define the surreal as precisely such a blurring in the individual mind between the categories of imagination and reality. '[T]he true nature of reality', Aragon writes, 'is just an experience like any other' – 'the essence of things is not at all linked to their reality . . . there are other experiences that the mind can embrace which are equally fundamental such as chance, illusion, the fantastic, dreams. These different types of experiences are brought together and reconciled in one genre, Surreality' (Aragon 2003: 1). Aragon's account of the surrealist pursuit of this new hallucinatory reality is echoed in Breton's *Manifesto*: 'I believe in the future resolution of these two states, dream and reality, which are seemingly so contradictory, into a kind of absolute reality, a *surreality*, if one may so speak. It is in the quest of this surreality that I am going' (Breton 2004: 14; emphasis in the original).

Carter's adoption in *Shadow Dance* of both an overwhelmingly male narrative perspective, and the iconography of the largely male surrealist movement, serves two subversive aims. The text, I will argue, seeks provocatively to mimic, in order to lay bare, misogynist patterns buried deep in the (male *and* female) psyche, and in that way challenge traditional and prescriptive notions of femininity as either passive and virtuous or threatening and castrating. This theme is illustrated by the dramatization of an uncanny return of the repressed, which is inextricably linked to an abject femininity, eliciting both fear and feelings of aggression in the male subject. Simultaneously, the representation of misogynist violations of the female body becomes part of Carter's surrealist aspiration to shock and disturb, as an end in itself. These two threads, I will suggest, can be seen both to reinforce and to contradict each other. The sexual aggression that characterizes the male protagonists' treatment of the female character Ghislaine in *Shadow Dance* bleeds into Carter's own *textual* aggression against cultural convention. The ultimate effect of this, I argue, is an ambivalent tightrope act in which Carter's text both performs a feminist critique and simultaneously risks becoming complicit in the very patriarchal logic it is trying to transcend, in which women exist only as metaphors, circumscribed by the myths the male imagination has constructed around them.

Carter's alignment with the historical avant-garde serves as a revolt both against what she perceived as the contemporary British 'realist' literary scene and against static cultural conventions, including prescribed versions of 'feminine' behaviour.[1] As Julia Kristeva argues, '[t]he surrealists always sought out unbearable, provocative, or erotic events to repel the bourgeois. . . . The choice of characters in surrealist poetic and prose texts was itself dictated by the notion of scandalous event' (Kristeva 2000: 118). In *Shadow Dance*, such surrealist scandal is perhaps most visibly embodied in the character Honeybuzzard, whose black humour and transgressive actions carry strong echoes of the cinema of Luis Bûnuel and Salvador Dalí. Their film collaborations *Un Chien andalou* (1929) and *L'Age d'or* (1930) employ a violent and erotic surrealist language of the unconscious in order to shock and disturb, a project which seems to have had a major influence on the young Carter. In a 1984 interview with Toril Moi, she attests to the profound influence these films – in particular the latter one – had on her writing in her early twenties (Moi 1984: 19). Honeybuzzard's sadistic cutting of Ghislaine's face bears an obvious resemblance to the infamous opening scene of *Un Chien andalou*, in which a man splits open a woman's eye with a razor. Moreover, Honeybuzzard's blasphemous murder of Ghislaine at the end of the novel closely follows the model of sacrilege and transgression set up in the closing scenes of *L'Age d'or*, in which Jesus Christ is cast as the murderous libertine Duc de Blangis of the Marquis de Sade's *The 120 Days of Sodom*.[2]

Honeybuzzard's blasphemous violence is on one level a symbol of Carter's own atheist and iconoclastic agenda, which underpins her oeuvre as a whole. However, while surrealist acts of erotic blasphemy (such as Honeybuzzard's) had enjoyed immense shock-value in the 1920s and 1930s, they had most certainly lost at least some of their revolutionary edge in 1966, when Carter wrote *Shadow Dance*. As Matei Calinescu observes, by the 1960s, the avant-garde had become absorbed by mainstream culture. 'The avant-garde, whose limited popularity had long rested exclusively on scandal', he writes, 'all of a sudden became one of the major cultural myths of the 1950s and the 1960s. Its offensive, insulting rhetoric came to be regarded as merely amusing, and its apocalyptic outcries were changed into comfortable and innocuous clichés. Ironically, the avant-garde found itself failing through a stupendous, involuntary success' (Calinescu 2006: 120–121). Therefore, one might argue, it is questionable whether the rhetoric of scandal and shock in *Shadow Dance* can offer any significant challenge to conventional morality for a post-1960s audience.

This blatant rhetoric of scandal is perhaps the most visible surrealist echo in *Shadow Dance*, but, as I will suggest, it is rather in its marvellous disruption of subjective reality that the novel most fully achieves surrealism's subversive aims. This estrangement effect is primarily produced through the novel's evocation of the uncanny. The revolt of *Shadow Dance*, therefore, is ultimately staged in the intimate spaces of the psyche. Moreover, in its dramatizations of the return of the repressed, Carter's novel brings the iconography of surrealism to bear on normative gender stereotypes, in this way opening up the possibility for a renewal of the subversive potential of surrealism itself. However, as I will show, the feminist subversion in *Shadow Dance* is highly ambivalent, as the novel oscillates between radical critique of patriarchy and complicity with the very patriarchal logic it is attempting to overthrow.

Uncanny Returns

The uncanny as a concept has been intimately associated with the core of the surrealist aesthetic project.[3] This term, according to Freud, relates 'to what is frightening – to what arouses dread and horror.' Not everything that is frightening is uncanny, however: '[t]he uncanny is that class of the frightening which leads us back to what is known of old and long familiar' (Freud 1955: 219, 229). To define the 'special core of feeling' that constitutes the uncanny (*das Unheimliche*), Freud carries out an analysis of the etymology of the German word *heimlich*, which, he concludes, can both mean homely, 'what is familiar and agreeable', and 'what is concealed and kept out of sight' (ibid., 224–25). Thus only the first signification of *heimlich* is the antonym of *unheimlich*, while the subsidiary definition actually shades into that of its opposite: '*heimlich* is a word the meaning of which develops in the direction of ambivalence, until it finally coincides with its opposite, *unheimlich*. *Unheimlich* is in some way or other a sub-species of *heimlich*' (ibid., 226). Freud explains this seeming paradox in the following way: 'this uncanny is in reality nothing new or alien, but something which is familiar and old-established in the mind and which has become alienated from it only through the process of repression . . . the *unheimlich* is what was once *heimlich*, familiar; the prefix "*un*" ["un-"] is the token of repression' (ibid., 241, 245). Hence, the uncanny is a commingling of the familiar and unfamiliar, or, as Kristeva writes, 'that which *is* strangely uncanny would be that which *was* (the past tense is important) familiar': in short, the uncanny is an unexpected return of repressed material (Kristeva 1991: 183; emphasis in the original). It is closely connected to a ' "compulsion to repeat" proceeding from the instinctual impulses and probably inherent in the very nature of the instincts – a compulsion powerful enough to overrule the pleasure principle . . . whatever reminds us of this inner "compulsion to repeat" is perceived as uncanny' (Freud 1955: 238). Hence, the uncanny experience is triggered by an encounter with something intimately familiar, which is perceived as strange because it has undergone repression.

The surrealists actively sought to disturb the distinction between the categories of the imagination and reality, a project that according to Hal Foster intimately connects their art and literature to the disruptive effects of the uncanny. This 'concern with events in which repressed material returns in ways that disrupt unitary identity, aesthetic norms, and social order' is, Foster writes, 'crucial to particular surrealist oeuvres as well as to general surrealist notions'. The surrealists, he continues, 'not only are drawn to the return of the repressed but seek to redirect this return to critical ends' (Foster 1993: xvii): they employ the unsettling effects of the uncanny as part of their revolutionary project. As Bethany Ladimer tells us, '[a]lthough for most modern revolutionaries the term "revolution" necessarily suggests *collective* action, which finds its origin in the subsuming of individual concerns to those of the group, surrealism was unique in that it consistently identified the starting point of social change with the liberation of the *individual* psyche' (Ladimer 1980: 175; emphasis in the original). In this sense, the surrealist exploration of the return of the repressed as a revolt against notions of a coherent self has a clear parallel in Kristeva's re-evaluation of revolt. In *The Sense and Non-Sense of Revolt*, Kristeva provides an etymology of the word revolt, suggesting that we bear in mind its Latin origin, the verb *volvere*, which means to 'turn' or 'return' (Kristeva 2000: 1). 'In urging us to recall these etymological traces of "return" embedded in the word "revolt" – all of which imply a non-linear temporality', Ashleigh Harris explains,

> Kristeva prompts a psychoanalytic Freudian reading of the term, in which she focuses on the 'return of the archaic, in the sense of the repressed but also the timelessness (*zeitlos*) of the drive' (Kristeva 2000: 12). . . . Revolt, then, becomes 'interrogation', and intimate act emerging, primarily, from within the singularity of experience, rather than from shared, communal and political experiences of time and history (Kristeva 2002: 13). (Harris 2011: 231–2)

The uncanny – the return of the repressed – brings with it the possibility of such 'intimate revolt' as it disrupts the subject's sense of a coherent identity. As Kristeva explains in *Strangers to Ourselves*, 'uncanniness maintains that share of unease that leads the self, beyond anguish, towards depersonalization. . . . [It] is a *destructuration of the self*' (Kristeva 1991: 188; emphasis in the original).

Shadow Dance repeatedly invokes the uncanny and dramatizes it in a surrealist manner that revolts, disturbs and unsettles. The plot of *Shadow Dance* revolves around a literal return: the once beautiful Ghislaine returns from a one-month stay in hospital, where she has been treated after having been knifed by her previous sexual partner, the charismatic but dangerous Honeybuzzard. Her face is now horribly disfigured by a deep scar, 'all red and raw as if, at the slightest exertion, it might open and bleed' (Carter 1994: 2). Ghislaine's scar 'drew her whole face sideways and even in profile, with the hideous thing turned away, her face was horribly lop-sided, skin, features and all dragged away from the bone' (ibid.). Although it was Honeybuzzard who scarred Ghislaine, the novel's protagonist, junk-shop owner and amateur painter Morris, knows that he was complicit in the crime, as he, after a disastrous love affair with her, 'gave' her to Honeybuzzard to 'teach her a lesson' (ibid., 34).

The narrative point of view of *Shadow Dance* is predominantly provided by Morris whose uncontainable and uncontrollable feelings of guilt, terror and anxiety perpetually threaten the boundary between reality and imagination in the text. The opening scene is a case in point, as Sarah Gamble has pointed out, since it is distorted by Morris's 'subliminal fears and fantasies . . . mak[ing] the line between subjectivity and objectivity almost impossible to draw. Thus, reader as well as character is drawn

into an environment within which the validity of everything is open to question'
(Gamble 1997: 48–9). The novel opens as Morris meets Ghislaine, for the first time
after her disfiguration, in the local bar:

> 'Morris!' she said.
> He, in a vacant muse, turned; and flinched away from her, from the touch of her
> hand on his arm, in a sudden terror.
> 'Hellooo, Morris', she said; her vowels moaned like the wind in the pines. 'I
> thought I might see you here'.
> 'Oh, God in heaven', he said in his mind, as if invoking protection against her.
> 'Shall I buy a drink for you, Morris? Have you no money? Always penniless,
> poor Morris'.
> He had half thought, half imagined what she would look like when he was
> forced to see her again but, meeting her with this unprepared suddenness, he
> could speak or think or look at anything but her face. (Carter 1994: 1–2)

'[A]n uncanny effect is often and easily produced when the distinction between
imagination and reality is effaced', writes Freud (Freud 1955: 244). An uncanny blurring of
the real and the imagined is present from the very start of *Shadow Dance*, and produces a
fundamental unsettling of Morris's sense of identity. As soon as Ghislaine walks through
the door, the atmosphere, as experienced though Morris's perspective, becomes suffused
with eeriness and dread, as if invaded by something ghostly: Ghislaine's emergence is
sudden and terrifying, her touch is repugnant, and her voice is that of a spectre returning
to haunt him. Her appearance in the bar causes Morris so much trepidation that he
instinctively invokes protection against her. The confrontation with 'her shattered beauty'
(Carter 1994: 3) induces panic in him: 'The noise in the public house banged at his head;
pulses behind his eyes began to throb and beat. The white walls waltzed around him and
he thought he might faint' (ibid.). A few pages later, when Morris thinks he has regained
a footing in reality, the crevice between the real and the imagined opens up again as he is
'suddenly gripped with the nauseating conviction that [his beer] tasted of her':

> He was drinking her down sacramentally; the taste of her metallic deodorant
> sweat and the foundation cream she smeared over her lips to make them pale
> and a chemical smell of contraceptives and her own sexual sweat. At once the
> memory of her naked, threshing about beneath him, homed to him like a pigeon
> and horrified him with its impropriety. He felt as though he had an erection at a
> funeral. He could not bear to drink from his glass again and flushed it behind a
> bowl of melting ice, to hide it.
> 'I mustn't get upset', he thought fearfully; he thought he might start screaming,
> with fear and hysteria, snatching up things and throwing them around. (ibid., 5)

As this passage illustrates, Morris is unable to distinguish between subjective experience
and objectivity reality, a perspective that perpetually threatens to push him into a state
of hysteria. Importantly, the above passage also displays the immanence of eroticism
in Morris's fear of Ghislaine, a connection which will become increasingly strong as
the narrative progresses.

In fact, Ghislaine's own claims to familiarity or normalcy appear to make her seem all the more estranged to Morris, as her pieces of commonplace conversation are construed as an uncanny commingling of the strange and the familiar. 'Isn't it funny', she says: 'It wasn't even properly spring when I went to hospital, the trees were only just a little bit green at the tips and it got dark so early. But now it's almost summer and everywhere is so lovely and waaaaarm' (ibid., 6). For Morris, this banal pronouncement is imbued with both the (once) comfortably homey and the frightening (-ly sexual). The 'lingering voice on the long vowel' is for Morris 'like an intimate caress. A caress from a witch-woman' (ibid., 6). It evokes a memory of the *heimlich*, as that which is 'intimate' and 'friendlily comfortable' (Freud 1955: 222), but that is returned as something eerie, witchlike, seductive and dangerous. Ghislaine becomes the locus of this ambiguity. The commingling of fear and eroticism in Morris's experience of the uncanny Ghislaine is betrayed by his response: '"The sap's rising", he said. His voice shook. Now, he wondered, why did I say "The sap's rising" to her? What will she think I mean?' (Carter 1994: 6). Apparently relating to Ghislaine's comment about the seasonal change in temperature, Morris's reply also conspicuously exhibits the eroticism inherent in the effect she has on him. Again, the surfacing of a sexual memory relating to Ghislaine utterly disturbs Morris's sense of control over himself.

Ghislaine's return from hospital sets up a dichotomy between the past and the present, the boundary between which is represented by Ghislaine's transformation: 'A month ago, she was a beautiful girl; how could such a girl not be beautiful? . . . She was a beautiful girl, a white and golden girl, like moonlight on daisies, a month ago. . . . To talk to her, simply, made you feel pampered, loved and wanted. Or had done until a month ago' (ibid., 2, 3, 5). Before the scarring Ghislaine represents, it would seem, the very idea of the *heimlich* – the homely and familiar, 'friendlily comfortable' (Freud 1955: 222) – a description which stands in stark contrast to the way in which she is portrayed after her release from hospital: returned she is a 'bride of Frankenstein . . . a horror-movie woman' (Carter 1994: 4) and her face is 'all sideways and might suddenly – at too large a mouthful of drink or a smile too unwisely wide or a face-splitting request for "bread and cheeeeeeese" – leak gallons of blood and drown them all, and herself, too' (ibid., 3). The scar itself, as Gamble notes, 'comes to represent a conceptual break between the past and the present; what Ghislaine was and what she is' (Gamble 1997: 49), the thrice repeated 'a month ago' (Carter 1994: 2, 3, 5), invoked in the description of what Ghislaine used to be like before the mutilation of her face, almost like an incantation, reinforcing the dichotomy between the present and an irrecuperable past.

Moreover, the automatic repetition of 'a month ago' contributes to an uncanny sense of hysteria or panic which infiltrates the narrative perspective as a whole. The histrionic prose of the opening section poses a threat to the very boundaries of the narrative itself, as it reveals something uncontainable and maddening at its core. The exaggeration and mania that tinges the description of Ghislaine is a case in point, and is worth quoting in some detail:

> She was a very young girl. She used to look like a young girl in a picture book, a
> soft and dewy young girl. She used to look like the sort of girl one cannot imagine

sitting on the lavatory or shaving her armpits or picking her nose. She had such a little face, all pale; and soft baby cheeks and a half-open mouth as if she was expecting somebody, anybody, everybody she met to pop a sweetie into it.

And she had long, yellow, milkmaid hair and her eyes were so big and brown they seemed to gobble up her face, as those of a bush baby do. They were as big as the eyes of the dog with eyes as big as cartwheels in the fairy story; and as brown as wood or those painted on Egyptian mummy cases. And her darkened lashes swept down over half her cheeks.

And she was so light and fragile and her bones so birdy fine and little and her skin was so light and translucent. You wondered how she had the strength to hold the great big, heave half-pint mug when she drank and you remembered how the red wine had seemed visible, running down the white throat of Mary, Queen of Scots.

. . .

She glanced at him over the rim of her glass, sharing sly secrets, and laughed her personalized, patented laugh – she must be the only girl, anywhere, who could laugh like that. The shimmery, constricted yet irrepressible giggle of a naughty little girl, such a young, lovely and wicked giggle. (ibid., 2, 6)

The language in this passage has acquired an overt fairy-tale aura (emphasized, again, by the repetition of 'a month ago'), which also deliberately blurs the distinction between reality and imagination. The sense of excess in this passage is related to an aggression that characterizes the violent imagery in the narrative as a whole: the affectation and exaggeration with which Ghislaine's apparent innocence is construed betrays strong resentment. The aggression is further reinforced by sudden slips contradicting the depiction of Ghislaine as innocent: her smile, while being 'tremulous' and 'shy', is simultaneously 'disingenuous' (ibid., 3), and soon after the description of her innocence she is referred to as '[r]otten' and 'phoney' (ibid., 4), wanting to 'weep and glitter with public tears and fatten her undernourished little self on them, her poor little vanity, all pale and thin with pinman Oxfam arms and legs' (ibid., 8). Furthermore, the description of Ghislaine's giggle as 'naughty' and 'wicked' – the import of which is implicitly sexual – testifies to Morris's desire to punish her.

I have argued elsewhere that Morris's fear of losing control when faced with Ghislaine is overtly linked to castration anxiety.[4] Hence, Ghislaine's scar is configured in Morris's imagination as a monstrous vagina threatening to 'open up and swallow her into herself, screaming, herself into herself' (ibid., 10), to 'leak gallons of blood and drown them all, and herself, too' (ibid., 3), to 'absorb him, threshing, into the chasm in her face' (ibid., 39). Castration anxiety is, according to Freud, a direct source in the uncanny experience (Freud 1955: 231–3), and it is the scar itself that most acutely represents the uncanny menace Ghislaine poses to Morris, both because it becomes the symbol of the horrifying change she has undergone and because of its sexual menace of engulfing or castrating him. Indeed, for Freud, the female genitalia are themselves uncanny: 'It often happens that neurotic men declare that they feel there is something uncanny about the female genital organs. This *unheimlich* place, however, is the entrance to the former *Heim* [home] of all human beings, to a place where each one of us lived once upon a time and in the beginning' (ibid., 245). Thus, for Freud, what determines the uncanny experience that accompanies the encounter with the female genitalia is a kind of 'homesickness' – a desire to return to an intrauterine existence within the womb (ibid.). It would consequently seem as if the uncanny is intricately bound up with the maternal (the original 'home'). 'Why is it that the maternal landscape, the *heimisch*, and the familiar become so disquieting?' Hélène Cixous asks in her essay on Freud's 'The Uncanny': 'The answer is less buried than we might suspect. The obliteration of any separation, the realization of the desire which in itself obliterates a limit' (Cixous 1976: 544). The fantasy of maternal plenitude, of an intimacy and unity before any separation or loss, in this way implies a complete loss of self, the total erasure of the boundaries of subjectivity, which is simultaneously desired and deathly for the subject.

As Foster has convincingly argued, surrealist art repeatedly evokes images of maternal plenitude as well as paternal punishment, both of which fantasies, as we have seen, are inextricably linked to an uncanny unsettling of the self (Foster 1993: 193). Indeed, as Foster argues, the surrealists consciously sought to produce a disruption of unitary identity in their art and literature for critical purposes (Foster 1993: xvii). In Marcel Raymond's words, the task was 'to unsettle man, to make him lose heart in the face of his life and the world, to put him in permanent contact with the irrational' (Raymond 1970: 318). This 'convulsion' of given notions of identity, to use the artist Max Ernst's term, through inducing a kind of hysterical sensibility in the subject, would upset expected and rational ways of seeing the world (Ernst 1948: 19). The uncanny – through the return of a repressed desire for plenitude – produces such a disturbance of the subject's sense of identity. The radical unsettling of the boundaries of the subject evokes both fear and pleasure, as it reminds the subject of a prior pre-linguistic space – before the separation from the maternal and the subsequent formation of autonomous identity. This 'return of the archaic' (Kristeva 2000: 12), which prompts fundamental self-interrogation through 'depersonalization' and 'a *destructuration of the self*' (Kristeva 1991: 188; emphasis in the original), is the version of revolt Kristeva is advocating.

Ghislaine's appearance in the pub at the start of *Shadow Dance* puts Morris in a fearful trance that threatens to obliterate his sense of a rational self. The action which makes him momentarily able to restore a feeling of rationality is his pronunciation of her name: after 'struggl[ing] vainly for words ... finally, thank God, he found he was able to speak her name. Her bare, naked name; but it would do for a start' (Carter 1994: 4). The articulation of her name temporarily breaks '[t]he bad spell on him', 'for he had always disliked and resented her name and he found he disliked and resented it still . . . He looked down at the top of her head in pure, remembered dislike' (ibid.). It is significant that it is reinstated *aversion* that 'rescues' Morris from the dread Ghislaine elicits in him. As a threat to his sense of a coherent subjectivity, the mere thought of encountering her makes him feel 'spectral and translucent, a figment of somebody else's imagination' (ibid., 107). The pronunciation of her name becomes a symbolic act of aggression which is a premonition of a succession of acts of violence throughout the narrative: the naming, and the dislike that accompanies it, temporarily puts Morris in symbolic and psychological control of Ghislaine – it makes her symbolically containable and less threatening. It is also an act of expulsion, of abjection, for his aggressive naming of Ghislaine enables Morris to reinstate the boundaries around his self. As we later learn, Morris 'could best accommodate the thought of Ghislaine as the subject for a painting, a Francis Bacon horror painting of flesh as a disgusting symbol of the human condition; that way, she became somehow *small enough for him to handle*, she dwindled through the wrong end of the telescope of art' (ibid., 19–20; emphasis mine). This fantasy too betrays his anxiety of not being able to contain and possess Ghislaine.

One of the sources of Morris's neurotic response to Ghislaine is his complicity in her mutilation – the very reason that she returns 'estranged'. Upon finding Ghislaine's murdered body at the end of the novel, Morris confesses that he had indeed 'wished it'; he had wanted Honeybuzzard to kill her (ibid., 178). His desire to violate Ghislaine is translated into a series of compulsive and symbolic repetitions of the violence Honeybuzzard subjected her to. Upon his return home from the bar on the night of Ghislaine's release from hospital, Morris repeats the mutilation of her face in an act of symbolic violence. With his wife Edna asleep in the next room, he, '[i]n a fever, . . . stared around the room as if it were a stranger's room' (ibid., 15): the uncanny has thus pervaded the very symbol of the *Heimlich* – the home. Seized with a compulsion, he 'could not stop looking at the bookshelf' (ibid., 15), where he has hidden a collection of erotic photographs he and Honeybuzzard took of Ghislaine before she was scarred. Intending to erase her face with ink in order to 'duly extinguish her', he is instead seized with a desire to scar her and proceeds to mark 'each image of her with a long scar from eyebrow to navel' (ibid., 17). Morris's aggression towards Ghislaine, subsequently repeated in a series of dreams in which he cuts her face with a shard of broken glass or a blunt kitchen knife, emanates from an urge to re-establish the boundaries of his subjectivity, which Ghislaine so clearly threatens.

Sexual/Textual Violence

As I have suggested elsewhere, the mutilated Ghislaine is suggestive of surrealism's many violated female forms, which more or less overtly evoke the threat of castration.[5] Ghislaine's vagina-like scar serves to literally inscribe her 'feminine condition' – her castration – on her face. As an emblem of castration, she represents both the frightful castratrix and the image of the wounded (castrated) woman, shackled by her self-imposed martyrdom. The image of the castrated woman is, it would seem, the ultimate source of all the evocations of the uncanny in *Shadow Dance*, and is rehearsed by Carter in order to deconstruct it. In *The Sadeian Woman* Carter would later write, '[f]emale castration is an imaginary fact that *pervades the whole of men's attitude towards women and our attitude to ourselves*, that transforms women from human beings into wounded creatures who were born to bleed' (Carter 2000: 23; emphasis mine). What Carter calls the 'social fiction of the female wound' is, in her analysis, thus essential in the construction of the patriarchal myth of woman as an inferior victim. Her rehearsal of this myth in *Shadow Dance*, as in the rest of her oeuvre, aims to lay bare the processes through which the objectification of women is constituted. In this manner, as Gamble argues, the novel is 'exhibiting exploitation' (Gamble 2006: 61) through the deeply engrained patriarchal attitudes that not only propel aggression towards women as both embodiment and threat of castration, but also cement the internalization by women of a myth of femininity as marked by victimhood.

The violence to which Ghislaine is subjected is symptomatic of a culture in which the notion of woman is connected with victimhood and passivity; this is the ugly reality Carter is attempting to diagnose and display in *Shadow Dance*, in order for it to be critiqued and ultimately transcended. According to Sage, the image of the suffering woman victim was a spectacle Carter 'feared and loathed and found hilarious', and her cruel treatment of this image in her writing in 'is a measure of her fear' (Sage 1994: 32–3). Thus, as Sage implies, the violation of Ghislaine in *Shadow Dance* perhaps signifies more than a sheer exhibition of destructive myths about femininity in patriarchy; it also seems to work as a channel for Carter's own aggressions and fears regarding a version of femininity she wants to deconstruct and destroy. Ghislaine symbolizes a submissive and even masochistic femininity, which makes her deliberately renounce her own agency and embrace the role of the victim. Carter, in *Shadow Dance* as well as in all her subsequent fiction, explicitly interrogates what she considers such complicity on women's part in their own subjection and objectification. The coldness and even resentment with which the unravelling of Ghislaine's destiny is rendered is symptomatic, I venture, of Carter's own anger and aggression towards woman as a symbol of submissiveness and victimhood.

In this way, *Shadow Dance* repeats surrealist gendered violence as a revolt against both conventional notions of femininity and what Carter perceived as the contemporary literary convention. However, while Carter's adoption of a surrealist iconography that hinges on representations of violence against women does produce the desired effects of shock and disturbance, it does not automatically mean that it succeeds in its aim to liberate gender stereotypes. A feminist interrogation of Honeybuzzard's and Morris's violations of the female body might suggest that they, and the novel itself, actually to some extent reinforce misogynist values rather than destroy them, especially since Carter herself seems not to have been critically reflecting on the potential problems that might arise when a female author embraces a rhetoric that has been almost exclusively produced by men. As Carter herself later would comment in 'Notes from the Front Line' (1983), as a young writer, she was 'suffering a degree of colonisation of the mind . . . there was an element of the male impersonator about this young person as she was finding herself' (Carter 1998: 38). Furthermore, in an interview with Olga Kenyon, she confesses that '[i]t took me a long time to identify patriarchal bias in my discourse' (quoted in Gamble 1997: 54). Even more unsettling, perhaps, is Carter's claim that at the beginning of her career she 'didn't see the point of feminism' (Clapp 1991: 26, quoted in Gamble 1997: 54). These comments suggest that Carter's use of surrealist imagery in *Shadow Dance* might not have included a critical awareness of the overwhelmingly male bias of the surrealist movement.[6] Indeed, this novel was written before the wave of feminist critique of surrealist misogyny in the 1970s, and it is possible that Carter considered the mutilations of the female body in surrealism as pure subversion and shock (which of course, on one level they are).

It is notable that Carter overtly invokes the writings of Frantz Fanon in her later assessment of her young self. Although Fanon's notion of the 'colonisation of the mind' is admittedly taken out of their original context here, Carter's own utilization of this particular language to describe her engagement with patriarchal discourses in her early fiction is significant. Fanon, in *Black Skin, White Masks* (1952) discusses the acceptance by the colonized of the construction of themselves as inferior. Through the productions of race in popular media, such as magazines, comic books and adventure stories, Fanon argues, one can observe in the colonized 'the formation and crystallization of an attitude and a way of seeing and thinking that are essentially white' (Fanon 1967: 148). The colonized person's unwitting adoption of a 'white' subject position implies the construction of him- or herself in relation and opposition to a black other. This act of 'othering' involves a measure of rejection and aggression, which, in Fanon's analysis, the colonized unconsciously turn back on themselves (ibid., 147). Translated into gender terms, then, for Carter this meant that as a young writer she would, by her own admission, 'posit a male point of view as a general one' (Carter 1998: 38). More than that, however, it might also suggest that Carter's textual aggression against norm and convention merges with the sexual aggression she is representing through Honeybuzzard's and Morris's misogynist treatment of Ghislaine. In this way Ghislaine becomes a metaphor for something Carter herself is rejecting, a version of femininity she desperately does not want to inhabit. But, in choosing to revolt against female passivity and submissiveness through the adoption of a male, even patriarchal, language, it is questionable whether the novel can actually renew the gender norms it is seeking to undermine.

The seemingly impenetrable male perspective is perhaps the most truly shocking aspect of *Shadow Dance*, and is, in my view, what complicates and ultimately compromises Carter's critique of normative constructions of femininity in this novel. As Gamble points out, by excluding the female characters from any narrative voice, 'they are rendered figments of a fevered male imagination, and . . . become silent receptacles for male desires' (Gamble 1997: 54). Carter's aim to expose and transform the power structures that engender aggression against the figure of woman as a passive, inferior and 'castrated' being, ultimately threatens to fold back on itself, as Carter herself risks becoming complicit in the same logic she is attempting to transcend, in which women exist only by virtue of the myths the male imagination has constructed for them. Thus, the novel's 'intimate revolt', through its invocation of the surrealist uncanny, is deeply ambiguous: both triumphant and complicit.

Notes

1 *Shadow Dance* is one of a number of British novels written in the 1960s that resisted conventional literary realism in various ways, and which can be seen to herald the experimentalism of the postmodern text. See, for example, Malcolm Bradbury, Chapter Six, 'The Sixties and After, 1960–1979', in *The Modern British Novel*.
2 For a more in-depth discussion of Honeybuzzard's transgressions, see Anna Watz, 'Convulsive Beauty and Compulsive Desire: The Surrealist Pattern of *Shadow Dance*' in Rebecca Munford (ed.), *Re-Visiting Angela Carter: Texts, Contexts, Intertexts*, 21–41.
3 See, for example, Hal Foster, *Compulsive Beauty*; Elizabeth Wright, "The Uncanny and Surrealism," in Peter Collier and Judy Davies (eds), *Modernism and the European Unconscious*; Margaret Cohen, *Profane Illumination: Walter Benjamin and the Paris of Surrealist Revolution*; David Lomas, *The Haunted Self: Surrealism, Psychoanalysis, Subjectivity*.

4 See Watz, 'Convulsive Beauty and Compulsive Desire: The Surrealist Pattern of *Shadow Dance*'.
5 See Watz, 'Convulsive Beauty and Compulsive Desire: The Surrealist Pattern of *Shadow Dance*'.
6 In later novels, such as *The Infernal Desire Machines of Doctor Hoffman* and *The Passion of New Eve*, Carter would employ a male narrative perspective critically, through the distancing device of irony. Morris's perspective, however, lacks such distancing irony.

Works Cited

Aragon, L. (2003) [1924], 'A Wave of Dreams', trans. Susan de Muth, *Papers of Surrealism* 1 (Winter 2003), http://www.surrealismcentre.ac.uk/papersofsurrealism/journal1/acrobat_files/deMuth.pdf. Accessed 27 December 2010.

Bradbury, M. (1994), *The Modern British Novel*, London: Penguin.

Breton, A. (2004) [1924], *Manifesto of Surrealism*, in *Manifestoes of Surrealism*, trans. Richard Seaver and Helen R. Lane, Ann Arbour: The University of Michigan Press, 2004, 1–47.

Calinescu, M. (2006), *Five Faces of Modernity: Modernism, Avant-Garde, Decadence, Kitsch, Postmodernism*, Durham: Duke University Press.

Carter, A. (1994) [1966], *Shadow Dance*, London: Virago.

—(1998) [1983], 'Notes from the Front Line', *Shaking a Leg: Collected Journalism and Writings* (ed.) Jenny Uglow, London: Vintage.

—(2000) [1979], *The Sadeian Woman: An Exercise in Cultural History*, London: Virago.

Cixous, H. (1976), 'Fiction and Its Phantoms: A Reading of Freud's Das Unheimliche (The "Uncanny")', *New Literary History*, Vol 7, No. 3 (Spring, 1976), 525–48.

Clapp, S. (1991), 'On Madness, Men and Fairy-Tales', *The Independent on Sunday* (June 1991), 26–7.

Cohen, M. (1995), *Profane Illumination: Walter Benjamin and the Paris of Surrealist Revolution*, Berkeley and Los Angeles: University of California Press.

Ernst, M. (1948), *Beyond Painting: And Other Writings by the Artist and His Friends*, New York: Wittenborn, Schultz.

Fanon, F. (1967) [1952], *Black Skin, White Masks*, trans. Charles Lam Markmann, New York: Grove Press.

Foster, H. (1993), *Compulsive Beauty*, Cambridge, MA: MIT Press.

Freud, S. (1955) [1919], 'The Uncanny', *The Standard Edition of the Complete Psychological Works of Sigmund Freud*, vol. 17, trans. James Strachey, London: The Hogarth Press and The Institute of Psycho-Analysis 219–52.

Gamble, S. (1997), *Angela Carter: Writing from the Front Line*, Edinburgh: Edinburgh University Press.

—(2006), 'Something Sacred: Angela Carter, Jean-Luc Godard and the Sixties', *Re-Visiting Angela Carter: Texts, Contexts, Intertexts* (ed.) Rebecca Munford, Basingstoke: Palgrave, 42–63.

Haffenden, J. (1985), *Novelists in Interview*, London: Methuen.

Harris, A. (2011), 'What Revolt in the Postcolony Today?', *Traversing Transnationalism: The Horizons of Literary and Cultural Studies*, Pier Paolo Frassinelli, Ronit Frenkel and David Watson (eds), Amsterdam: Rodopi, 225–49.

Kenyon, O. (1992), *The Writer's Imagination: Interviews with Major International Women Novelists*, Bradford: University of Bradford Print.

Kristeva, J. (1991), *Strangers to Ourselves*, trans. Leon S. Roudiez, New York: Columbia University Press.

—(2000), *The Sense and Non-Sense of Revolt: The Powers and Limits of Psychoanalysis*, trans. Jeanine Herman, New York: Columbia University Press.

—(2002), *Intimate Revolt: The Powers and Limits of Psychoanalysis*, trans. Jeanine Herman, New York: Columbia University Press.

Ladimer, B. (1980), 'Madness and the Irrational in the Work of André Breton: A Feminist Perspective', in *Feminist Studies* 6, no. 1 (Spring 1980), 175–95.

Lomas, D. (2001), *The Haunted Self: Surrealism, Psychoanalysis, Subjectivity*, New Haven: Yale University Press.

Moi, T. (1984), 'Pornografi og fantasi: om kvinner, klaer og filosofi', *Vinduet* 4 (1984), 17–21.

Raymond, M. (1970) [1933], *From Baudelaire to Surrealism*, translator unknown, London: Methuen.

Sage, L. (1994), *Angela Carter*, Plymouth: Northcote House.

Watz, A. (2006), 'Convulsive Beauty and Compulsive Desire: The Surrealist Pattern of *Shadow Dance*', *Re-Visiting Angela Carter: Texts, Contexts, Intertexts* (ed.) Rebecca Munford, Basingstoke: Palgrave, 21–41.

Wright, E. (1990), 'The Uncanny and Surrealism', in Peter Collier and Judy Davies (eds), *Modernism and the European Unconscious*, Cambridge: Polity Press.

12

The Art of Speculation: Allegory and Parody as Critical Reading Strategies in *The Passion of New Eve*

Kari Jegerstedt

Recent years have witnessed a shift in Carter criticism away from the more traditional focus on Carter's 'politics' towards a more sustained preoccupation with her 'poetics'. This shift is an important reorientation, not only because it broadens the scope and field of Carter criticism, but also because it might shed new light on the already well-established tradition of political explications.[1] In Carter's work 'politics' and 'poetics' are intrinsically intertwined. Thus, insofar as most political analyses have tended to focus on what her texts *say* rather than what they *do*, valorizing the content of the utterance over the utterance itself, important aspects of Carter's innovative reworking of the Western imagination are lost.

The tendency to privilege content over practice has also hampered the discussions of allegory and parody, the two literary conventions or narrative modes most frequently associated with Carter's work. The many readings of Carter's quintessential anti-mythic novel, *The Passion of New Eve* (1977), are a case in point. Although widely recognized as one of Carter's allegorical novels, the specificities of allegorical writing are seldom mentioned in the actual analyses of the text; and when they are, allegorical elements are most often seen as covert representations of the novel's (hidden) 'message'.[2] Likewise parody, which permeates the overall tone and structure of the novel, tends to be reduced to a form of ridicule – mainly linked to Mother's (admittedly rather absurd) version of 'feminism'.[3]

Instead of investigating how allegory and parody work, the critical reception of *The Passion* has focused on whether or not the novel inscribes viable alternatives to the hegemonic conceptions of gender and femininity that it, according to most critics, sets out to debunk. However, such alternatives have proven difficult to find, thus leading its reception into a kind of deadlock: where one critic finds a positive alternative to existing gender norms (for example in the love relationship between Evelyn and Tristessa), another critic points out that the very same 'alternative' merely re-inscribes yet another 'mythical' representation (be it the Platonic hermaphrodite, or the playing out of femininity as masochism).[4] Arguably this 'deadlock' has been rather fruitful, spurring a critical dialogue that produces ever new (and interesting) readings. Even more importantly, it has increased the critical awareness of how pervasive and deep-seated gendered constructions are, constantly challenging the reader's own reflection and creativity. Yet at the same time this 'deadlock' is symptomatic of a certain prejudice in dealing with literary texts, asking them to offer solutions to political and philosophical problems (and criticizing them when they don't), instead of engaging with the particular ways in which signification is produced, including the text's own interpretative and self-reflexive procedures, its form and structure, its distinctive work with and within (literary) language. Due to the lack of involvement with these more formal aspects, a large part of Carter's aesthetic and political import is made to seem less radical than it actually is.

In this essay I argue that a detailed analysis of the complex interplay between parody and allegory in *The Passion* – especially as it relates to Freudian psychoanalysis – not only opens for reconsideration the main themes in the novel, but also calls for a reassessment of Carter's so-called demythologizing practice. In this essay I argue that a detailed analysis of the complex interplay between parody and allegory in *The Passion* – especially as it relates to Freudian psychoanalysis – not only opens for reconsideration the main themes in the novel, but also calls for a reassessment of Carter's so-called demythologizing practice. 'Reading is just as creative an activity as writing and most intellectual development depends upon new readings of old texts,' Carter states in 'Notes from the Front Line' (Carter 1997: 37). And her much quoted claim that she is investigating 'the social fictions that regulate our lives' (Carter 1997a: 38), 'transforming actual fiction forms to both reflect and to precipitate changes in the way people feel about themselves' (Carter 1997: 42), suggests that her writing must be conceived as a practice of *reading*, striving to destabilize Western hegemonic narratives from within. Parody and allegory play an important part in this reading strategy and situates Carter's 1977 novel within a distinctly postmodern practice of what Ross Chambers has called oppositional (or appropriative) critique, proceeding, most typically, in a 'de Certeaudian' manner, 'making use of dominant structures for "other" purposes [than they were meant for] and in "other" interests' (Chambers 1991: xiii). Indeed, *The Passion*'s redeployment of Freudian discourse, inserting it in 'fiction form', reorients not only Freud's 'purpose' and 'interests', but the 'purpose' and 'interests' of allegory as well, loosening it from its historical function as a didactic genre serving to reveal 'truths and ideals' and setting it in play within the formulae of 'speculative fiction' – meaning, as Carter explains, exactly that: 'the fiction of speculation, the fiction of asking "what if?" … a system of continuing inquiry' (Katsavos 1994: 14). Thus both Freud and allegory get a new twist: the speculative question asked in *The Passion*, where Evelyn is castrated and turned into the perfect woman, Eve, can, in fact, be construed as a parodic-allegorical literalization of a Freudian theme: 'What if woman really *was* a "castrated man"?'.[5] But how are we to read this question: in what ways does it serve as the basis for 'a system of continuing inquiry', especially as it concerns the specifically *feminist*, demythologizing aspects of the novel being not only, as Carter claims, an explicit thematization of 'the social creation of femininity' (Carter 1997a: 38), but also dedicated to change, a form of 'applied linguistics' serving to create 'a means of expression for an infinitely greater variety of experience than has been possible heretofore', precisely through 'new readings of old texts' (ibid., 42)?

Constituting a work with(in) language and texts, the use of parody and allegory in
The Passion do in fact account for the interpretative 'deadlock' pervading its reception,
debating whether Carter's so-called alternative representations are 'truly' alternative or
not: like all 'oppositional' practice, parody and allegory *necessarily* re-inscribe dominant
figures of thought. As Chambers remarks, oppositional criticism – which takes as its
premise that 'new' representations are always the function of existing power structures,
thus the solution is to work not only within but *with* those structures, effecting changes
in the way they signify – is always complicit, constantly having to negotiate the fact
that the very 'condition of there *being* change is, at the same time, the very condition
that constrains *the nature* of change' (Chambers 1991: xx). According to Hutcheon this
double coding as both complicity and critique is at the heart of 'the postmodern paradox',
since herein, she argues, lie also the political limits of postmodernism. Postmodernism
can only critique systems, never step outside them, thus circumscribing action on the
social level. Even if it may 'offer art as the site of political struggle by its posing of
multiple and deconstructive questions', since 'it never escapes its double coding . . . it
does not seem able to make the move into political agency' (Hutcheon 2002: 157).

The notion of oppositional reading thus apparently leads us straight into another
'deadlock', impeding the possibility of feminist art having direct, political consequences.
However, Hutcheon's prioritizing of social action – advancing that fiction and art should
prescribe the direction for action and change in 'the real world' – forecloses another
alterative: the possibility of reading art and fiction as *acts in themselves*, altering and
expanding the institutions and systems of representations that they work within. Within
this context, postmodern 'ambiguity', asking 'multiple and deconstructive questions'
without providing answers or clear directions for thoughts/action, is not a political
evasion but the very prerequisite for involving its readers/viewer in the (solidary)
act of *joint* creativity, posing questions 'designed to produce a sense of alienation and
discomfort in the reader so that newness may enter and alter a defamiliarized world'
(Salih 2004: 4).

Parody might be seen as a prime defamiliarizing device, since it exploits the fact that
representations can be subjected to radical 'trans-contextualisations' (Hutcheon 2000),
repeated in contexts that are alien to them, even in contexts that they have been meant
to exclude. Thus parodic trans-contextualization also makes it possible to question the
very system that governs the construction of representations. As Judith Butler argues,
parody reveals that what is represented as 'original' and 'natural' is always already
imitation, or copies, of ideals and norms – that is of phantasmatic entities (Butler 1999:
41).[6] Parody then not only opens already existing structures of signification for new
possibilities of meaning, but challenges, even changes, the ways they work. But how
does allegory play into this picture; in what ways can it, as a reading strategy, inform
not only a reading *of* but also the reading *in The Passion*?

Allegorically Speaking

To treat *The Passion* as an allegory is first of all to pay heed to the way the novel situates
itself as text or literature. The novel makes use of several conventions traditionally

associated with narrative allegory, such as the typical allegorical quest plot. Evelyn is the allegorical hero, thrown into chaos (New York), then setting out on a journey (Westwards, to 'find' himself) through dreamlike landscapes (the desert, Beulah, Zero's farm, Tristessa's glass mansion) where he encounters a series of challenges (imprisonments, a new sexual identity, abuse, falling in love) that must be dealt with while all the time heading towards the 'final inconclusiveness' exemplary, according to Maureen Quilligan, of all narrative allegories' ending (Quilligan 1979: 13). The novel leaves Eve(lyn) on the coast of California with a small boat that is also a coffin, to give birth to a child whose nature we never get to know. In this way, the novel not only situates itself within a specific generic tradition but, in doing so, also asks its readers to take part in a very specific interpretative game. Indeed, one of the central paradigms in its critical reception, that the ending of *The Passion* points to a radically open future, the (re- or de-gendered) meanings of which cannot as yet be represented,[7] concurs with the tendency of allegories to end just before 'an apocalyptic explosion of meaning' (ibid., 220).

This call for interpretation is expanded by the fact that allegory is not simply a plot structure, but always a relationship to another, or several other, text(s). If allegory, like parody, experienced a renaissance with postmodernism, becoming the major mode through which an earlier repertoire of representations and forms were reworked, it is, as Craig Owens argues in 'The Allegorical Impulse', precisely because of postmodernism's preoccupation with reading (Owens 1992). Like parody, allegory is first and foremost a relationship to another text, providing a structure through which it is 'read'. The number of texts attended to and engaged with in the richly wrought intertextual web of *The Passion* is, however, quite overwhelming, producing, as Susan Rubin Suleiman puts it, 'a dizzying accumulation [of narrative possibilities] that undermines the narrative logic by its very excessiveness' (Suleiman 1990: 137). Yet, these various multiplications/ subversions are not only dizzying, they are also the function of a distinctly allegorical structure, which, moreover, inscribes them in specific interpretable forms. Following Northrop Frye's claim that we have an allegory when a text 'obviously and continuously' refers to another system of signification, most often a set of religious or philosophical ideas (Frye 1990: 91), it is in fact possible to limit the allegorical prerequisites for *The Passion*'s many excesses to three religious/philosophical systems: the Bible ('the passion of new Eve' and the myths of the Creation and the Fall); the alchemical tradition (the novel's structuring according to the alchemical stages: *nigredo*, *albedo*, *rubedo*) and psychoanalysis (the coming into being of woman through 'castration' and the notion of the return of the repressed).[8]

Of course, these references do not make up the novel's 'true meaning'. Allegorical narratives must, as Quilligan points out, be distinguished from *allegoresis*. In contrast to *allegoresis*, which is an hermeneutic interpretative practice, narrative allegories, that work through the literalization of the concepts and ideas of its pretexts, making characters function as personifications of abstract figures of thought, do not search for 'hidden meanings', but play out its meaning on the surface of the text itself. However, the allegorical text's relationship to its pretexts does serve as 'the key to its interpretability' (Quilligan 1979: 23), that is: it structures its *readability*; the very fact that it can be interpreted and, at the same time, that it can be interpreted in several ways but is not open for just any determination.

Interestingly, the systems of signification that the novel inhabits are all narratives of transformation and change, whether in the form of salvation (the Bible), the making of gold or the betterment of the soul (alchemy), or in the notion of a cure (psychoanalysis). Thus, as Lorna Sage suggests, *The Passion* may indeed be read, precisely, as an 'allegory of change' (Sage 1996: 45). Yet as such, the novel reads equally well as a meta-fictional reflection on a genre: allegories are, by their very nature, narratives of change. Indeed, as Gay Clifford points out, it is exactly because allegories wish to express 'change and progress' that their action 'often takes the form of a journey [or] a quest', which then 'becomes the metaphor by which a process of learning for both protagonists and readers is expressed. In the course of their adventures the heroes of allegory discover which ideals are worth pursuing and what things are obstacles of value and disvalue' (Clifford 1974: 11). Thus *The Passion* seems to confront us with a series of redoublings, where the notion of change operates on several levels at the same time – the thematic (allegory *of* change), the structural (allegories *as* narratives of change), and the intertextual, or pretextual, level (the novel's allegorical inscriptions of the Bible, alchemy and psychoanalysis as narrative of change) – highlighting the issue of change as the major preoccupation in the novel.

Yet the reader who approaches *The Passion* as a traditional allegory of/as change will run into several problems. Most importantly these problems concern how to locate the text's 'ideals' or exactly *what*, in fact, Eve(lyn) learns. As Elaine Jordan observes, to the extent that 'readers often assume that Eve (. . .) is a role model for a new woman' and an 'ideal', they are missing out on what is going on: Eve(lyn) is a passive character who 'is put through certain phases of action for the instruction of the reader'; '[i]t is the action and the commentary on it which signify' (Jordan 1992: 122). Although Jordan does not talk about allegory here, her reading invokes other typical allegorical conventions. Both didacticism ('the instruction of the reader') and 'the incorporation of commentary and interpretation into the action' are well-known generic characteristics of narrative allegories (Clifford 1974: 5), and important elements in the novel's redeployment of the allegorical form. However, shifting the perspective from what Eve(lyn) learns to what the readers learn by way of 'instructions' does not solve the problem; the most pressing issue in the criticism of *The Passion* is whether we can speak of any changes, or any possibilities for change, at all.

The issue of change is given another twist if we turn away from the didactic elements of allegory and focus instead on how allegory functions in a demythologizing practice – of which *The Passion*, according to Carter, is a prime example – especially as it concerns her stated intent to investigate how certain 'truths' are produced against a background of 'myths' and ideological conceptions circulated as if they were 'facts', 'the real thing' (Carter 1997: 38). Here 'truths', following Simone de Beauvoir and Roland Barthes, are given a 'mythical' quality; thus they cannot be subsumed under the traditional conception of allegories pointing to 'real', or 'true', truths. Rather, the 'obvious and continuous' references to the Bible, alchemy and psychoanalysis serve to order a set of historically constructed, culturally specific 'truths' in a certain way, not only inscribing them within pre-given narratives of 'change' from which the novel, as we shall see, creates *new* fictions, but also laying them 'bare' for investigation through the process of *literalization*.

Literalization is *the* chief allegorical device. As Quilligan observes, narrative allegories constantly valorize the literal over the figural, not the least through their preoccupation with personifications. This preoccupation accounts for the 'obsession with words' found in narrative allegories, where meaning is typically construed as word-play, inquisitive uses of puns etc. (Quilligan 1979: 31), making allegories in fact function as investigations into 'the literal truth inherent in individual words, considered in the context of their whole histories as words' (ibid., 33). Allegories then become a specific way of working with and within texts and language, favouring, as Gregory Ulmer points out, 'the material of the signifier over the meanings of the signifieds', and functioning within 'an "epistemology" of performance – knowing as making, producing, doing, acting, as in Wittgenstein's account of the relation of knowing to "the mastery of a technique"' (Ulmer 1983: 94–5). Yet literalization may also function inquisitively in parody insofar as the taking of words at *face value* represents a form of intentional 'misreading', serving to expose the more or less unconscious implications that reside in the rhetoric of the parodied discourse or text. Reading literally in this way, parody converges with allegory in a shared, but differential, effort to uncover 'the literal truth inherent in individual words'. And it is typical of the use of parody and allegory in *The Passion* that they are constantly intertwined, allegory always being parodic, and parody allegorical, thus displacing the opposition between parody and allegory conceived as a difference between revealing 'faults' or 'truths' and opening, instead, for a creative, interventionist investigation not only of words but of discursive systems, considered to generate 'myths' circulating as 'facts'. At this point parody and allegory also meet speculation, posing the speculative 'what if?' question as a parodic-allegorical literalization of a Freudian theme: 'What if woman really was a castrated man?'. Indeed, this question may be seen to structure the whole plot, such that Evelyn's transformation into Eve can be read as a consistent literalization of the Freudian narrative of how femininity develops – or in Freud's own words: how a woman 'comes into being' (Freud 1991: 149) – as it is presented (for example) in his essay 'Femininity'.

'What if Woman Really was a Castrated Man?'

According to Freud's essay 'Femininity', a woman does not exist *a priori* but is the effect of a complicated psychosexual development through which she 'develops out of a child with a bisexual disposition' (ibid.). Indeed, Freud argues, in her pre-Oedipal phallic phase the little girl even *is* 'a little man' (ibid., 151). She derives pleasure from her clitoris, her little 'penis-equivalent', in the same way as the boy derives pleasure from his penis, and, like him, she takes her mother as her object of love and of her (incestuous) fantasies. The turning point in the little girl's development, the very moment she becomes, as it were, 'a girl', arises with her specific form of the castration complex – the realization that she lacks 'the boy's far superior equipment' and with it, her 'acknowledgement' of 'inferiority' (ibid., 160). Blaming this unfortunate 'fact' on her mother, the little girl turns away from her in hatred. From now on the girl's development is governed by penis-envy, which is why she turns to her father, searching for the longed-for object.

Thus begins her journey towards mature, 'normal' womanhood, which is only reached when the girl/woman's desire for a penis is replaced by the desire to have a child. In Freud this transition or exchange – penis/child – is equalled with 'an ancient symbolic equivalence'; hence his conclusion that a woman's 'happiness is greatest if later on this wish for a baby finds fulfilment in reality, and especially so if the baby is a little boy who brings the longed-for penis with him' (ibid., 162).

Evelyn's transformation into Eve closely echoes Freud's text and does so, precisely, through literalizing it. Eve(lyn) not only develops from a 'child with a bisexual disposition', cleverly denoted by his very name – Evelyn is both a male and female name – he is, quite literally (in his 'phallic phase') a *little man*: 'slender and delicately made' (Carter 1982: 55).[9] The castration which marks the turning point in his development is a literal act, also making literal the mother's supposed responsibility for the girl's lack of a penis/phallus: Mother effectively 'cut[s] off all [his] genital appendages with a single blow' (ibid., 70). Thus begins Eve(lyn)'s development into 'normal' womanhood. Starting in the video room in Beulah were s/he is exposed to various imagery of culturally sanctioned femininity, including 'every single Virgin and Child that had ever been painted in the entire history of Western European art' (ibid., 72), it evolves as a gradual acceptance of and growth into motherhood – happy to escape it at the sterile Zero's farm ('it was a great relief to me to know I would not be betrayed to motherhood in this vile place' (ibid., 102)), ready to embrace the possibility in his/her first encounter with Tristessa ('I felt a sensation within me as though the neck of my new womb moved' (ibid., 125)) – and culminates at the shores of California where Eve(lyn) declines the offer to have his former male genitals (temporarily stored in a portable miniature fridge) back, opting instead for the future as a mother. Again Freud's rhetoric of the equivalence penis/child as a 'symbolic exchange' where the desire to have a baby replaces the desire to have the male genital organ, is made literal. Eve(lyn)'s development into a woman unfolds, in other words, as an allegorical literalization of Freudian discourse on femininity, making Eve(lyn) the very personification of this discourse.

This literalization of Freud's text is not, however, only allegorical but also parodic. It serves, first, to highlight certain phallocentric aspects of Freud's discourse, thus coding the meaning of the narrative differently recalling Mikhail Bakhtin's claim that parodies 'transpose the values of the parodied style, to highlight certain elements while leaving others in the shade' (Bakhtin 1981: 75). *The Passion* dramatizes, through literalization, how within Freudian discourse femininity is constructed on a male model, making woman a special case of man, a product of his desire. The woman Eve(lyn) becomes is, after all, nothing but a 'Playboy center fold', his 'own masturbatory fantasy' (Carter 1982: 75), the ironic twist being that s/he is forced to be, live and feel like this fantasy, becoming, as it were, his own other. Thus the novel might well be read, as Marleen S. Barr has suggested, as 'one of these power fantasies [which plays] (sometimes vengefully) with patriarchy' (Barr 1992: 9).

Secondly, 'Evelyn' is not an obvious allegorical name and only becomes a personification, the literal representation of a discourse, through an intricate narrative game. Evelyn's castration is namely literal also in the 'letteral' sense: Along with his penis Eve(lyn) looses the appendage to his name, 'lyn' – his/(her) little 'penis-equivalent'? – thus becoming Eve. Later Eve(lyn) even speculates that Mother's guerrillas 'had utilised my tender body because they couldn't resist the horrid pun of my name, with all its teasing connotations' (Carter 1982: 73) – that is: both bisexual and 'castratable'. What is more, his name/sex-change, these parallel forms of castration, transform him into the quintessential woman in modern Western culture; the very first woman who is equally made from the body of a man, thus linking the biblical and the psychoanalytic narrative. The name Evelyn, then, serves the function of a pun, a play on words, or rather a play on letters, which poses as a narrative-grammatological investigation into 'the literal truth inherent in words', but parodically, since the 'truth' in the name/word 'Evelyn' is *made up*. It is, in other words, a fictive wordplay. The 'allegorical' name Evelyn does not in itself point to a figure in psychoanalysis (even if it bears resemblance to the biblical Eve), but is the effect of a certain parodic-allegorical reading of it, making the Freudian narrative of femininity itself function as a fiction – rather than a 'hidden message' – in a semantic game.

Yet, through this move, psychoanalysis comes to function as a (fictional) mode not only *in*, but also *of*, the novel's investigation of cultural 'truths', its speculative 'system of continuing inquiry'. The different characters Eve(lyn) meets on his/(her) journey are, for example, all personifications of different psychoanalytic images of gender: Leilah (whose name comes from the Arabic Layla, meaning 'night') is the literal embodiment of Freud's infamous 'orientalist' claim that female sexuality constitutes a 'dark continent'. Evelyn also treats her like that, bending over her 'like a doctor' (perhaps in parody of Freud himself) 'in order to examine more closely the exquisite negative of her sex' (Carter 1982: 27), thus acting the role of explorer. Leilah moreover incarnates feminine narcissism, 'absorbed in the contemplation of [her own] figure in the mirror' (ibid., 28); and she is linked to the hysteric. The inscription on her apartment building, *introite et hic dii sunt* (which Evelyn again confronts in Beulah (ibid., 25, 52)), is the motto Freud used for his first writings on hysteria.[10] Mother (with a capital M) is both the phallic, castrating mother and 'the destination of all men' (ibid., 58), the forever haunting spectre of Oedipal desire: one of her names being Iokaste, she urges Evelyn to come back to 'mama' (ibid., 63), to '[e]mbrace [his] fate like Oedipus – but more brave than he' (ibid., 67). The one-legged, one-eyed Zero (nothing) is another Oedipus figure, 'symbolically' castrated like Oedipus himself, while Zero's envious and bickering wives pose as personifications of Freud's discourse on the effects of penis envy (among other things). Indeed, as Eve(lyn) notes, they are not women at all but 'case histories' (ibid., 99). Tristessa (sadness) personifies all kinds of things: Foremost s/he is the personification of femininity as suffering but also the woman in courtly love – elevated, unattainable, 'the recipe for perennial dissatisfaction' (ibid., 6) (another psychoanalytic theme); further s/he also symbolizes Evelyn's necrophilia and, perhaps most interestingly, the psychoanalytic discourse on fetishism, embodying the simultaneous having and lacking the male genital organ. Moreover, Eve(lyn)'s function as the personification of Freudian discourse is duplicated as Freud's language reverberates in Eve(lyn)s own pondering on the nature of sexual difference: 'Masculine and feminine are correlatives which involve one another,' Eve(lyn) thinks, 'the quality and its negation are locked in necessity. But what the nature of masculine and the nature of feminine might be, whether they involve male and female . . . that I do not know. . . . [S]till I do not know the answer to these questions. Still they bewilder me (ibid., 149).[11]

Of course, these personifications do not only embody psychoanalytic images and discourse but are overdetermined: Leilah is also Lilith, Adam's first wife, she is *nigredo*, the first stage in the alchemical process, and she is the Sphinx, 'a strange, bird-like creature, plumed with furs' (ibid., 20), guarding the city where Oedipus (Evelyn) will face his destiny; Mother personifies the monstrous Other and serves additionally to critique a certain form of feminism; Zero is the murderous patriarch, evoking the figure of Charles Manson; the MGM-star Tristessa is the epitome of the Hollywood image of woman, and so on. Yet insofar as the main images of gender and femininity inscribed in the novel are shown to be products of male fantasies, psychoanalysis plays an important part in the interrogation of these figures. It provides the novel with a method of reading, linking symbolic representations to desire and thus to the unconscious.

In fact, there are no 'women' in *The Passion* at all, only variously embodied effects of masculine desire (or of what is culturally produced as masculine desire). The two main 'female' characters in the novel, Eve(lyn) and Tristessa, who are both also men, are of course the most obvious examples of this mechanism. Echoing Eve(lyn)'s own transformation, Tristessa has 'made himself the shrine of his own desires, [has] made of himself the only woman he could have loved' – which is also why 'a real woman' could never 'have been so much a woman' as her/him (ibid., 129). But also Leilah, another 'perfect woman', is perfect precisely to the extent that she is 'like the moon', only giving 'reflected light', mimicking Evelyn's desire, and thus becoming 'the thing [he] wanted of her' (ibid., 34). Even Mother, the prototypical 'feminist', is a figment of Evelyn's imagination, a mirage of his hidden dreams. As an object of desire, 'the destination of all men', Mother, Evelyn observes, has 'always been waiting for me, where I'd exiled her, down in the lowest room at the root of my brain' (ibid., 58), in other words in his own unconscious.

The different personifications of 'woman' in *The Passion* thus literalize different effects of masculine desire. As such they constitute various elaborations of what can be said to be the novel's allegorical thesis of femininity, namely that 'woman is indeed only beautiful insofar as she incarnates most completely the secret aspirations of man' (ibid., 129, my emphasis).[12] Psychoanalytic theory is both part and party to this investigation; it provides the theory of the unconscious – enabling the novel to make use of it new and non-hegemonic ways – and, at the same time, it provides one of the discourses that is thus critically read. As such the novel's parodic-allegorical deployment of psychoanalytic discourse in its investigation of cultural 'truths', reiterates Luce Irigaray's claim that psychoanalysis *is*, precisely, the discourse of truth, or more specifically, '[a] discourse that tells the truth about the logic of truth: namely, that *the feminine occurs only within models and laws devised by male subjects*. Which implies that there are not really two sexes, but only one' (Irigaray 1985: 86, italics in the original).

Violent Games

As a parodic-allegorical literalization of Freud, the novel challenges readings that claim that Eve(lyn)'s choice at the end is the effect of a 'political enlightenment' (Makinen 1997: 163). Yet what happens then to the notion of 'change'? Is *The Passion* in any way 'an allegory of change'? It is a widespread notion that the *critical* import of *The Passion* inheres in the way cultural representations are linked, not only to unconscious desires, but to their material, historical effects, injuring women (Pitchford 2002; Wyatt 2000; Day 1998) – and, I would like to add, also injuring men. The characters in Carter's novel are all imprisoned in violent games, where abusers and abused alike are equally lonely and unhappy or mutually dependent on each other. Zero's power relies on the brutal subjection of his wives but admits that he is '[t]he lowest point . . . nullity' (Carter 1982: 102); they, on the other hand, could easily escape but decide to stay, 'pretend[ing] to believe, for his sake, that a weekly injection of his holy if sterile fluid kept them from all the ills of the flesh and they would have been unable to survive without it' (ibid., 100). It is as if suffering itself is a magic pull which functions only to keep systems going, hierarchies in place, and people at bay. As Eve(lyn) notes about Tristessa: 'He suffered terribly from his memories, but he had only invented them to make him suffer' (ibid., 152). Yet if these cathexes are precisely the effects of unconscious desires, how can this vicious circle be broken?

The Passion does not answer this question; quite the contrary, it seems to be locked in the same deadly game itself, probing, like Eve(lyn), further and further into the maze. As Paulina Palmer notes, while the novel presents 'a brilliantly accurate analysis of the oppressive effects of patriarchal structures, [it runs] the risk of making these structures appear even more closed and impenetrable . . . discounting all possibilities for change' (Palmer 1987: 180). If the novel does not present alternatives to the figures it inscribes – only critically analysing them, dramatizing their phallocentric assumptions and destructive effects – then is it at all possible to say that the novel's parodic-allegorical reworking of cultural representations is critical without at the same time preserving – even, as Palmer argues, strengthening – the very same destructive signifying systems?

Indeed, the novel's allegorical structure might in fact *contribute* to this dilemma, keeping its characters/personifications trapped by their names. Zero will continue to be zilch, reduced in death to a wooden leg floating around in a swimming pool (Carter 1982: 142). The dying Tristessa will return to 'the sinuous principle of his notion of femininity' (ibid., 156), an 'uroborous', a 'dead-end'. Even Leilah and Mother, who do actually change, cannot escape their mythic resonances. Leilah comes back as the freedom fighter Lilith, another mythic figure and as such 'ageless', capable of 'outliv[ing] the rocks', seemingly uninterested in Eve(lyn)'s suggestion to put away all symbols and wait for time to create 'a fresh iconography' (ibid., 174). The retired Mother divides her existence into two: An old, vodka drinking Tiresias-like woman 'with hair like a nest of petrified snakes' (ibid., 190), and 'a figure of speech [who] has retired to a cave beyond consciousness', thus ready to show herself again, as an effect of the unconscious (ibid., 184). Even Eve(lyn)'s choice of motherhood at the end of the novel merely concludes the novel's parodic-allegorical literalization of Freud's text, challenging the traditional conception that allegories serve as didactic illustrations of ideal behaviour describing positive processes of change for their protagonist. Change, the novel seems to suggest, is an extremely difficult business to come about.

Yet it is precisely in the novel's parodic-allegorical redeployment of psychoanalytic thought that change *can* be said to occur. It does not, however, occur by giving us alternative representations, but through playful interventions in the gendered implications of psychoanalytic thought, comprising not only a 'reading' but a strategic '*mis*-reading' of them.[13] Indeed, the very speculative/allegorical question 'what if woman really was a castrated man?' is *already* a displacement of the Freudian discourse on femininity, its 'purpose' and 'interests', since it does not purport to say anything about woman as such but serves as the basis for an exploration of *masculine* desire focusing on the phallocentric assumptions in Freudian discourse itself – *its*, as it were, unconscious. The novel's allegorical thesis of femininity, that 'woman is only beautiful insofar as she most completely incarnates the secret aspirations of man' (ibid., 129), might thus be seen to hide an *alternative* question: 'what *are* the secret aspirations of man?' Or, to borrow a formulation from Gayatri Spivak: 'what is man that the itinerary of his desire creates such a text?' – the text of woman's castration (Spivak 1987: 186, 191).

Tracing Male Desire

In her analysis of different castration images in a selection of Carter's work, Jean Wyatt suggests that the answer to this question, 'why does man (including Freud himself) need to represent woman as castrated?' (Wyatt 2000: 63), is so that man can hide *his own* lack. This is what Tristessa's performances dramatize, Wyatt argues, drawing on Lacan's concept of femininity as masquerade. Tristessa 'is costumed as "lack-of-being".' She is equal to the "secret aspirations of man" . . . because she can act out man's lack – so he need not assume it' (ibid., 64). In other words, the secret aspiration of man is to uphold 'the fiction that man can embody the phallic ideal' (ibid., 63).

Wyatt points to important aspects of Tristessa's allegorical function, noting how her behaviour 'takes on significance as elaborate rituals of mourning over some loss too fundamental to name' (ibid., 64). Yet since she sees Eve(lyn) and Tristessa simply as 'mirror images', she misses the importance of the quest-plot in which Tristessa is merely *one* of the personifications (and challenges), albeit a central one, that Eve(lyn) meets on his/(her) way. Moreover, if Eve(lyn), like Tristessa, functions not only as the 'notion of femininity as a male construct', but is the very embodiment of 'masculine desire', how does the fact that he is *himself* (literally) castrated during the course of the action serve as an elaboration of what the secret aspirations of man 'are'?

Insofar as the quest plot serves as a tracing of the itinerary of masculine desire, femininity as masquerade plays a significant role in this tracing. Indeed, Eve(lyn)'s first stop, his relationship with Leilah, is an effective deployment of this Lacanian trope. A case in point is the many scenes which portray Leilah dressing up in front of the mirror creating an image of the woman, 'this formal other', she only later becomes: 'Her beauty was an accession. She arrived at it by conscious effort', thus bringing 'into being a Leilah who lived only in the not-world of the mirror and then became her own reflection' (Carter 1982: 28). Her masquerade, however, does not uphold 'the fiction that man can embody the phallic ideal' (Wyatt 2000: 63), quite the contrary. Since Leilah's masquerade is a mimickry of *Evelyn's* desire, what she in fact mimics is *his lack*, thus forcing him to confront his own castration: '[I]t was my own weakness, my own exhaustion that she had, in some sense, divined and reflected for me that had made her so attractive to me,' Evelyn notes, but thus she has also 'mimicked me so well she had also mimicked the fatal lack in me that meant I was not able to love her because I myself was so unlovable' (Carter 1982: 34).

Read according to the Lacanian dynamics set up in these scenes – parodically playing out the sexual relationship as a comedy which casts woman as lack-in-being and man as lack-in-having – Evelyn decides to leave, not only because of Leilah's pregnancy, but precisely because he is forced to confront the question of his own castration. The outcome of sexual comedy is that man's '*own desire* for the phallus will throw up its signifier in the form of a persistent divergence towards "another woman," who can signify this phallus under various guises' (Lacan 1982: 84). Ironically, this persistent drive's repeated reorientations towards another woman will in the course of the novel's quest-plot lead Evelyn first to Mother (the original lost object that the subject forever vainly tries to replace in all relationships), then to himself as woman (the ultimate fantasy of woman as, indeed, castrated), only to end up with another woman who, like Leilah – and like Eve(lyn) him/(her)self at the time – masquerades as a woman, but *with a difference*, since Tristessa is also a man, thus playing out femininity as the fetishist notion of both 'being' and 'having' the phallus or, rather, as a simultaneous lack-in-having and lack-in-being.

Hence the trajectory of male desire (his secret aspirations) can be seen to follow a fetishist dynamic, seeking to *preserve* the notion of woman's phallus (woman as the phallic mother; woman as man; woman as both woman and man) even when, or precisely when, she is presented as castrated man – an effort which, of course, is constantly undermined. In this trajectory Evelyn's desire *and* lack are metonymically displaced through a continuous transformation of the drive, eventually pointing to the hollowness and illusory character of the myth of the Platonic hermaphrodite as 'the whole and perfect being' (Carter 1982: 148). However, this trajectory only makes up the *forward* manifestations/transformations of the drive and is, as such, a decoy. As Evelyn points out, 'the world, in time, goes forward and so presents us with the illusion of motion, though all our lives we move through the curvilinear galleries of the brain towards the core of the labyrinth within us' (ibid., 39); '[t]he destination of all journeys is their beginning' (ibid., 186). In fact, the whole quest-plot, the itinerary of 'male' desire, might be seen as a journey the 'other way', backwards, downwards, towards 'original silence and darkness' (ibid., 25), 'the source we have forgotten' (ibid., 39), towards 'the core of the labyrinth within us' (ibid.). And, the core of the labyrinth within (the still male) Evelyn fantasizes in Beulah, is nothing but the womb: 'a room with just such close, red walls *within me*' (ibid., 58, my emphasis).

Indeed, Evelyn's whole journey can be seen as a repeated quest back to the womb, figured first by Leilah, 'the dark room' made flesh (ibid., 27, 39), then by Beulah, 'the inwards parts of the earth' (ibid., 47) the centre of which is, precisely, a 'simulacra of the womb' (ibid., 52), a 'round, red-painted, over-heated, red-lit cell' (ibid., 63), and Mother, 'the destination of all men, the inaccessible silence, the darkness that glides, at the last moment, always out of reach' (ibid., 58), until Eve(lyn) is finally 'fitted . . . up with a uterus of [his] own' (ibid., 9) and becomes pregnant by Tristessa, then travels through the womb-like subterranean grotto, 'walls of meat' (ibid., 186), by the Pacific Ocean, where (s)/he is born anew, finally ready to sail the ocean, 'mother of mysteries' (ibid., 191), the amniotic fluid of all species, to give birth. It is as if the driving force in Eve(lyn)s narration, 'descend lower, descend lower . . . go further' (ibid., 49, 150, 186), towards 'the core', towards 'the source', 'within us', 'within me', is neither his/(her) desire for Tristessa (to whom the narrative is 'dedicated'), nor the 'female' desire for a penis/ child (which is the novel's allegorical pretext), but a form of 'womb-envy' – a *masculine* desire that the penis can be exchanged for a child, which is, quite literally, precisely what happens in the novel's closing pages.

The novel can then be seen to appropriate psychoanalytic theory as a fantasy of masculine autogenesis, displacing Freud's 'ancient symbolic equivalence' between penis/child – which he used to explain the development of normal womanhood – into a fictive elaboration of male womb envy. Insofar as the trajectory of masculine desire, 'the secret aspirations of man', takes part in a dynamics of wish-fulfilment, castration is precisely the price Evelyn has to pay in order both to *have* and *become* mother – the ultimate satisfaction of 'Oedipal desire'. As such, the parodic-allegorical literalization of Freud indeed functions as an investigation of the 'literal truth inherent in words', making Irigaray's claim that psychoanalysis 'tells the truth about the logic of truth', that there is only one sex, signify through an acoustic pun on the word woman, where Eve(lyn), as the personification of Freud's text, poses as 'womb-man' (and thus also the perfect companion to Tristessa, woe-man).

Yet the novel is not only an appropriation of Freud's discourse on femininity, but a re-appropriation of its repressed elements as well. Positing possible causes why the male child develops narcissistic scars, Freud argues that: '[t]he child's sexual researches, on which limits are imposed by his physical development, lead to no satisfactory conclusion . . . . His own attempt to make a baby himself, carried out with tragic seriousness, fails shamefully' (Freud 1989: 21). The germ for a theory of womb-envy is thus already present in Freud's own writing but he never follows up on it; instead he makes the desire to have a baby – the very equation penis/baby – signify as female penis-envy. As Eva Feder Kittay notes on Freud's apparent 'forgetfulness':

> While Freud discusses the possibilities of resolving the wound to the girl's self-esteem in literally producing the penis from her body in the form of a male child, Freud has no discussion of what happened to the wounded self-esteem of the boy who wanted to produce babies. . . . Instead Freud transformed the narcissistic wound suffered by the boy into a fear of castration rather than an unfulfilled desire to give birth and nurture a child from one's own body. (Kittay 1998: 177)

By linking literal castration to the getting of a womb and thus to wish-fulfilment, 'the secret aspirations of man', *The Passion* atones for this 'slippage' and produces the possibility of man resolving the wound to his self-esteem through the literal exchanging of the penis for the production of a child from his own body in 'a symbolic exchange'.

In this way the novel's parodic allegory of Freudian psychoanalysis illustrates Spivak's suggestion of how the Freudian text may be rewritten by 'making available the idea of womb envy as something that interacts with the idea of penis envy to determine human sexuality and the production of society' (Spivak 1996: 58). The idea of 'womb envy' explored in *The Passion* is an intervention in psychoanalytic discourse and the effect of a process of reading; an engagement with Freudian thinking and method which subtly subverts core psychoanalytic concepts such as castration, femininity as masquerade, fetishism and wish-fulfilment through parodic-allegoric literalizations, *not* a theory of what men can be said to have. Yet again – perhaps – 'womb envy' is not such a far-fetched idea after all and, at least, something (Freudian) psychoanalysis can be said to have. Thus the novel not only inscribes Freud's narrative with a 'female difference', opening his discourse up for alternative uses, but transforms the uses of allegory as well – both for a 'female imagination' and for a feminist project.

Notes

1   See for example *Re-Visiting Angela Carter* edited by Rebecca Munford (2006), one of the most recent collections of Carter criticism and symptomatic of this shift. Munford explicitly situates the collection as 'the beginnings of a response' to Alison Easton's oft quoted call for more 'close textual work' on Carter's writing and 'imaginative procedures', asserting that they are 'part of a wider political examination' of the Western cultural tradition (Munford 2006: 16).

2   See for example Day (1998). He argues that all of Carter's writing must be understood 'in the manner of a traditional "allegory of ideas" ' (Day 1998: 8), yet in the actual readings, allegory is hardly mentioned, not to say analysed. As concerns *The Passion* as allegorical text, the only thing Day notes is that 'the metaphor of alchemy and its associated figure of the hermaphrodite are to be central to the allegory of *The Passion of New Eve*', showing Carter's sympathies 'with the rational disquisitions and conflicts of history' (ibid., 131).

3   See for example Palmer (1997), who claims that '[t]he portrayal of Mother and the radical feminist community she rules is an anti-feminist caricature' (Palmer 1997: 29), and Makinen, whose more positive reading of Mother comes at the expense of parody: 'even though [Mother] may be supposed to embody a "consolatory nonsense", the complexity of her characterization turns her into an enormously enjoyable and awe-inspiring violator' (Makinen 1997: 161).

4   A case in point is the different interpretations made by Suleiman and Schmidt. According to Suleiman, Eve(lyn) and Tristessa's love is subversive to the precise extent to 'which it is impossible to say who is woman and who is man, where one sex or one self begins and the other ends', thus constituting 'one of the most extraordinary sensual and bewildering love scenes in recent literature' (Suleiman 1990: 139–40). Schmidt, on the other hand, argues that this very same scene only serves to re-enforce gender binaries: 'Even in the apparent freedom of play-acting they cannot escape the social constructions of femininity and masculinity. Eve's and Tristessa's playful role-change during their love-making still equates active pursuit with masculinity and docile submission with femininity' (Schmidt 1989: 65).

5   The posing of the 'what if-question' in *The Passion* resembles that of another of Carter's so-called speculative fictions from the 1970s, *The Infernal Desire Machines of Dr. Hoffmann* (1972), which similarly constitutes a parodic-allegorical literalization of a Freudian theme: 'What if there really was a war between the reality principle and the pleasure principle?' – played out in the novel through *absurdum*.

6   Carter actually presents a miniature version of Butler's groundbreaking theory of parody and gender performativity, two years before the publication of *Gender Trouble* (1990), when she tells Anna Katsavos that 'I was having a conversation with

a friend of mine about a gay couple we knew, and I said their relationship seemed to be sometimes a cruel parody of heterosexual marriage. My friend thought for a while and said, "Well, what's a heterosexual marriage a parody of then?" It's the same sort of question put here. What's the original? And it's a very good question' (Katsavos 1994: 16).

7 See for example Day who argues that 'Eve and her child may . . . set out in history on a course as yet unmapped' (Day 1998: 129); Simon who claims that 'the ending of the text looks to the future as a wide, open mysterious space of uncertainty, awaiting the birth of the new' (Simon 2004: 148), Makinen who writes that Eve(lyn) 'can set out into a future where her child – the fruit of a transsexual and a transvestite – will grow up with entirely new concepts of masculinity and femininity, since the old ones have proved redundant' (Makinen 1997: 163), and Schmidt who points out that the paradoxical ending where 'the narrator who very probably dies must yet have survived to tell her tale' reveals that 'the course of the heroine's future journey cannot yet be foretold, since new symbols (of which Eve has had but a glimpse) have yet to be created on a social level. Thus she cannot be given a concrete point of view from which to tell her story. What becomes of her remains an open question' (Schmidt 1989: 74).

8 In the novel these systems of signification are constantly intertwined: We meet them in the opening pages where we are introduced to a New York that has disintegrated to 'an alchemical city. . . . chaos, dissolution, nigredo, night', although the city is built to preclude 'the notion of Old Adam' (that is, as a 'city of visible reason'), simply because 'the darkness had lain, unacknowledged, within the builders' and all 'Old Adam want to do is, to kill his father and sleep with his mother' (Carter 1982: 16). In other words: Old Adam and Oedipus are merged in the same figure and their return, the return of the repressed, coincides with the first stage of the alchemical process, nigredo or primordial chaos. This intertwinement is fairly consistent throughout the novel. For another striking example, see Beulah which (in addition to a whole host of other associations: Blake, the womb, etc.) is both the place of (the biblical) Eve's birth and of the Oedipal encounter between Evelyn and Mother; moreover, Beulah is described as 'the interior' both in terms of 'the inward parts of the earth' (ibid., 47) – where alchemical processes of transformation where supposed to take place (Schwartz-Salant 1995: 2) – and in terms of 'the mazes of the brain itself, . . . all processing downward' (Carter 1982: 56) – as in the notion of the unconscious.

9 The reference to Evelyn's slender frame is made shortly before his sex change, when he is dressed up like one of the guerrilla members. Thus he is made to look like a girl, further underscoring the theme of bisexuality: 'now I was dressed like this girl, I looked like this girl's sister, except that I was prettier than she' (Carter 1982: 55).

10 The quote, which can be translated as 'come in, for here the Gods live', is from Heraclitus; Freud, however, gets it from Aristotle. See Freud's letter to Fliess, December 4th 1896, in J. M. Masson (1985: 205).

11 Compare with Freud, who states in the beginning of the essay that 'what constitutes masculinity or femininity is an unknown characteristic which anatomy cannot lay hold of' (Freud 1991: 147), and concludes at the end that '[t]hat is all I have to say to you about femininity. It is certainly incomplete and fragmentary' (ibid., 169). Compare also with Freud's remarks on the interlocking qualities of the libido: 'There is only one libido, which serves both the masculine and the feminine sexual functions. To itself we cannot assign any sex; if, following the conventional equation of activity and masculinity, we are inclined to describe it as masculine, we must not

forget that it also covers trends with a passive aim. Nevertheless the juxtaposition 'feminine libido' is without any justification' (ibid., 165–6).

12 This 'thesis', which may be characterized as surrealism's 'credo' of femininity, is a quote from Benjamin Péret's *Anthologie de l'Amour Sublime*. I am grateful to Anna Fruchart Watz, who was able to locate this quote for me. It testifies to Angela Carter's lifelong fascination with surrealism, although critical of its gender politics; see for example Carter's essay with the telling title 'The Alchemy of the Word', linking, perhaps, surrealism to the alchemical theme in *The Passion* (Carter 1997b: 512).

13 These strategic misreadings operate in various ways: There is, for example, a quite interesting inversion of 'castration' when Zero exposes Tristessa's hidden genitals. In an almost exact replica of Mother ('the Castratrix of the Phallocentric Universe' (Carter 1982: 67)) who 'cut[s] off all [Evelyn's] genital appendages with a single blow' (ibid., 70), Zero ('the avenging phallic fire') takes 'the knife from his boot, thrust[s Tristessa] down with a foot in her belly and slit[s] the g-string with one sweep of his stiletto' (ibid., 127). The 'castration' of Tristessa is however radically disjoined from any notion of losing a genital organ, quite the contrary: '[o]ut of [Tristessa's] vestigial garment sprang the rude, red-purple insignia of maleness', forcefully depriving her/him of her/his identification as/with woman (ibid., 128). Zero's misogynist, homophobic act ironically places 'the event of castration' where it belongs, as a violent, compulsory disciplining of gendered identity.

Works Cited

Bakhtin, M. (1981), *The Dialogic Imagination*, Austin: University of Texas Press.

Barr, M. S. (1992), *Feminist Fabulation*, Iowa: University of Iowa Press.

Butler, J. (1999), *Gender Trouble* (2nd edition), New York and London: Routledge.

Carter, A. (1982), *The Passion of New Eve*, London: Virago.

—(1997a), 'Notes from the Front Line', *Shaking a Leg. Collected Journalism and Writings*, London: Chatto & Windows.

—(1997b), 'The Alchemy of the Word', *Shaking a Leg, Collected Journalism and Writings*. London: Chatto & Windows.

Chambers, R. (1991), *Room for Maneuver. Reading Oppositional Narrative*, Chicago and London: University of Chicago Press.

Clifford, G. (1974), *The Transformations of Allegory*, London: Routledge & Kegan Paul.

Day, A. (1998), *Angela Carter. The rational glass*, Manchester and New York: Manchester University Press.

Freud, S. (1989), *Beyond the Pleasure Principle,* trans. James Strachey, New York and London: Norton.

—(1991), 'Femininity', *New Introductory Lectures on Psychoanalysis*, trans. J. Strachey, Pelican Freud Library Vol. 2, London: Penguin Books.

Frye, N. (1990), *Anatomy of Criticism*, London: Penguin.

Hutcheon, L. (2000), *A Theory of Parody. The Teachings of Twentieth-Century Art Forms*, Urbana and Chicago: University of Illinois Press.

—(2002), *The Politics of Postmodernism* (2nd edition), London and New York: Routledge.

Irigaray, L. (1985), *This Sex which is Not One*, trans. Catherine Porter, Ithaca, New York: Cornell University Press.

Jordan, E. (1992), 'The Dangers of Angela Carter', *New Feminist Discourses: Critical Essays on Theories and Texts* (ed.) Isobel Armstrong, London: Routledge.

Katsavos, A. (1994), 'An Interview with Angela Carter', *The Review of Contemporary Fiction* 14:3 (Fall): 11–17.

Kittay, E. F. (1998), 'Mastering Envy: From Freud's Narcissistic Wounds to Bettelheim's Symbolic Wounds to a Vision of Healing', *Gender & Envy* (ed.) Nancy Burke, New York and London: Routledge.

Lacan, J. (1982), 'The Meaning of the Phallus', *Feminine Sexuality: Jacques Lacan and the école freudienne*, trans. J. Rose (ed.) Juliet Mitchell and Jacqueline Rose, New York and London: Norton.

Makinen, M. (1997), 'Sexual and textual aggression in *The Sadeian Woman* and *The Passion of New Eve*', *The Infernal Desires of Angela Carter* (eds) Joseph Bristow and Trev Lynn Broughton, London and New York: Longman.

Masson, J. M. (ed.) (1985), *The Complete Letters of Sigmund Freud to Wilhelm Fliess, 1887–1904'* Cambridge: Harvard University Press.

Munford, R. (2006), 'Angela Carter and the Politics of Intertextuality', *Re-Visiting Angela Carter. Texts, Contexts, Intertexts* (ed.) R. Munford, Houndmills and New York: Palgrave Macmillan.

Owens, C. (1992), 'The Allegorical Impulse, Part 2', *Beyond Recognition: Representation, Power, and Culture*, Berkeley, Los Angeles and Oxford: University of California Press.

Palmer, P. (1987), 'From "Coded Mannequin" to Bird Woman: Angela Carter's Magic Flight', *Women Reading Women's Writing* (ed.) Sue Roe. Brighton: The Harvester Press.

—(1997), 'Gender as performance in the fiction of Angela Carter and Margaret Atwood', *The Infernal Desires of Angela Carter* (eds) Joseph Bristow and Trev Lynn Broughton, London and New York: Longman.

Pitchford, N. (2002), *Tactical Readings. Feminist Postmodernism in the Novels of Kathy Acker and Angela Carter*, Lewisburgh: Bucknell University Press.

Quilligan, M. (1979), *The Language of Allegory*, Ithaca and London: Cornell University Press.

Sage, L. (1996), *Angela Carter*, London: Northcote House.

Salih, S. (2004), 'Introduction', *The Judith Butler Reader* (eds) S. Salih with J. Butler. Malden, Mass: Blackwell.

Schmidt, R. (1989), 'The Journey of the Subject in Angela Carter's Fiction', *Textual Practice* 3(1): 56–75.

Schwartz-Salant, N. (1995), 'Introduction', *Jung on Alchemy* (ed.) N. Schwartz-Salant, London: Routledge.

Simon, J. (2004), *Rewriting the Body. Desire, Gender and Power in Selected Novels by Angela Carter*, Neue Studien zur Anglistik und Amerikanistik Bd. 90, Frankfurt am Main: Peter Lang.

Spivak, G. (1987), 'Displacement and the Discourse of Woman', *Displacement. Derrida and After* (ed.) Mark Krupnick, Bloomington: Indiana University Press.

—(1996), 'Feminism and Critical Theory', *The Spivak Reader* (eds) Donna Landry and Gerald MacLean, New York and London: Routledge.

Suleiman, S. R. (1990), *Subversive Intent*, Cambridge and London: Harvard University Press.

Ulmer, G. L. (1983), 'The Object of Post-Criticism', *The Anti-Aesthetic: Essays on Postmodern Culture* (ed.) Hal Foster, Port Townsend: Bay Press.

Wyatt, J. (2000), 'The Violence of Gendering: Castration Images in Angela Carter's *The Magic Toyshop, The Passion of New Eve*, and "Peter and the Wolf"', in (ed.) Alison Easton, *Angela Carter: Contemporary Critical Essays*, New York: St. Martin's Press.

13

Blending the Pre-Raphaelite with the Surreal in Angela Carter's *Shadow Dance* (1966) and *Love* (1971)

Katie Garner

In an article in *New Society* from 1978 entitled 'Poets in a Landscape', Angela Carter briefly mentions the Pre-Raphaelite Brotherhood as a way of questioning one aspect of perceived cultural differences between French and English artists:

> English artists are supposed never to congregate together in groups the way that French artists do. Indeed, it is the proud boast of modern masters like Kingsley Amis and Margaret Drabble that the whole point of the thing is the bourgeois individualism with which it is done. Nevertheless, form groups they always have, in fact, ever since Shakespeare and Jonson at the Mermaid Tavern; the Pre-Raphaelite brotherhood, the Camden Town Group, the Bloomsbury Group. (Carter 1997b: 183)

Couched between Shakespeare and Bloomsbury in a list of (intentionally) quintessential 'English' answers to French bohemia, the Pre-Raphaelites are at once typically 'English', and also subversive of any English trend. Many critics have noted how the French arts (notably surrealism, but also French film and cinema) exert a strong influence on Carter's early novels, and both *Love* (1971) and *Shadow Dance* (1966), have been read as 'surrealist' texts (Gamble 2006; Suleiman 2007; Suleiman 1990: 136–140; 162–3). For Sue Roe, *Love* is 'Carter's Surrealist poem for the forlorn daughter' (Roe 2007: 80), while the 'playful postmodern use of a surrealist painter's eye' in *Shadow Dance* was examined first by Jane Hentges and more recently by Anna Watz to reveal a debut novel with strong ties to the surrealists' key principles of mutability, transgression and automatism (Hentges 2002: 44; Watz 2006: 21–41). Less remarked upon, however, is the extent to which members of the famous English Pre-Raphaelite Brotherhood – as well as their works, muses and associates – mingle with trends from across the channel in Carter's early work. In both *Shadow Dance* and *Love*, Carter's *bricolage* brings together English and French artists in order to 'assemble', as she put it, 'all sorts of new vehicles' (Haffenden 1985: 92). The violence and fragmentation suffered by the female (muse) is all the more shocking in these novels due to their almost double interrogation of both surrealist and Pre-Raphaelite visions of the female body.

As artistic movements, the expanse between Pre-Raphaelitism and surrealism is vast; each originated in a different country and in a different century, and not surprisingly, both have very different aesthetic ideologies. For Carter, surrealism's 'entire aesthetic was based on an appreciation of the marvellous' (Carter 1997c: 431). Surrealism revelled in the wholly imaginable and was defined by André Breton, the movement's leader and philosopher, as fuelled by a desire to dispose of the perceived contradictions between 'life and death, the real and the imagined, past and future . . . high and low' (Breton 1972: 123). In stark contrast, nineteenth-century English Pre-Raphaelitism longed for a return to nature and the authenticity of art before Raphael (1483–1520). Yet the Brotherhood also stressed the importance of working from real life; indeed, as Tim Barringer notes, it is precisely this combination 'of a yearning for the past with an intensely modern, mid-nineteenth century realism', that constitutes the 'paradox at the heart of Pre-Raphaelitism' (Barringer 1998: 8).

However, to imply such a straightforward contrast between Pre-Raphaelitism and surrealism is perhaps initially misleading. Both trends are considered *avant-garde*, and both have a tendency to defy theorization as distinct movements. Carter vehemently emphasized that 'surrealism . . . was never a school of art, or of literature, as such' (Carter 1997e: 507) and Pre-Raphaelite commentators, too, are apt to caution against the dangers of portraying a united 'brotherhood' (Bullen 1998: 1). With similar alacrity, Barringer emphasizes that 'there never was, in fact, a single identifiable Pre-Raphaelite style' (Barringer 1998: 14), and Carter's brief refusal to recognize any truth in assumptions about innate differences between the organization of French and English artists in 'Poets in a Landscape' suggests a universal (rather than essentialist) view of the construction and communication of aesthetic trends. Indeed, there is open evidence of cross-channel correspondence between Pre-Raphaelitism and surrealism. In 1936, Salvador Dalí submitted an article in praise of the Pre-Raphaelites to the surrealist journal, *Minotaure* (1933–39), edited by Breton. In 'Le Surréalisme spectral de l'éternel féminin préraphaélite' ('The Spectral Surrealism of the Pre-Raphaelite Eternal Feminine'), Dalí declared himself 'dazzled by the flagrant Surrealism of English Pre-Raphaelitism' (Dalí 1998: 311). His fascination lay chiefly in what he saw to be the conflation of terror and desire embodied in their female models:

> The Pre-Raphaelite painters give us and make radiant for us women who are all at once the most desirable and most frightening in existence; for this has to do with beings one would feel the greatest terror and anxiety at the idea of having to eat them: these are the carnal phantasms of childhood's 'false memories', it is the gelatinous meat of the most shameful sentimental dreams. The Pre-Raphaelites place on the table the sensational dish of the eternal feminine livened up with a touch of highly respectable 'repugnance'. (ibid., 311–2)

Dalí's dark 1930s vision presents a Pre-Raphaelitism both Freudian and cannibalistic, containing an incongruous mix of childhood and sexual desire, beauty and repulsion, and death and the eternity of the signifier. The end result, a 'sensational dish of the eternal feminine', seems reminiscent of Carter's scarred Ghislaine in *Shadow Dance*, who embodies the same mixture of repulsion and desire for the text's protagonist, Morris, with her face like 'ice-cream' or a 'bowl of blancmange' (Carter 2004: 16, 23). Dalí's description draws attention to the affinities between surrealism and

Pre-Raphaelitism: both were masculine-dominated and patriarchal art groups; both were interested in (violating) the female body; both were concerned with – despite the Pre-Raphaelites' capacity for realism – myth and dreams.

Carter was well aware that the surrealists flagrantly disassembled female body parts in collage or sculpture, and often depicted women in sadomasochistic settings. As she wrote retrospectively in 1978, 'the surrealists were not good with women. That is why, although I thought they were wonderful, I had to give them up in the end' (Carter 1997e: 512). In the works of the Pre-Raphaelites, female suffering is less immediately apparent, but nevertheless present in the tales surrounding the paintings of the excessive takings of laudanum, illness and melancholia of their female muses, epitomized in the life of Elizabeth Siddall, the artist, model and later wife of Dante Gabriel Rossetti (Rodgers 1996: 21–3). As Griselda Pollock summarizes, 'the dominant tropes of Pre-Raphaelite literature have functioned to secure a regime of sexual difference' (Pollock 2003: 157). Art critics, Pollock suggests, have been all too eager to establish a discourse around Pre-Raphaelite aesthetics as a site/sight where 'woman functions as a sign whose signified is masculine creativity' (ibid., 161). The surrealists, too, celebrated the female body as creative sign and flaunted it by suspending a female mannequin from the ceiling of their headquarters, the *Centre des Recherches Surréalistes* in Paris (Suleiman 1990: 20–1). If Carter's early fiction punctuates surrealist circumstances with occasional nods to Pre-Raphaelite fathers, then, it may be for no other reason than to expound the universal ahistoricity of her fundamental critique: that all nineteenth- and twentieth-century art is underlined by a monolithic antifeminist approach involving some cost to the female body.

Shifting the focus onto the Pre-Raphaelites is not intended to be an argument against, or indeed to lessen, the strong influence of surrealism on Carter's early novels. As Watz convincingly argues, Carter's debt to surrealism has been distinctly underplayed (Watz 2010: 1). Rather, asking questions about the intertextual function of Pre-Raphaelite images amidst otherwise surrealist narratives can provide a new perspective on the heavily sadomasochistic frames of *Shadow Dance* and *Love*. Pre-Raphaelite subtexts exert a substantial influence on both plot and character in these novels; in *Love* particularly, the narrative's (re)vision of the Pre-Raphaelite aesthetic offers a more positive rendering of female subjectivity than is possible from within a strictly surrealist frame. In her appraisal of Carter's intertextual methods, Rebecca Munford proposes that Carter's work 'occup[ies] a position of in-betweenness which mirrors the dissonances and fissures between style and substance in her own texts' (Munford 2006: 12–13). By considering Pre-Raphaelitism and surrealism together, Carter's use of each dissonant aesthetic style becomes a polar contributor to, and creator of, this trademark intertextual 'in-betweenness' – an effect built as much on visual as textual subtexts.

Shadow Dance and the Pre-Raphaelite Aesthetic

For Julie Sanders, *Shadow Dance* confirms Carter's 'fascination with the Pre-Raphaelites' (Sanders 2006: 124). Indeed, the complexities born of allegiances within an artistic brotherhood are at the core of *Shadow Dance* and its portraits of Honeybuzzard, the enigmatic dandy, and the guilt-ridden painter, Morris, and their artistic and emotional co-dependency. More specifically, the novel's Pre-Raphaelite influence shows itself in the form of similes (where the painting described or named has a real, identifiable source), as well as more subtle permeations which support the novel's themes of problematic or shared desire. Morris spies Honeybuzzard posing in stolen costumes from a London playhouse, resembling 'Janey Morris as Guinevere, with a mouth like a sad pomegranate, cheeks hollowed, shadowed with infinite weariness, infinite experience' (Carter 2004: 78). The allusion looks to William Morris's only easel painting, a portrait of his future wife as *La Belle Iseult* (1857–8), and given the erroneous title of 'Queen Guinevere' until 1986 (Marsh 1986, 2011). Undertaken by Morris during a period in which he was much encouraged and influenced by Rossetti, the painting's medieval subject, attention to detail and focus on a central female figure all espouse Pre-Raphaelite principles. In Carter's rendering, Jane Morris owns lips like a pomegranate in a manner reminiscent of Dalí's vision of the Pre-Raphaelite muse as a fleshly banquet – though the simile also recalls Rossetti's own later depiction of the same model holding the mythical fruit close to her face in *Proserpine* (1874). Honeybuzzard's imaginary Pre-Raphaelite masquerade as Janey Morris highlights his androgyny and theatricality, while simultaneously exposing – through the introduction of Guinevere – the latent cuckoldry Morris initially feels at the intrusion of Honeybuzzard's new girlfriend, Emily, into their artistic ménage. But most importantly, the intertextual perspective invites a parallel between the onlooker to the Pre-Raphaelite tableau, Carter's own Morris Grey, and the Victorian writer, poet, painter and craftsman, William Morris (1834–96).

Carter's description of Jane Morris as the suffering muse, weary and 'sad' with 'hollowed cheeks', co-opts William Morris into the Pre-Raphaelite aesthetic and its strange, incongruous mix of beauty, sickness and desire. Both Morris and Edward Burne-Jones became associated with the Pre-Raphaelite Brotherhood in the 1850s, sometime after its foundation by Rossetti, William Holman Hunt and John Everett Millais in 1848. Morris's central role in the foundation of Morris, Marshall, Faulkner and Company in 1861 signalled a more commercial shift in his work towards Arts and Crafts production, but, for Carter, these later artworks nevertheless remained representative of a decaying beauty. In 'Overture and Incidental Music for *A Midsummer Night's Dream*' (1982), the underpinnings of trees seem 'all soggy and floral as William Morris wallpaper in an abandoned house' (Carter 2006b: 275). This makes Morris's wallpapers a fitting backdrop for *Shadow Dance*, throughout which Morris Grey is 'at home' in 'such an atmosphere of hope decayed' (Carter 2004: 25). For Carter, William Morris is a prime example of the English artist – the forest in 'Overture' is '*the* English wood' – and also of the English Utopian dreamer (Carter 2006b: 275; emphasis in original). In 'So There'll always be an England' (1982), another piece of 'English' journalism from the same year, William Morris again provides the intertextual decor for Carter's sardonic observation of the human desire to dream: 'We will have our personal Utopias, our own versions of *News From Nowhere*' (Carter 1997d: 187). One of Morris's most popular and well-known literary works, *News From Nowhere* (1890) idealized a socialist, medievalist and agrarian utopia where all work was creative and pleasurable. Carter's Morris in *Shadow Dance* is another Utopian dreamer, who is, as Marc O'Day identifies, 'prey to all kinds of dreams and fantasies', including an indulgence in the possibility that he is the last man on earth (O'Day 2007: 60). When Morris realizes that the Struldbrug – the old woman whom he fears he and Honeybuzzard have frightened to death during a junk raid on an abandoned house – is still very much alive, the food in the tired cafe, previously 'not like real food at all but some miraculous product of modern synthetic technology' (Carter 2004: 30), becomes a vision of resplendent medieval naturalism: 'the marzipan petals on the fondant cakes shook out in gay green life. Deep notes of joy rang from the cream horns. . . . The ham rolls bounded like ecstatic piglets from their cellophane pens' (ibid., 161). Morris's prior vow to stop indulging in nostalgic 'fantasies' is forgotten as a joyous vision of natural plenitude erupts in front of him and echoes the same turn away from machinery and artificial production that William Morris advocated in *News from Nowhere* (ibid., 160).

In fact, the Victorian William Morris shadows Morris throughout the novel. In the kitchen of the same abandoned house in the aptly named 'William Square' (ibid., 73; 74) that houses the Struldbrug, Morris finds 'old Woodbine packets in William Morrisy greens and purples in curly and ornate squiggles' (ibid., 88). He later purchases the same brand of Woodbine cigarettes twice, from the dying tobacconist's wife (ibid., 126), and the greengrocer (ibid., 172). Through the ornamented packet and Morris's subsequent purchases, the cigarettes (broadly associated with 1960s bohemianism) become fused with the outputs of the 1860s Arts and Crafts movement, to convey the sense that all art is a product of one circular, and repetitive human 'addict[ion]' (ibid., 74). With the reoccurring Morrisean cigarette packet, Carter mocks and undermines the drive for naturalism inherent to both Arts and Craft and Pre-Raphaelite design.

But it is the image of the suffering Pre-Raphaelite muse which reoccurs again and again in *Shadow Dance,* and colours Carter's portrayal of Morris's sensitive and 'Victorian' wife Edna, who has a particular 'Pre-Raphaelite glow' (ibid., 45). In another of Morris's extended fantasies, his imagination paints the dark-haired Edna in the style of John Everett Millais (1829–96):

> 'Compassion', Millais would have called her, with her upturned face and incandescent eyes and long hands joined like the ears of a butchered rabbit. In a pompous gilt frame, she would have been exhibited at the Royal Academy and afterwards reproduced in the *Illustrated London News*, to subsequently grace a thousand humble walls up and down the country. (ibid., 50)

As Watz has observed, the juxtapositions in Ghislaine's horrifically scarred face make her a valid avatar of the surrealist version of woman (Watz 2006: 22), but Edna is the novel's Pre-Raphaelite muse. Such saintly poses as Carter describes were highly fashionable in the latter half of the nineteenth century, owing largely to Rossetti's commemorative portrait of Elizabeth Siddall, *Beata Beatrix* (1863). Millais, on the other hand, did not paint a 'Compassion', but his late piece, *A Disciple* (1895), shows a dark-haired model with an 'upturned face' and joined hands that strongly resemble Carter's description. It is the unexpected analogy of the ears of the 'butchered rabbit' which seem to add a vaguely surrealist element of violence to the otherwise strong religious iconography. This juxtaposition – between the images of a compassionate saviour and a victimized rabbit – taints the description with a problematic hypocrisy, which is reinforced by the opposition between the 'pompous gilt frame' and the selflessness essential to pure 'compassion'. In this instance, the novel's surrealist commitments perpetuate a foregrounding of violence which infiltrates the pseudo-Millaisian frame. Though Edna and Ghislaine are aligned with different artistic models, the effect of the comparisons remains the same. Indeed, this consistency is the point: in *Shadow Dance*, woman always suffers through, or for, visual art.

Importantly, such consistency is less a violation of Pre-Raphaelite authenticity, and more a subtle exposé of the Brotherhood's contribution to real instances of female suffering; indeed, this aspect of Pre-Raphaelitism is thrown into new relief in Carter's prose in a manner facilitated by the novel's foregrounding of surrealist violence. For Carter, Pre-Raphaelitism can be as 'repugnant' as surrealism, which, again, echoes Dalí's sentiments in *Minotaure*:

> These carnal concretions of excessively ideal women, these feverish and panting materialisations, these floral and soft Ophelias and Beatrices produce in us, as they appear to us through the luminescence of their hair, the same effect of terror and unequivocal alluring repugnance of that of the soft belly of a butterfly seen between the luminescences of its wings. (Dalí 1998: 312)

It is Edna's extreme 'compassion' – her 'compulsive urge to love' (Carter 2004: 43) – and her own excessive idealism, that repel Morris. In their bedroom, Edna reminds Morris of 'St Ursula, the virgin, smiling at the rapists; painted by Burne-Jones rather than Millais for in the heat she grew waxen and moist-looking at once' (ibid., 120). Pre-Raphaelite references expand outwards as Carter draws on the artists' differences in style, rather than any shared aesthetic. Burne-Jones is associated with a 'waxen' artificial mysticism, which the text measures against Millais' celebrated capacity for realism. Such a succession of Pre-Raphaelite frames facilitates an ironic distancing and, again, makes way for the suggestion of violence: that rape can occur within marriage. *Shadow Dance* tentatively begins to explore ways in which Pre-Raphaelitism and surrealism can work in tandem in order to hint at a wider, and more sinister, critique of male artistic practice than one founded on the masochism of one movement alone.

Love and John Everett Millais

Surrealist artworks bring violence against the female form to the surface (or, more specifically, to the canvas), but the infamous tales of the mental and physical ill-health of the Pre-Raphaelite muses are more hauntingly absent from their paintings themselves. The most strident example of a Pre-Raphaelite female model's suffering for the sake of art lies, of course, behind Millais' famous painting, *Ophelia* (1851–2).

Millais' model was Elizabeth Siddall (1800–1859), the lover, and later wife of Rossetti, who lay in a bath of water heated by lamps positioned beneath to pose for the portrait. Engrossed in his subject, Millais failed to notice when the candle-lit lamps went out and Siddall subsequently contracted a severe case of pneumonia from which her health never fully recovered. What such contexts for Pre-Raphaelite works convey is a dual subjectivity for the Pre-Raphaelite muse, as both the artist's saviour – the vital

Figure 13.1 John Everett Millais, *Ophelia* (1851–2), Tate Britain, United Kingdom © Tate, London 2011.

source for his art – and the victim of it. The tale of the composition of Millais' *Ophelia*, in which the female muse's function as victim is made shockingly real, is closely linked to the narrative climax of Carter's fifth novel, *Love*, through repeated allusions to the both the painting itself and its violent historical contexts.

Consistent with the pairing of Pre-Raphaelite art with violence in *Shadow Dance*, Millais' *Ophelia* enters *Love* at one of the text's most violent moments. A heated game of chess between Lee and Annabel, the novel's dysfunctional young husband and wife, provokes Lee to 'force [Annabel] to kneel and beat her until she toppled over sideways' (Carter 2006a: 40). The episode leaves Annabel 'strangely joyous' and Lee stricken with guilt; quick to take advantage, Annabel immediately makes a request for a moonstone ring as an apology (ibid.). Instead, Lee purchases 'a print of Millais' "Ophelia" in a second-hand shop because Annabel often wore the same expression' (ibid.). With Millais' print, Lee presents Annabel with an aestheticized vision of herself as the 'mad girl' and demonstrates his attempt to read her through the established and commercialized discourse of the image of the hysteric (ibid., 3). As Elisabeth Bronfen would put it, Lee uses Millais' image to 'dream the death' of Annabel, *Love*'s beautiful woman (Bronfen 1992: xi). Here it is Lee who is aligned with the role of the Pre-Raphaelite artist, for whom the sensual beauty of his muse is enhanced by (or perhaps even a product of) her restrictive, unhealthy female body.

Few critics have responded to the influence of Millais' *Ophelia* on the ending of *Love* and Annabel's spectacular suicide; those that do, tend to see the reference to Millais as part of Carter's wider engagement with Shakespeare's female characters. For Christina Britzolakis, Millais' print functions as a signpost for the novel's essentially Shakespearian 'script of the numb and passionless "beautiful hysteric" who haunts male subjectivity with the spectre of disorder' (Britzolakis 1997: 48). I would argue that the Millais image exerts a strong presence over *Love* in its own right, as it is the earlier memory of the print which colours Annabel's submission to death. It is Millais' watery image, showing Ophelia on the boundary between life and death, 'laid out like a corpse, but still singing her songs of madness' (Barringer 1998: 62), which Carter uses to emphasize Annabel's same gradual transition at the novel's climax, when, 'like Ophelia, she gladly lay down on the river and waited for it to carry her away as if she was as light and will-less as a paper boat' (Carter 2006a: 107). Lorna Sage was the first to point towards Carter's fascination with Millais' work, or, more specifically, with his image of Ophelia:

> One of the images that haunts her fiction, one of the most poignant and persistent borrowings, is the image of crazy, dying Ophelia, as described by Gertrude in Shakespeare's Hamlet, and (possibly even more) as painted by Millais: waterlogged, draped in flowers, drifting downstream to her virgin death. (Sage 1994: 33)

As Sage hints, the same image of Ophelia, 'waterlogged', continually reoccurs throughout Carter's oeuvre; when Joseph rolls himself into the pond on the Down in *Several Perceptions* (1968), his 'hair floated out upon the water like that of drowned Ophelia' (Carter 2006a: 66). Similarly, Julie Sanders has noted how Tiffany emerges as a vision of Ophelia with 'a bit of wallflower stuck in her hair . . . and her hands full of flowers' towards the end of *Wise Children* (1991) (Sanders 2006: 122). In the most extended treatment of Carter's Pre-Raphaelite intertexts to date, Sanders (also picking up on Sage's observation above) clarifies that 'in the visual arts' representation of this off-stage event [Ophelia's drowning] the choice is frequently taken to freeze the moment earlier in the narrative, before Ophelia drowns or becomes fully conscious of her watery fate' (ibid., 123). Because Ophelia's death never occurs onstage in *Hamlet*, the identification of Annabel with an Ophelia drowning in her own orchestrated gas leak positions Annabel – and Carter – in correspondence with Millais, not Shakespeare.

There are striking similarities between the depiction of Ophelia in Millais' image, and Carter's description of what Britzolakis has termed Annabel's 'elaborate "makeover"' (Britzolakis 1997: 45):

> [S]he chose a long, plain, white dress of cotton with a square-cut neck and long, tight sleeves. In the mirror of the changing room in the shop, she glimpsed the possibility of another perfect stranger, one as indifferent to the obscene flowers of the flesh as drowned Ophelia, so she had her hair dyed to dissociate her new body from the old one and then she got her face painted in a beauty shop. She was surprised to see how cold, hard and impersonal this new face was. (Carter 2006a: 100)

Annabel's meticulous construction of Ophelia's white dress and light hair colour are copied from Millais's painting, and reproduced with a critical eye that replicates the Pre-Raphaelite artist's attention to detail. What is more, the pun on 'dyed', and the 'cold' commerciality of the 'beauty shop' move art into the world of financial exchange where beauty can be bought, and Millais' image becomes a deathly parody of modern self-fashioning. The Pre-Raphaelite muse is no longer ethereal or abstract, but part of a purchasable system: a critique that plays off Carter's appreciation of Millais as a realist. The description also indicates that Annabel reads Millais' art 'against the grain', not as Lee perceived it (as showing a face which matches Annabel's own), but as depicting 'obscene flowers of the flesh', radiating obscenity rather than beauty, and a carnal rather than natural sexuality (Pearce 1991: 5–11).

Repeating the multiple reproductions of Edna's 'Compassion' in *Shadow Dance*, Carter again draws attention to how modern print production means that anyone can own an *Ophelia*. This fragments the subjectivity of the Pre-Raphaelite muse and, *pace* Walter Benjamin (1999), divorces the image from the autonomy of the artist, as a second-hand print is the product of a transfer of power, from the artist to the consumer. By assuming the pose of Ophelia, then, Annabel is not assuming the position of Millais' model, Elizabeth Siddall (nor the Pre-Raphaelite muse *per se*, or even Shakespeare's Ophelia), but adopting the anonymity which the muse has acquired in twentieth-century culture. In *Love*, the two bifurcated artistic versions of woman Carter constructs in *Shadow Dance* (in the surrealist Ghislaine and the Pre-Raphaelite Edna) become fused in Annabel, who exploits both perspectives to parody the masculine reading of images of the female body. Indeed, as Sarah Gamble has argued, in *Shadow Dance* it is through Edna, not Ghislaine, 'that the possibility for female empowerment can be glimpsed, however faintly' because Edna shows a degree of 'sexual independence' by sleeping with Henry Glass (Gamble 1997: 56). Morris and Lee read Edna and Annabel as Pre-Raphaelite women, but importantly, both are exposed as misreadings, for the Pre-Raphaelite woman no longer stands for anything fixed or stable, but for the instability of commercial poses that can be assumed – and undercut – by the contemporary woman. In other words, Carter infects the mythic status of the Pre-Raphaelite muse with a distinctly surrealist mutability.

It is, then, Annabel's blend of Pre-Raphaelite and surrealist values that add to her unfathomable and often threatening persona. When Lee, Buzz and Annabel sleep together (innocently, it must be added, for sexuality is transgressive in the novel), she 'drowned both brothers in her Pre-Raphaelite hair' (Carter 2006a: 82). In contrast to the passive connotations in Edna's Pre-Raphaelite symbolism, Annabel's identification with the Pre-Raphaelite muse can openly threaten the men in *Love*: it is the brothers, rather than Ophelia, who are in danger of drowning. *Love*'s Pre-Raphaelite imagery builds on the foundation of Edna's earlier faint sexual autonomy to provide Annabel with an empowering femininity. The self-fashioning Annabel accesses through Millais' art, together with the (not unrelated) unsettling presence of the Pre-Raphaelite muse in the age of mechanical reproduction, offer Annabel an adverse increase in artistic subjectivity.

Towards a Surrealist Ophelia

Millais' painting of Ophelia-in-death continued to occupy Carter's mind long after the writing of *Love*. In a letter addressed to Lorna Sage in 1989, Carter described a recent boat trip along the London canals in terms which invoke the composition of Millais' oil:

the canals are wonderful . . . You get this Ophelia-style view of the canal bank, huge juicy plants & flowers & grasses; and we saw herons, & a king-fisher . . . the East End ... is now one really one vast nature reserve, mile after mile of abandoned factories returning to the wild. (Sage 1994: 57)

What signals Carter's Ophelia-style view as Millaisian, rather than Shakespearean, is her overwhelming concern with describing the landscape of Ophelia's suicide (never depicted in *Hamlet*). The description also capitalizes on Ophelia's viewpoint, to the effect of making her 'pale body laid out like a corpse' in the painting strangely absent (Barringer 1998: 62). What Carter describes is Ophelia's view outwards, rather than the onlooker's gaze onto her body. With the corpse left out, there is a disquieting lack of negativity in Carter's description, and the 'Ophelia-style' view instead implies freedom (from the city) and an opportunity for escape: a return 'to the wild'. By generating an idea of Ophelia as the viewer and surveyor, the description performs the same subtle adaptation (Ophelia-as-surveyor) that it is necessary for Annabel to perform in order to survey her own portrait-in-death from both inside and outside the frame. After all, Annabel, we are told, 'did not even think of herself as a body but more as a pair of disembodied eyes' (Carter 2006a: 30). While Carter's construction of Annabel as effectively 'disembodied' leads Sue Roe to conclude that Annabel does not exist as a subject (or body) in the text, this seems difficult to marry with the positive voyeurism which Carter attaches to the image of Ophelia. Rather, through the adapted Millaisian image, Annabel's suicide is associated with this same idea of a 'return' to the 'real' world at the end of the novel. Her outlines may well 'cease to define her' but such outlines did not define Annabel in life, either: she has always appeared 'blurred' (ibid., 108, 3).

The surreal dimensions of Millais' Pre-Raphaelite image are slowly drawn out in the narrative of *Love* in a fashion similar to Carter's description of the canal. Millais spent eight months painting the landscape of Ewell in Surrey and held further painting sessions with Siddall afterwards back in his London studio. *Love*'s structure partly imitates this landscape-to-portrait process of composition, as the narrative follows the changes on the walls of Lee and Annabel's bedroom, from white to 'very dark green' (ibid., 6). When Annabel positions herself in the bedroom of the flat to die, she is surrounded by her own painting of 'landscapes of forests, jungles and ruins . . . trees with breasts, winged men with pig faces and women whose heads were skulls' (ibid., 6–7). Lee's observation that Annabel 'could have stepped into the jungle on the walls and not looked out of place beside the tree with a breast or the carnivorous flowers' gives both a forewarning of the novel's final dénouement and reinforces Lee's habitual reading of Annabel through artistic images (ibid., 101). Her position as the creative artist of the work is bypassed and Lee equates her purely with the *objet d'art*. Yet, once more, Carter exposes Lee's reading of Annabel's art as a perilous misreading and misinterpretation; her drawing of a tree he 'seriously misconstrued as, perhaps, a tree of life when it was more nearly related (for him at least) to the Upas Tree of Java, the fabulous tree that casts a poisoned shade' (ibid., 31). What Lee cannot see is that Annabel owns the mastery allocated to the artist and gradually confines him in *her* frame, so that 'the room belonged to Annabel; she had painted her ambivalent garden on the walls and installed Lee in the midst of it whether he matched her colours or not' (ibid., 64). Elaine Showalter suggests that in Millais' *Ophelia* 'the artist rather than the subject dominates the scene' (Showalter 1985: 85) and, through the meticulous detailing of Annabel's preparations for her suicide (and Lee's inability to understand her artistic vision), Carter ensures that the same is true of Annabel's replica.

Though indebted to 'Romanticism', Annabel's paintings on the wall owe little to Pre-Raphaelite typology and are overall more broadly surrealist in style (ibid., 6). Tellingly, Annabel's 'favourite painter' was the surrealist painter and specialist in collage, Max Ernst (1891–1976) (ibid., 30). Echoing *Love*'s violent themes, Ernst's own collage novels not only depicted women in sadomasochistic settings, but also enacted the male artist's cutting up and repositioning of woman through their very artistic method. In Ernst's 'The Lion of Bellefort', from *Une Semaine de bonté* (1934) a woman is bound with ropes to a torture device (Turpin 1993: 19), and 'Culture physique, or La mort qu'il vous plaire' from *La Femme 100 têtes* (1929) depicts a naked woman placed underwater in a giant fish tank guarded by a male figure (ibid., 15). Yet in more traditional mediums, Ernst painted a series of dark green forests and one piece in particular, *La Joie de Vivre* (1936), has much in common with Annabel's dark green forest, as well as a title which echoes the irony of Lee's exclamation, '*Le jour de gloire est arrivé*', upon seeing Annabel's bodily transformation (Carter 2006a: 102).

Ernst's dark depiction of dense undergrowth, coiling vines and strange half-plant, half-human shapes seem to match Carter's descriptions of Annabel's work, and also

Figure 13.2 Max Ernst, *La Joie de vivre* [The Joy of Life] (1936), Scottish National Gallery of Modern Art. Purchased with the assistance of the Heritage Lottery Fund and the Art Fund 1995 © ADAGP, Paris and DACS, London 2012.

echo the 'huge juicy plants' from Carter's Ophelia-style trip down the London canals. When Annabel steps into her constructed frame she is surrounded by her surrealist forest, but adopting a Pre-Raphaelite pose. It is in this final image, then, a true fusion of Millais and Ernst, that *Love* positions Annabel as the maker of *bricolage*, a Pre-Raphaelite Ophelia painted in 'her own ambivalent garden' that revises Ernst's surreal forests (ibid., 64).

Like Morris in *Shadow Dance*, Annabel's identity as an artist complicates her aesthetic allegiances. Both Pre-Raphaelite and surrealist perspectives inform her ways of seeing, and nowhere is this more apparent than when she surveys herself internally and externally in the course of arranging her final portrait: 'She wanted to look perfect on her deathbed. But then she thought a minor imperfection would make the spectacle even more touching' (ibid., 103). One of the Pre-Raphaelites' less radical aims was to 'produce thoroughly good pictures' (Rossetti 1895: 153) and Annabel broadly follows their aesthetic in her desire to 'look perfect'. However, with the addition of the 'imperfection' – the chipping of her nail polish as she tapes up the room ready to create the gas leak – 'a random act of chance' is added to her final portrait, recalling the 'principles so much prized by the Surrealists' and praised earlier in the novel (Carter 2006a: 34). The perfection of Annabel's 'painted' face (ibid., 100) is reminiscent of Carter's comments elsewhere concerning Frida Kahlo, who, as part of her artistic practice, also 'loved to paint her face' (Carter 1997a: 433). Also often cast as a 'Mexican Ophelia', Kahlo was 'a Surrealist discovery rather than a Surrealist' with an ambiguous relationship to the surrealist movement, admitting 'I never knew I was a Surrealist until André Breton came to Mexico and told me I was one' (Herrera 1989: xiii, 256, 230). In praise of Kahlo's self-portraits, Carter wrote:

> The painted face is that of a woman working at transforming her whole experience in the world into a series of marvellously explicit images. She is in the process of remaking herself in another medium than life and is becoming resplendent. The flesh made sign.
>   The wounded flesh. (Carter 1997a: 434)

Annabel, too, returns from the beauty shop 'resplendent', like Kahlo, in her self-portraiture, and finally remakes herself into another medium than life, becoming 'a marvellous crystallisation retaining nothing of the remembered woman but her form' (Carter 2006a: 101).

However, this resplendence is short-lived, and unlike Kahlo's, Annabel's self-portrait quickly disintegrates. Not only is her body preyed upon by flies, but Buzz's suggestion that Lee assume a 'victorious pose' over her corpse is indicative of Annabel's lack of ownership over her own work (ibid., 109). If Carter celebrates the work of the female artist, she also celebrates the celerity with which her art can be destroyed. Annabel has 'failed in the attempt to make herself [a] living portrait' (ibid., 100), and despite the sense of an alternative, positive process of rebirth Carter creates around the Ophelia-style view, and its offer of a return to the unprohibited wild, her proposal of a counter-image can also be read as affirming a lack of negativity in the death of the feminine body for the male onlooker. As Bronfen argues, 'the threat that death and femininity pose is recuperated by presentation, staging absence as a form of re-presence, or return, even if or rather precisely because this means appeasing the threat of real mortality, of sexual insufficiency, of lack of plenitude and wholeness' (Bronfen 1992: xii). Yet, as Bronfen goes on to emphasize, 'the "re" of return, repetition or recuperation suggests that the end point is not the same as the point of departure, although it harbours the illusion that something lost has been perfectly regained' (ibid.). A repetition is never just a repetition, and Carter's creation of an Ophelia-style view in Annabel's perspective must be recognized as a feminist (re)visioning of the Pre-Raphaelite muse and the female model more broadly; moreover, the creativity involved in such a revision is embodied in Annabel's turn away from 'look[ing] perfect' and her acceptance of a surrealist fault to create a new shocking effect (Carter 2006a: 103). While the influence of a Pre-Raphaelite constructive practice is substantially present in *Love* and *Shadow Dance*, it is in this realm of aesthetic 'in-betweenness' – the intertextual space created by blending the Pre-Raphaelite with the surreal – that Carter offers an important profile of the female artist's struggle for creativity.

Works Cited

Barringer, T. (1998), *The Pre-Raphaelites: Reading the Image*. London: Weidenfeld and Nicolson.

Benjamin, W. (1999) [1936], 'The Work of Art in the Age of Mechanical Reproduction' in (ed.) H. Arendt *Illuminations*, trans. H. Zorn. London: Pimlico, 211–44.

Breton, A. (1972) [1930], *Second Manifesto of Surrealism* in *Manifestoes of Surrealism*, trans. R. Seaver and H. R. Lane. Ann Arbour: University of Michigan Press, 117–94.

Britzolakis, C. (1997), 'Angela Carter's Fetishism' in J. Bristow and T. L. Broughton (eds) *The Infernal Desires of Angela Carter: Fiction, Femininity, Feminism*, Harlow: Addison Wesley Longman, 43–58.

Bronfen, E. (1992), *Over Her Dead Body: Death, Femininity and the Aesthetic*, Manchester: Manchester University Press.

Bullen, J. B. (1998), *The Pre-Raphaelite Body: Fear and Desire in Painting, Poetry, and Criticism*, Oxford: Clarendon Press.

Carter, A. (1997a) [1989], 'Frida Kahlo' [Preface, *Images of Frida Kahlo*] in J. Uglow (ed.) *Shaking a Leg: Journalism and Writings*, London: Chatto and Windus, 433–8.

—(1997b) [1978], 'Poets in a Landscape', in J. Uglow (ed.) *Shaking a Leg: Journalism and Writings*, London: Chatto and Windus, 181–5.

—(1997c) [1987], 'Pontus Hulten: The Arcimboldo Effect', in J. Uglow (ed.) *Shaking a Leg: Journalism and Writings*, London: Chatto and Windus, 430–1.

—(1997d) [1982], 'So There'll Always Be an England' in J. Uglow (ed.) *Shaking a Leg: Collected Journalism and Writings*, London: Chatto and Windus, 185–9.

—(1997e) [1978], 'The Alchemy of the Word' (1978) in J. Uglow (ed.) *Shaking a Leg: Collected Journalism and Writings*, London: Chatto and Windus, 507–12.

—(2004) [1966], *Shadow Dance*, London: Virago.

—(2005) [1968], *Several Perceptions*, London: Vintage.

—(2006a) [1971], *Love*, London: Vintage.

—(2006b) [1985], 'Overture and Incidental Music for *A Midsummer Night's Dream*' in A. Carter, *Burning Your Boats: Collected Stories*, London: Vintage, 271–83.

Dalí, S. (1998), 'The Spectral Surrealism of the Pre-Raphaelite Eternal Feminine' ['Le Surréalisme spectral de l'éternel féminin préraphaélite'] in H. Finkelstein (ed. and trans.) *The Collected Writings of Salvador Dalí*, Cambridge: Cambridge University Press, 310–4.

Ernst, M. (1936), La Joie de Vivre [The Joy of Life], Scottish National Gallery of Modern Art, Edinburgh, United Kingdom.

Gamble, S. (1997), *Angela Carter: Writing From the Front Line*, Edinburgh: Edinburgh University Press.

—(2006), 'Something Sacred: Angela Carter, Jean-Luc Goddard and the Sixties' in R. Munford (ed.) *Re-Visiting Angela Carter: Texts, Contexts, Intertexts*, Basingstoke: Palgrave, 42–63.

Haffenden, J. (1985), *Novelists in Interview*, London: Methuen.

Hentges, J. (2002), 'Painting Pictures of Petrification and Perversion: Angela Carter's Surrealist Eye in *Shadow Dance* and *The Magic Toyshop*', *Études brittaniques contemporaines*, 23, 43–53.

Herrera, H. (1989), *Frida: A Biography of Frida Kahlo*, London: Bloomsbury.

Marsh, J. (1986), 'William Morris's Painting and Drawing', *Burlington Magazine*, 128:1001, 569–75.

—(2011), '*La Belle Iseult*', *Journal of William Morris Studies*, XIX:2, 9–19.

Millais, J. E. (1851–2), *Ophelia*, Tate Gallery, London, United Kingdom.

—(1895), *A Disciple*, Tate Gallery, London, United Kingdom.

Morris, W. (1858), *La Belle Iseult*, Tate Gallery, London, United Kingdom.

—(2009) [1890], *News From Nowhere: or, An Epoch of Rest*, Oxford: Oxford University Press.

Munford, R. (2006), 'Angela Carter and the Politics of Intertextuality' in R. Munford (ed.) *Re-Visiting Angela Carter: Texts, Contexts, Intertexts*, Basingstoke: Palgrave, 1–20.

O'Day, M. (2007), ' "Mutability is having a field day": The Sixties Aura of Angela Carter's Bristol Trilogy' in L. Sage (ed.) *Flesh and the Mirror: Essays on the Art of Angela Carter*, 2nd edn, London: Virago, 43–77.

Pearce, L. (1991), *Woman/Image/ Text: Readings in Pre-Raphaelite Art and Literature*, Hemel Hempstead: Harvester Wheatsheaf.

Pollock, G. (2003), *Vision and Difference: Feminism, Femininity and the histories of art*, 2nd edn, London: Routledge.

Rodgers, D. (1996), *Rossetti*, London: Phaidon.

Roe, S. (2007), 'The Disorder of *Love*: Angela Carter's Surrealist Collage' in L. Sage (ed.) *Flesh and the Mirror: Essays on the Art of Angela Carter*, 2nd edn, London: Virago, 78–114.

Rossetti, D. G. (1863), *Beata Beatrix*, Tate Gallery, London, United Kingdom.

—(1874), *Proserpine*, Tate Gallery, London, United Kingdom.

Rossetti, W. M. (1895), *Dante Gabriel Rossetti: His Family-Letters, with a Memoir*, 2 vols, London: Ellis.

Sage, L. (1994), *Angela Carter*, Plymouth: Northcote House.

—(2007) (ed.), *Flesh and the Mirror: Essays on the Art of Angela Carter*, 2nd edn, London: Virago.

Sanders, J. (2006), 'Bubblegum and Revolution: Angela Carter's Hybrid Shakespeare' in R. Munford (ed.) *Re-Visiting Angela Carter: Texts, Contexts, Intertexts*, Basingstoke: Palgrave, 111–33.

Showalter E. (1985), 'Representing Ophelia: Women, Madness and the Responsibilities of Feminist Criticism' in P. Parker and G. Hartman (eds) *Shakespeare and the Question of Theory*, London: Methuen, 77–94.

Suleiman, S. R. (1990), *Subversive Intent: Gender, Politics and the Avant-Garde*, London: Harvard University Press.

—(2007), 'The Fate of the Surrealist Imagination in the Society of the Spectacle' in L. Sage (ed.) *Flesh and the Mirror: Essays on the Art of Angela Carter*, 2nd edn, London: Virago, 115–32.

Turpin, I. (ed.) (1993), *Ernst*, London: Phaidon.

Watz, A. (2010), 'Angela Carter and Xavière Gauthier's *Surréalisme et Sexualité*', *Contemporary Women's Writing* 4.2, 114–33.

Watz [Fruchart], A. (2006), 'Convulsive Beauty and Compulsive Desire: The Surrealist Pattern of *Shadow Dance*' in R. Munford (ed.) *Re-Visiting Angela Carter: Texts, Contexts, Intertexts*, Basingstoke: Palgrave, 21–4.

Part Three

Mythologies

14

Genesis and Gender: The Word, the Flesh and the Fortunate Fall in 'Peter and the Wolf' and 'Penetrating to the Heart of the Forest'

Hope Jennings

If there is any one myth that Angela Carter repeatedly returns to as she goes about her 'demythologising business' (Carter 1997b: 38), it is the creation story in Genesis and the accompanying Christian myth (or doctrine) of the Fall.¹ Carter views Genesis as one of the more insidious patriarchal narratives, since within Western culture it has had such a significant impact on the construction of gendered subjectivities as well as socio-sexual roles and/or relations; she exposes in her numerous rewritings of this myth the ways in which Genesis articulates and constructs a repressive fear of female sexuality in order to police female (and often male) desires. The Fall, as her work suggests, is also analogous to psychoanalytic models of the origins of sexual differentiation and maturation, particularly Freud's theory of the castration complex. Likewise, both Julia Kristeva and Hélène Cixous offer corresponding readings of Genesis in psychoanalytic terms: Eve's economy of desire or pleasure, represented by her transgression of eating the forbidden fruit, is perceived as a threat to the Law of the Father, which relies on a masculine or phallic unity that represses female difference in the name of the One God (or, the one sex, 'man'). We see this same scenario played out in two of Carter's short stories, 'Peter and the Wolf' (1982) and 'Penetrating to the Heart of the Forest' (1974), both of which challenge the myth of the Fall through their emphases on the female flesh as representative of an economy of desire that disrupts the repressive authority of the paternal law or word. Furthermore, in both stories Carter offers male perspectives that (unlike Freud's male subject) refuse to reduce the other's (or 'woman's') difference, thus providing an 'other' discourse of sexual relations. Although she remains sceptical of the possibility of divorcing Genesis from its misogynist heritage, Carter's revisionist (rather than strictly deconstructive) approach towards the biblical creation myth in these two stories provides another example of her repeated attempts at negotiating the terms of (female) transgression and desire.

Both patriarchal and feminist readers view Eve as a decidedly subversive figure, whose desires are capable of transgressing those socio-cultural laws dictating gendered identities and behaviour. Throughout the long literary tradition of predominantly male readings of Genesis, it is 'woman', or Eve, who plays the most crucial role in evolving receptions of the tale, since within the deep structure of the biblical text the 'feminine' serves as an anomalous, mediating element permitting various constructions of 'man' and his others (Milne 1993: 154–5). In other words, Genesis positions Eve/woman as a disruptive presence that must be contained in her threat to a patriarchal order's desire for masculine or phallic unity. As Pamela Norris observes in her comprehensive study, *The Story of Eve*, if the woman is to blame for the breaking of taboos and man's expulsion from paradise, then to maintain the (patriarchal) social order Eve and her daughters are necessarily 'cursed', safely consigned to their desexualized roles as 'suffering' child bearers; thus, the Virgin Mother arises out of the Christian theology of original sin and redemption, where Mary as suffering mother redeems Eve's 'terrible flesh'. Overall, as Norris also points out, the vast corpus of rabbinical commentaries and Christian exegeses surrounding Gen. 1-3 set up a conflict between male reason and female passion, situating 'woman' as the dangerous other, and thus justifying the need to repress female bodies and desires.

However, the obsession with controlling and repressing female sexuality creates a strong impulse towards the forbidden, inevitably exposing the ways in which male fantasies or narratives, due to the unravelling of their inner logic, do not always succeed in containing female desires. As Kristeva argues, Eve's transgression in eating the forbidden fruit could be representative of Adam's sublimated desire to transgress the law; the responsibility for the man's shame or guilt is then shifted onto the woman in an attempt to rationalize men's powerlessness to resist their own forbidden desires (Kristeva 1986: 143). Accordingly, if 'woman' is positioned as the embodiment of a patriarchal order's unconscious desires, then she is also emblematic of the return of the repressed; this in turn bestows upon the female subject immense powers of disruption, whereby she has the potential to destabilize the rigid boundaries a patriarchal order constructs in the effort to keep out or suppress what is threatening to its rationale. This power of feminine disruption consequently lends itself to various feminist appropriations of the myth, which attempt to offer a more productive reading of the biblical text that recovers and asserts a feminine form of knowledge that might bring into play more reciprocal relationships between the sexes.

Dating back to Christine de Pizan's *L'Épistre au Dieu d'amours* (1399), the majority of 'feminist' readings of Genesis have been aimed at freeing the text from its androcentric biases through a confrontation with those translations or scriptural interpretations that emphasize a relationship of distorted inequality between the sexes.[2] In other words, if we accept this reformist argument, it is not the biblical text that is the problem, but a history and tradition of male-centred readings (mis)informing our understanding of the original egalitarian messages intended to be discovered therein.[3] On the other hand, Pamela J. Milne questions whether the Bible can be liberated from its patriarchal heritage; though Genesis attempts to present a universalistic perspective, it is written from the male point of view since the story's logic presents the primal human as male. Furthermore, as Milne argues, even if the mythic theme of the Fall posits sexual differentiation as bringing mutual joy and pain to both men and women, it is ultimately used to shift the guilt of the Fall/sin away from God and 'man', onto 'woman' and the serpent. For Milne, then, a feminist reformist approach is unlikely to succeed in ridding the text of its androcentric biases. Thus, if we accept that the biblical text is thoroughly embedded in patriarchal discourse, then tactics of deconstruction might provide the most viable means of confronting the underlying phallocentricism of Genesis, while also allowing for the possibility of effectively changing our relations to a text that cannot be rejected due to its profound and continuing influence on Western thought (Milne 1993: 147, 149, 158–9, 162–3).

Kristeva also insists on reading the story of Eve and Adam as an unquestionably patriarchal narrative, as it attempts to suppress the (female) flesh in its privileging of the (male) word, or God's Law, indicating women's subsequent exclusion from the symbolic order. In Kristeva's interpretation of the biblical text, Eve's disobedience in going against God's prohibition opens up an alternative feminine space of fleshly desires, placing her outside the law since she fails to submit to its demand for the rejection of sensual pleasure. Thus, as Kristeva goes on to argue, the Genesis narrative structures women's knowledge as corporeal, 'aspiring to pleasure', yet in its desire for masculine unity, represented by a monotheistic God, the text suppresses this female knowledge. The word, then, relies on excluding women from its symbolic economy, since by designating 'woman' to the realm of the flesh, 'man' is granted the sole privilege of engaging in the discourse of the law. Paradoxically, the integrity of the law/word is kept in place by that threat of feminine desire: if 'man' is in possession of the law, his power over it is sustained by creating one who does not have it and desires to seize it. In other words, the male is threatened with castration, necessitating the repression of female bodies and desires. As a result, sexual differences are inscribed according to a code of oppositions and the relationship between the sexes becomes one of envy, fear and hostility (Kristeva 1986: 140–5, 151–4).

Kristeva's analysis of this scenario explicitly connects monotheistic principles to core precepts found in 'Freudianism', acknowledging that neither of them can be separated from their patriarchal heritage. Carter also conflates monotheistic and psychoanalytic narratives to examine how they attempt to construct 'woman' as other and thus outside the symbolic order, marginalizing and silencing female identities and desires. By exposing this repression of the (female) flesh, as well as any feminine knowledge, from the paternal word/law, Carter works towards opening the 'forbidden book' (Carter 1996b: 288) of women's bodies, which the creation myth endeavours so hard to keep closed. She achieves this by 'entering the female body into a structuring discourse' (Wyatt 2000: 62), and for Carter, the Fall is indeed fortunate because it moves us outside the mythic (hence oppressive) and undifferentiated space of paradise, allowing women's bodies, desires and voices to enter into history (and by extension individuated, socio-cultural specific subjectivities). As Carter reminds us in *The Sadeian Woman*: 'Flesh comes to us out of history' (Carter 2000: 11). Furthermore, her texts present the Fall as a form of grace, as opposed to sin, overturning much of the rationale underpinning the myth in a way that potentially allows for a productive alliance between the sexes based on a respect rather than repression of sexual differences.

The premise of an impassable abyss existing between the sexes is reinforced by Freud in his formulation of the castration complex (Kristeva 1986: 145), which he asserts is the defining moment in the (male) child's 'fall' into knowledge of sexual difference. According to Freud, the boy's 'terror of castration . . . is linked to the sight of something', which is actually 'nothing'; in other words, when he first catches sight of the female genitals, he can only interpret the girl's lack of a penis as a horrifying absence (Freud 1990b: 322), and thus a threat or reminder of his possible castration. Subsequently, although his fear of castration is necessary to resolve his oedipal complex, the boy's attitude towards the female sex will later develop into either 'horror of the mutilated creature or triumphant contempt for her' Freud 1990c: 272). Freud seems to see no other possible relation to the 'other' sex.

As for the little girl, Freud claims 'she is cast out of her fool's paradise' the moment she realizes she must relinquish her desire for the penis, which she recognizes as 'the superior counterpart of [her] own small and inconspicuous organ' (ibid., 309, 314). She is compelled to give up her original identification or love-object (the mother) for her father, and accept his child (his law/the phallus) as a substitute for the penis she may never obtain (Freud 1990a: 309). It would seem, then, that the little girl is a little Eve, forced to denounce her desire/pleasure (for the flesh/penis and/or maternal body) and submit to the Law of the Father (a phallic economy). However, what if the little girl was never introduced to this law, and what if the boy refused to play by these rules? If we remove Freud's 'law of castration', what happens to the notion of sexual difference as a relationship of antagonism, where the boy feels fear/contempt towards the girl for her 'lack', and the girl is mired in her inferiority and envy for what she has been convinced is lacking (in her)?

'Peter and the Wolf' explores these questions, rewriting the Freudian scene of the boy's discovery of sexual difference and the girl's 'failure' to leave her delusional paradise, imagining both in the context of the Fall. Or, for the wolf-girl in this story, there is no Fall, since she remains in her state of prelapsarian grace (unconsciously) drawing the boy, Peter, into her innocence of the law, whereby he experiences 'the vertigo of freedom' (Carter 1996b: 291). Carter challenges the privileging of sight in the psychoanalytic reduction of anatomical differences by setting up two crucial moments in her text centred on the boy's observation of the female genitalia/body. Contrary to Freud's description of this moment, when Peter is confronted with 'the thing he had been taught most to fear' (Carter 1996b: 284), he sees what is present rather than what is absent. As Jean Wyatt observes, Carter 'answers Freud's "no thing" with a complex whorl of fleshly things, his "nothing" with a material "infinity"', and by doing so, the text avoids reducing 'female difference to a logic of the same' (Wyatt 2000: 61).

The wolf-girl is truly 'other' in the sense that she is a borderline, liminal creature, neither animal nor human. When the pack of wolves invades the house to reclaim the girl, terror overwhelms the entire family, since 'that which they feared most, outside, was now indoors with them' (Carter 1996b: 288). However, before the wolves 'rescue' their fosterling, Peter observes the distinguishing mark of her human femaleness; when the wolf-girl crouches upright 'she offer[s] . . . a view of a set of Chinese boxes of whorled flesh that seemed to open one upon another . . . drawing him into an inner, secret place in which destination perpetually receded before him, his first, devastating, vertiginous intimation of infinity' (ibid., 287). In that moment Peter experiences the 'sensation of falling' yet initially remains unconscious of any fear, drawn into the sight of 'her girl-child's sex' while viewing 'her intimacy clearly, as if by its own phosphorescence' (ibid.). In other words, the boy 'falls' into the girl's otherness, but without horror or contempt, without seeing the absence of a penis as an indication of something lacking; rather, in this passage Carter insists there may be another way of seeing, that there is in fact something to see, something that offers plenitude and plurality.

This different way of seeing, however, is never presented as a simple alternative, since Peter's first 'vertiginous' contact with the other is merely an 'intimation' of difference, and he must struggle against becoming indoctrinated by the Law of the Father. As for the wolf-girl, she returns to her 'fool's paradise', if she ever left it; she 'closed up her forbidden book without the least notion she had ever opened it or that it was banned' (ibid., 288). Peter, on the other hand, has been allowed a glimpse into that book, but because it is a text that is 'banned', he becomes 'consumed by an imperious passion for atonement' and studies with the village priest (ibid., 289). Carter indicates here that even if the child sees differently from the prescribed vision, he or she must still negotiate his or her relationship to the symbolic order, which determines one's entrance into adulthood and its constructions of language and time. Peter's journey from child to adult, then, does not simply centre on his discovery of sexual difference, but on how he learns to interpret that difference. He is forced to negotiate his identity in relation to the safe familiarity or acceptance promised by the law/word and to that which exists outside the law, the strange 'devastating' intimacy of the flesh/other.

Peter is allowed a second glimpse of the wolf-girl, or more appropriately, wolf-woman, when seven years later he leaves home to join the seminary, eager yet anxious 'to plunge into the white world of penance and devotion' (ibid., 289–90). He encounters the wolf-woman on the other side of the river where he has camped, and this vision provides him with passage into another world that has nothing to do with guilt and sin. The wolf-woman now seems more animal than human, as a kind of primal mother with cubs feeding from her 'dangling breasts' (ibid., 290). Rather than feeling revulsion, Peter is overcome with the same sense of 'awe and wonder' (ibid., 284) he experienced when he first saw the wolf-girl as a child. Luce Irigaray argues that this 'awe and wonder' is crucial to forming an 'ethics of sexual difference', whereby the sexes are 'always meeting as though for the first time' so that 'one will never exactly fill the place of the other' (Irigaray 2001: 238). Peter not only refuses to reduce this female other to the reflection of his projected desires and fears, but while watching her lap water from the river, he appreciates how she herself has no awareness of any reflection: 'she had never known she had a face and so her face itself was the mirror of a different kind of consciousness . . . just as her nakedness, without innocence or display, was that of our first parents, before the Fall' (Carter 1996b: 290). Her knowledge is corporeal, or 'informulable' (Kristeva 1986: 140), and in the face of this 'other' knowledge, Peter longs to cross over to the other side of the river and 'join her in her marvellous and private grace' (Carter 1996b: 290).

For Cixous, who employs the myth of the Fall to structure a different discourse of relationships between self and other, grace is an experience of coming to know the other through a 'delicate movement of detachment' (Cixous 2002: 236), or rather, in non-appropriative terms, which she claims can only be received after the Fall. This is because in the undifferentiated space of Eden there is no acknowledgement of otherness, since for Adam and Eve before the Fall they have no understanding of their (sexual) difference. Their innocence, which has no knowledge of loss or death, is meaningless, and Cixous insists that the only meaningful innocence is marked by an 'absolutely guilty' knowledge of the other's irreducible difference, but without trying to repress that difference; in this way we might receive the grace of a 'second innocence' in which we are innocent (not guilty) of appropriating the place of the other (ibid., 234–6). For example, Peter is 'guilty' in his knowledge of the wolf-woman, yet he never attempts to deny her otherness. When she runs off 'into the bright maze of the uncompleted dawn', into the story belonging to her, 'a child suckled by wolves, perhaps, or of wolves nursed by a woman' (Carter 1996b: 290–1), Peter does not appropriate that story or try to impose his own meanings onto its strangeness; he is determined to make his way 'into a different story' (ibid., 291). He refuses to look back on his childhood as a lost paradise, which has become a savage, impersonal, oppressive place that he has managed to escape. Through this movement of departure, he begins to progress forward in a newly discovered innocence of the world, free to construct his future without the burden of sin or shame. Moreover, Peter's second unexpected encounter with the wolf-woman, in which he accepts the vision of her 'animal' beauty as a gift of grace, demonstrates the possibility of embracing the other's difference. In both key moments of Carter's story, Peter experiences without fear the fall into an infinity of possible identities and relations, revealing how 'the vision of real difference, taken in without denial or defensive categorisation, opens the mind to the previously unsignified, springing the subject free from established categories of thought' (Wyatt 2000: 61).

This process of transgressing the boundaries of established orthodoxies and/or myths, in order to find a different way of seeing and relating to the irreducible differences of the other, is perhaps one of Carter's most enduring themes, and is encountered in an earlier story that is equally intent on disrupting Freud's specular theory of castration. 'Penetrating to the Heart of the Forest' also presents a newly invented Adam and Eve who refuse to pay loyalty to the (phallic) law; the moment of recognition (of sexual difference) is again located in the male gaze, and similar to Peter's vision this gaze looks on the other with awe and wonder. Moving beyond the impenetrable silence of the wolf-girl, however, Carter opens up a space for the articulation of female desires in order to provide not simply an alternative relation to the law but perhaps a complete dismantling of it. In this text, Eve's perceived transgression primarily derives from her discourse with the serpent, with that which is outside the law. Carter implies that Eve's desire is threatening because she does not desire the phallus (law) but rather the flesh/ fruit, which is 'desired to make *one* wise' (Gen. 3:6), promising a (fleshly) knowledge of pleasure. Ultimately, the text poses the question: If a woman does not desire the phallus, if her desire is for something outside the law, then what precisely sustains a phallic economy in its definition of women's bodies as castrated or lacking?

As Cixous argues, contra Freud, it is not anatomical sex that determines differences between men and women but how they negotiate their desires. Cixous claims that 'every entry to life finds itself *before the Apple*' (Cixous 1988: 15); it is only when one is confronted with situating him or herself in relation to pleasure, to the body, that one might gain a necessary knowledge of the flesh that initiates our growth into full, responsible human beings. Similar to Kristeva's interpretation, Cixous reads the Genesis text as one of the most significant examples of how patriarchal narratives attempt to exclude from the symbolic order a feminine knowledge. The figure of Eve is representative of how 'woman' is the one who has 'to deal with [this] question of pleasure' (ibid.), since the creation story describes 'a struggle between the Apple [the flesh] and the discourse of God [the word]' (ibid., 16). God's word, as Cixous goes on to illustrate, not only attempts to subordinate the flesh to the spirit/mind, but because it is mediated by Adam to Eve, she is allowed no direct relation to God; whereas the Apple presents itself to Eve as an unmediated interior, so that the 'genesis of woman goes through the mouth, through a certain oral pleasure, and through a non-fear of the inside' (ibid.). Thus for Eve, God's threat that 'you will die' has no meaning; it is an abstraction that has no relevant connection to her direct knowledge, which is corporeal, revealing that what is at stake in the law/word is a conflict between absence and presence (ibid.).

Although Carter's story is concerned with discovering a different discourse outside the Law of the Father, the text follows a movement from the margins or boundaries of the law to a secret interior, which is figured as a maternal space where the children gain knowledge of fleshly pleasures. Their fall into such 'guilty' knowledge, however, is experienced as a form of grace, since both regard each other with renewed innocence, and without fear or the desire for appropriating the other's difference. Carter positions the girl as a somewhat aggressive Eve, the initiator of this entrance into the realm of desire, while the boy passively follows her lead in accepting the forbidden; yet his acceptance opens up into 'a multiple, universal dawning' rather than enclosing them in sin and shame (Carter 1996a: 66). Although Carter follows a close reading of Genesis in her characterization of Adam and Eve, picking up on those elements in the biblical text where Eve comes across as far more active due to her curiosity, by dismantling the notion of original sin she offers a very different interpretation of the Fall. If sin is a matter of the flesh, as patriarchal interpreters of Genesis often assert, then Carter indicates this is a particularly insidious myth since it not only conveys a 'savage denial of the complexity of human relations' (Carter 2000: 6) but also prohibits any reciprocity between the sexes.

'Penetrating to the Heart of the Forest' opens with the description of an edenic landscape: a pristine, untouched territory; a vast valley 'like an abandoned flower bowl' surrounded by mountains; and in its centre a dense forest (Carter 1996a: 58). Within this forest is a 'malign' tree, 'whose fruits could have nourished with death an entire tribe'; though no one has seen this tree, its presence 'categorically forbade exploration' of the forest (ibid., 59). At least Dubois, a widower and father of the twins, Madeleine and Emile, explicitly forbids any exploration of the forest. Initially, Madeleine and Emile are infantile versions of Eve and Adam, and Dubois is an absent god whose only demand is that his children remain locked in their innocent and undifferentiated purity. As the twins grow older, they begin to desire knowledge of the forbidden forest and begin exploring its outskirts; thus, Carter exposes the ways in which the law creates a desire for the very thing it prohibits.

Significantly, at the age of thirteen, and marking the onset of puberty, the children decide to penetrate the heart of the forest, going further 'into the untrodden, virginal reaches of the deep interior' (ibid., 61), determined to eventually reach its 'navel' (ibid., 62). Although Emile and Madeleine refuse to believe in the threat of the mythical tree, they are fearlessly curious about it, driven by the sense that their world seemed incomplete, lacking 'the knowledge of some mystery' (ibid., 62–3). What they discover in the forest is 'a vegetable transmutation', where previously recognizable forms of natural wildlife undergo 'an alchemical change', presenting an array of fantastical variations (ibid., 65). As they journey towards that 'central node of the unvisited valley' (ibid., 62), the forest seems to envelop them like a womb, the changes in the landscape progressively taking on distinctly feminine maternal features. One tree proffers fruit like oysters, another has breasts from which the children drink a milky liquid (ibid.). Their exploration of this maternal terrain, the very thing their world has been lacking, is marked by a lush exoticism that returns them to a fleshy origin that pre-exists the father's law, initiating a discovery of their own flesh.

Madeleine and Emile are also introduced to the tension of power relations as they gradually become 'less twinned' in relation to each other (ibid., 65). For instance, when they bathe together in a river, Emile can no longer ignore his sister's nakedness, and is overcome by a momentary 'unfamiliar thrill of dread' (ibid.). Madeleine, sensing her brother's anxiety, is now motivated by a desire 'to make him do as she wanted, against his own wishes', and in turn is thrilled by her new-found power over Emile (ibid.). Just as we see in 'Peter and the Wolf', though, it is not so much the children's discovery of sexual difference, but how they comprehend those differences that informs their relations to each other. Their journey into knowledge is fraught with danger, with necessary risk, as Cixous would urge, because without risking the disruption of the other, there is no meaningful, or at least productive, experience of grace or love. The twins eventually learn to negotiate their sexual differences and desires beyond the restrictions of the paternal law, and it is Madeleine who forces them to deal with the question of pleasure through her disobedience. She insists that everything they discover must remain secret, convincing Emile of the need to conceal something from their father. Emile at first believes that his sister, after being bitten by a 'fanged flower' (ibid.), has 'received some mysterious communication from the perfidious mouth that wounded her' (ibid., 64), as if Madeleine, like Eve, has been holding discourse with a (wise) serpent. He discovers in his sister 'the ultimate difference of a femininity'; yet he does not view her with dread or contempt but rather desire for 'this difference [that] might give her the key to some order of knowledge to which he might not yet aspire' (ibid.).

For Emile, this awakening of desire is unsettling not only because he recognizes something lacking within himself, thus penetrating to the heart of desire, but also because he accepts this lack rather than project it onto his sister. He respects that Madeleine's difference gives her access to a specifically feminine knowledge, and because her irreducible difference is something 'he might not yet aspire' to understand, he merely hopes to receive this 'other' knowledge as a gift of grace. Consequently, Emile's non-appropriative desire figuratively opens up an alternative space in which the (maternal) flesh supersedes the demands of the (paternal) law. Overall, Carter enacts a disruption of the phallocentricism embedded in Genesis, and in privileging this maternal space, she exposes where the maternal and/or female body has been repressed by the patriarchal narrative.

When the children reach the centre of the forest, they find a small inner valley with a fresh-water pool (which has no visible source and is the navel/womb they have been seeking). Beside the pool they discover the supposedly malign tree, which seems to exhibit both masculine and feminine attributes, and is thus representative of an erotic alliance between the two, displaying elongated 'flowers tipped with the red anthers of stamens' and 'clusters of leaves' that 'hid secret bunches of fruit, mysterious spheres of visible gold' marked by 'a round set of serrated indentations exactly resembling the marks of a bite made by the teeth of a hungry man' (ibid., 66). Madeleine, in a burst of laughter, because the threat of death now seems absurd, eagerly accepts the fruit as a gift from the forest. The image of her eating the fruit is presented through Emile's eyes, and unlike the traditional depiction of Adam's distrust and displeasure with Eve's act of disobedience, he experiences a moment of ecstasy while observing his sister's specifically feminine pleasure, which dares to laugh at the law by rejecting its prohibition of the forbidden (flesh). Emile views the juice dribbling down his sister's chin, her 'newly sensual tongue' licking her lips, in silent appreciation, and when she offers him the fruit: 'Her enormous eyes were lit like nocturnal flowers that had been waiting for this especial night to open and, in their vertiginous depths, reveal . . . the hitherto unguessed at, unknowable, inexpressible vistas of love' (ibid., 67).

Daring to step outside the law, then, experiencing a fall into fleshly knowledge might not lead to sin or shame, but 'vistas of love'. Madeleine and Emile, like Peter and the wolf-woman, seem to have achieved that difficult proximity, coming together as if for the first time and without the fear of being consumed by the other. Their sense of awe and wonder allows them 'a space of freedom or attraction, a possibility of separation or alliance' (Irigaray 2001: 238). They choose an alliance through the consummation of their desires, as Carter's story simply and abruptly ends: 'He took the apple; ate; and, after that, they kissed' (Carter 1996a: 67). Even the taboo of incest is rejected in this garden of earthly delights, and in overturning the myth of original sin, the text explores through the unsanctioned desires of incest, as both a literal and metaphorical device, the possibilities of sexual relations operating outside the law. Carter's rewriting of Genesis suggests the need for escaping the limits of the patriarchal narrative while seeking out an alternative discourse of sexual differences that does not remain loyal to the paternal law in its repression of the 'feminine'. Madeleine and Emile's willingness to risk the prohibitions of the law indicates an economy of transgression that opens the way to a discourse of fleshly (feminine) pleasure, one that resists and subverts the monolithic unity of the law's privileging of phallic desire.

In spite of the feminist revisionary approach towards the Genesis myth in 'Penetrating to the Heart of the Forest' and 'Peter and the Wolf', indicating a slight shift away from Carter's self-proclaimed 'demythologising business', she remains rigorously self-critical of her own remythologizing impulses. Even if her texts seek out possibilities for transgression and subversion, she primarily does so through a necessary confrontation with their limits, as seen in the various reincarnations of Eve and Adam that appear across the body of her work: Melanie and Finn in *The Magic Toyshop*, Marianne and Jewel in *Heroes and Villains*, and of course Eve/lyn in *The Passion of New Eve* are set up as originary couples or figures, all of them struggling (and perhaps failing) to escape the old gendered scripts and/or oppressive influence of a monstrous God (or Goddess); in *Nights at the Circus* Fevvers and Walser must both experience a fall before they can achieve grace (or, the consummation of their desires); and the obsession with origins in *Wise Children* indicates the fallen world of

Dora and Nora's illegitimacy and their accompanying desire to gain access into the 'lost paradise' of legitimacy they believe their father's recognition and love might confer upon them. In each of these texts, the subject's attempts at transgressing or escaping the tyranny of the paternal law are fraught with difficulties, since in the world outside fiction and fantasy, subversion (as Carter often demonstrates) does not always work as some utopian leap of the imagination, but is a long and complicated process, a struggle perhaps against one's own interior colonization. It is precisely this ongoing struggle that Carter negotiates in her texts, seeking out ways in which the articulation of disruptive desires are capable of productively challenging our most potent cultural myths, as well as reimagining and rewriting gendered identities.

Notes

1   We should keep in mind that nowhere in Genesis 1-3 is there mention of 'original sin'; this element has been superimposed upon the Hebrew text by the New Testament. As a result, the Christian myth of the Fall has come to dominate our cultural perceptions of the Hebrew creation story in Genesis. Furthermore, though there is no mention of Eve after Genesis 5, there exists a wealth of Jewish apocrypha and post biblical exegeses that address themselves to her character. These commentaries also have had a large influence in constructing gender relations according to social schemas that rely on biological justifications for women's 'inferiority', dichotomously categorizing male and female attributes. An extensive compilation and analysis of these commentaries can be found in Kvam *et al.* (1999).
2   Pizan embraces the Fall as a 'fortunate' event; by doing so, she attempts to overturn a history of misogynist interpretations of Eve, arguing that Eve was 'made of very noble stuff', in God's image as much as Adam, and that 'she never did play Adam false' having offered him the forbidden fruit in complete innocence. Pizan then challenges anyone who 'would search . . . in the Bible just to prove me wrong', since the Bible itself supports her egalitarian reading; rather it is religious doctrine that has distorted Eve/woman's reputation, only providing examples of corrupt and immoral women in order to instruct young schoolboys 'so they'll retain such doctrine when they're grown' (Kvam *et al.* 1999: 236–40). For a wide range of contemporary revisionist readings see Brenner (1993).
3   See Trible (1973) which had a significant influence on feminist re-readings of Genesis.

Works Cited

Brenner, A. (ed.) (1993), *A Feminist Companion to Genesis*, Sheffield: Sheffield Academic Press.

Carter, A. (1996a) [1974], 'Penetrating to the Heart of the Forest', *Burning Your Boats: Collected Short Stories*, London: Vintage, 58–67.

—(1996b) [1982], 'Peter and the Wolf', *Burning Your Boats*, 284–91.

—(1997a) [1983], 'Anger in a Black Landscape', *Shaking A Leg: Collected Journalism and Writings*, London: Chatto & Windus, 43–52.

—(1997b) [1983], 'Notes from the Front Line', *Shaking A Leg*, 36–43.

—(2000) [1979], *The Sadeian Woman*, London: Virago Press.

Cixous, H. (1988), 'Extreme Fidelity', in Susan Sellers (ed.) *Writing Differences: Readings from the Seminar of Hélène Cixous*, Milton Keynes: Open University Press, 9–36.

—(2002), 'Grace and Innocence', in M. Joy, K. O'Grady and J. L. Poxon (eds), *French Feminists on Religion: A Reader*, London: Routledge, 233–36.

Freud, S. (1990a) [1931], 'Female Sexuality', in Elisabeth Young-Bruehl (ed.), *Freud on Women: A Reader*, New York: Norton, 321–41.

— (1990b) [1922], 'Medusa's Head', in Young-Bruehl (ed.), 272–3.

—(1990c) [1925], 'Some Psychical Consequences of the Anatomical Distinctions Between the Sexes', in Young-Bruehl (ed.), 304–14.

Irigaray, L. (2001), 'Sexual Difference', in Philip Rice and Patricia Waugh (eds), *Modern Literary Theory: A Reader, 4*th *edition*, London: Hodder and Stoughton, 236–38.

Kristeva, J. (1986) [1974], 'About Chinese Women', in Toril Moi (ed.), *The Kristeva Reader*, Oxford: Blackwell, 138–59.

Kvam, K. E., Schearing, L. S. and Ziegler, V. H. (eds) (1999), *Eve and Adam: Jewish, Christian, and Muslim Readings on Genesis and Gender*, Bloomington: Indiana University Press.

Milne, P. J. (1993), 'The Patriarchal Stamp of Scripture: The Implications of Structuralist Analyses for Feminist Hermeneutics', in Athalya Brenner (ed.), *A Feminist Companion to Genesis*, Sheffield: Sheffield Academic Press, 146–72.

Norris, P. (1998), *The Story of Eve*, London: Picador.

Trible, P. (1973), 'Depatriarchalizing in Biblical Interpretation', *Journal of the American Academy of Religion* 41(1), 30–48.

Wyatt, J. (2000), 'The Violence of Gendering: Castration Images in Angela Carter's *The Magic Toyshop, The Passion of New Eve*, and "Peter and the Wolf"', in Alison Easton (ed.), *Angela Carter: Contemporary Critical Essays*, Basingstoke: Macmillan, 58–83.

15

'Ambulant Fetish': The Exotic Woman in 'Black Venus' and 'Master'

Sarah Artt

Rebecca Munford, in her 2004 article 'Re-presenting Charles Baudelaire/Re-presencing Jeanne Duval' states '[c]ertainly, there is a sense in which Carter's exuberant intertextual interweaving of a decadent poetic raises uncomfortable questions about her potential complicity with a male-centred aesthetic structured around the objectification of the female body' (Munford 2004: 2). It is these uncomfortable questions that I wish to address here in my discussion of two of Carter's short stories – the well-known 'Black Venus' story which imagines the consciousness of Baudelaire's mistress, Jeanne Duval and an earlier, less examined story, 'Master' which tells of an anonymous tribal girl sold to a white big game hunter in the jungle. To date, there has been little critical attention paid to 'Master' and further investigation of this story is long overdue, particularly as it constitutes a radical intervention by Carter in terms of positioning the reader to simultaneously inhabit positions of power and weakness in relation to the image of the exotic woman.

In re-appropriating the exotic woman of early orientalist discourse, of the anthropological postcard, through the image of the silent, abused girl of 'Master' and indeed of Jeanne Duval herself about whom we know so little – a woman who was literally painted out by Gustave Courbet[1] and whose portrait languished anonymously among Edouard Manet's unfinished works[2] – in re-appropriating these particular images Carter's writing ascribes agency to these previously silent and powerless female figures. These women – Jeanne in 'Black Venus' and the 'girl who did not know her own name' (Carter 1995a: 77) of 'Master' – once the object of the gaze, gain a degree of autonomy in Carter's rewriting. In the earlier story, 'Master', action is predictably violent – it is the only possible solution to the brutality of the situation in which the 'pubescent girl, as virgin as the forest that had borne her' (ibid.) finds herself when she is bought by the anonymous white hunter. The woman in 'Master' becomes the jaguar and undergoes a magical transformation in order to escape the brutal power of patriarchy – a trope that Carter revisits in many of the stories originally published in *The Bloody Chamber* (such as 'The Tiger's Bride' and 'The Company of Wolves'). In 'Black Venus', Duval survives Baudelaire to return to the Caribbean where she attains success selling his manuscripts and living off her savings. The story concludes with Jeanne continuing to sell herself and to 'dispense, to the most privileged of the colonial administration, at a not excessive price, the veritable, the authentic, the true Baudelairean syphilis' (Carter 1995b: 243). This final revelation acts as a kind of revenge where Jeanne is allowed to revisit upon the colonial administration the disease that in real life contributed to the early death of both herself and Baudelaire. This too is a kind of magical transformation which rewrites history and allows Duval greater agency.

What I also wish to argue here is that in both these stories, to quote Christine Britzolakis who writes about 'Black Venus', 'Carter's narrative perspective enacts an oscillation of identification and desire in which the permeability of fantasy (including its literary male-authored inscriptions) across the boundaries of gender plays a large part' (Britzolakis 2000: 183). This notion of the 'oscillation of identification' is key to my analysis of the way in which Carter allows the exotic woman to return the gaze and allows her reader to occupy alternate positions – that of the object of the gaze and the bearer of the look à la Laura Mulvey, who initially theorized this position in relation to classical Hollywood cinema. This mode of seeing and being seen can also be applied to Western art (in many ways, it is derived from the spectacle of the nude woman in classical art who does not meet the viewer's gaze) particularly when we consider the image of the exotic woman on a nineteenth-century postcard (anthropological/'authentic' or posed/oriental fantasy) or in a neoclassical painting of the nineteenth century that depicts the East (works by Jacques Louis David, Ingres, Jean-Léon Gérôme and John Singer Sargent all fall into this category). Much has of course been written about Carter's fiction and its engagement with the woman's image as it is reflected, whether it is the 'annihilating' ceiling mirror of 'Flesh and the Mirror', the multiplied, pornographic mirror of 'The Bloody Chamber' or the 'rational glass' of 'Wolf-Alice'. The spectacle of the female protagonist seeing herself in the mirror is always a watershed moment in Carter's work where the reflecting surface and the reflected image become important tools for self-awareness. Carter's deployment of this imagery re-appropriates the reflected image of the woman and divests it of its associations with classical depictions of feminine vanity. By imagining a consciousness for Jeanne Duval, the reader experiences how Duval sees herself and how she perceives Baudelaire's 'reflections' of her in his poetry. The girl in 'Master' cannot see her reflection, but her eyes like those of the jaguar – emblem of her tribe – enable her to see in the dark. Her perception is imagined as profoundly different from that of Master, and through this perception of herself, as her body changes to become more and more like the jaguar, the reader apprehends her powerful transformation and mode of escape. Both Jeanne and the girl, in a way, achieve self-actualization through escape that is also linked to self-awareness of the body. Jeanne's awareness of how her dancing fascinates the poet and later how her body becomes a vessel of the 'authentic' contagion provide a means to keep her from poverty. Though she is selling herself, Carter gives Jeanne a critical eye that mocks the poet's pretensions: '"Sucker!" she said, almost tenderly, but he did not hear her' (Carter 1995b: 233).

Carter's repurposing of the traditional image of female vanity – the woman admiring her own reflection or her own body becomes the woman seeing herself anew – contrasts with the 'visual seduction' of orientalism. Jeanne's inner monologue as she dances for Baudelaire – 'she sulked, sardonically, through Daddy's sexy dance,' (Carter

1995b: 234) – and the girl's realization that 'her fingernails were growing long, curved, hard and sharp . . . she could tear his back when he inflicted himself upon her' (Carter 1995a: 80), imply a kind of self-examination. Neither is an emotional participant in their objectification and further examination of the body and its actions brings about a kind of freedom. Jeanne knows it is only her allure that keeps Baudelaire paying for her keep, but she resents him and is bored by his views of her sensuality (which is far from inherent as he supposes). As the girl begins to hurt Master with her claws, she rapidly becomes the true, animal predator finally capable of vanquishing the hunter.

Rana Kabbani, in *Imperial Fictions*, discusses Gustave Flaubert's representation of the Orient based on his travels (and his encounters with dancers and courtesans):

> The onlooker is admitted to the Orient by visual seduction; he encounters the woman in a state of undress . . . in a state of pleasing vulnerability. *He* is not vulnerable: he is male, presumably in full dress, European, rational . . . and *armed with language* – he narrates the encounter in a reflective, post-facto narrative; he *creates* the Orient. (Kabbani 2008: 73; emphasis added)

This notion that the male European observer is 'armed with language' fits very well with the representations that Carter offers – the jaguar girl and Jeanne are not armed in this way: the girl in 'Master' is without formal language 'for though she could move her lips and tongue and so reproduce the sounds he made, she did not understand them' (Carter 1995a: 77); and later, 'her screams were a universal language; even the monkeys understood that she suffered when Master took his pleasure, yet he did not' (ibid., 79). The girl in 'Master' becomes increasingly feral and cat-like throughout the story and the absence of language underscores this. Soon, she can no longer form the words but only purrs (ibid., 80). Even her screams, the 'universal language' of pain, go undeciphered or ignored by the colonial European eye. Master never sees her as anything more than a possession, not even a pet, though he foolishly teaches her to shoot – a sign that he discerns her physical similarity to himself – or merely a sign that he regards killing as a universal skill: 'slaughter was his only proclivity and his unique skill' (ibid., 76).

Jeanne Duval in 'Black Venus' fares somewhat better:

> Her granny spoke Creole, patois, knew no other language, spoke it badly and taught it badly to Jeanne, who did her best to convert it into good French when she came to Paris and started mixing with the swells but made a hash of it, her heart wasn't in it, no wonder. It was as though her tongue had been cut out and another one sewn in that did not fit well.Therefore you could say, not so much that Jeanne did not understand the lapidary, troubled serenity of her lover's poetry but, that it was a perpetual affront to her. He recited it to her by the hour and she ached, raged and chafed under it because his eloquence denied her language. It made her dumb, a dumbness all the more profound because it manifested itself in a harsh clatter of ungrammatical recriminations and demands . . . (Carter 1995b: 239)

Jeanne's vocabulary is more extensive than that of the girl in 'Master', but their difficulties are similar. Where the silent girl struggles to fit her tongue around the words Master teaches her, Jeanne is silenced through her lack of education. The elaborate poetry she inspires mocks her dialect speech; she is denied access to the words she inspires, to their full meaning and impact. Carter writes in the above passage that Jeanne feels this gap very keenly – she knows that something is missing and this provides the reader with a sense of the character's self-awareness. Though silent or ungrammatical, the exotic woman's position is acknowledged. It is clear that the characters are aware of what is happening to them – they feel the slights and abuses – though no one (except the reader) is there to try to understand it.

Because the exotic woman is denied access to meaning through language in these stories, she expresses herself through movement instead. Though the girl in 'Master' does not dance, her association with the jaguar links her strongly with the sinuous, animal images of Jeanne Duval in 'Black Venus'. The girl in 'Master' becomes a predator the moment she begins to examine Master's guns and thinks of herself as 'death's apprentice' (Carter 1995a: 79). Her metamorphosis into the true jungle cat is gradual – first, she discovers she can see in the dark; soon, she can no longer abide cooked meat and must eat it raw; her fingernails grow long and curved and she begins to wound Master when he rapes her; then, she cannot take the feeling of water on her 'pelt'; finally, her tears dry up and she can no longer speak– there is only her great rumbling purr (Carter 1995a: 80). Jeanne is also 'my monkey, my pussy cat, my pet' (Carter 1995b: 232) to Baudelaire, linking her with the many sensuous images he creates for her in the Black Venus cycle of poems, as well as those where he writes about the sensual movements of the cat. Through this sinuous association with the cat and the snake, the animals often associated with Egypt in the orientalist iconography of Western painting, both Duval and the jaguar girl can be linked with the image of the oriental dancer.

Exotic Dancer

Munford states that 'exotic and sexually alluring, Duval is aligned with the figure of the veiled Oriental woman who embodies mythological inscriptions of the East as the "dark continent" – a concept that would later be equated with the unknown and unknowable *terra* of the female body in Freudian theory' (Munford 2004: 5). This veiled woman must be differentiated from the modest Muslim woman or even the exotic priestess (such as the white-robed female figure in John Singer Sargent's 1880 painting *Fumée d'Ambre Gris*) we see depicted throughout the nineteenth century by Western artists and early photographers. The veiled woman that we can associate with Jeanne Duval must be the figure of the oriental dancer, veiled only in the most translucent way, the woman who wears her wealth on her body in the form of coins and jewellery, such as the figures depicted in Jean-Léon Gérôme's paintings *An Almeh Performing a Sword Dance* (c. 1870) and *Dance of the Almeh* (c. 1875).[3] Both paintings show dancers draped in translucent veils and gold coin jewellery. The woman in the sword dance painting wears a green veil on her face, and a transparent chemise over her arms and stomach as she dances balancing a sword on her head, while around her neck is a heavy necklace of large gold coins. In *Dance of the Almeh*, the dancer also wears a translucent chemise, which leaves her stomach and part of her breasts exposed. She also wears clinking gold bracelets and a headdress with gold coins. The parallels with Jeanne's performance for Baudelaire in 'Black Venus' are clear – though all Jeanne's jewellery is paste:

> This dance, which he wanted her to perform so much and had devised especially for her, consisted of a series of voluptuous poses, one following another; private-room-in-a-bordello stuff, but tasteful, he preferred her to undulate rhythmically rather than jump about and shake a leg. He liked her to put on all her bangles and beads when she did her dance, she dressed up in the set of clanking jewellery he'd given her, paste, nothing she could sell or she'd have sold it. Meanwhile, she hummed a Creole melody, she liked the ones with ribald words about what the shoemaker's wife did at Mardi Gras or the size of some fisherman's legendary tool but Daddy paid no attention to what song his siren sang, he fixed his quick, bright, dark eyes upon her decorated skin as if, sucker, authentically entranced. (Carter 1995b: 233)

When Gustave Flaubert travelled to Egypt in the early 1850s, he became fascinated with the legendary dancer Kuchuk Hanem, describing her in the following terms:

> When she bends, her flesh ripples into bronze ridges. Her eyes are dark and enormous. Her eyebrows black, her nostrils open and wide; heavy shoulders, full, apple-shaped breasts (her black hair, wavy, unruly . . . for a bracelet she has two bands of gold, twisted together and interlaced. (Karayanni 2005: 49)

The similarities between this description and the image of the exotic woman as she appears in 'Master' and 'Black Venus' are striking. In 'Master', Carter writes: 'She wore a vestigial slip of red cotton twisted between her thighs and her long, sinuous back was upholstered in cut-velvet, for it was whorled and ridged with the tribal markings incised on her when her menses began – raised designs like the contour map of an unknown place' (Carter 1995a: 77). This image offers a literal representation of the unknowable, exotic female body with the phrase 'the contour map of an unknown place' hearkening back to Munford's phrase 'the unknowable terra of the female body in Freudian theory' (Munford 2004: 5). Of course, the woman's body is unknowable only for the hunter – the reader knows her more intimately through the way she reacts and the ways she looks at herself. In 'Black Venus' we have Carter's prose with Baudelairean inflection:

> She danced naked. Her necklaces and earrings clinked. As always, when she finally got herself up off her ass and started dancing she quite enjoyed it. . . . She bent over backwards until the huge fleece of a black sheep, her unfastened hair, spilled onto the Bokhara. She was a supple acrobat; she could make her back into a mahogany rainbow. (Carter 1995b: 234–5)

Jeanne is here performing a series of poses she knows please her benefactor, though she takes little pleasure in her own performance and watches her body and its reflection with detachment, even wondering 'if she was going to have to dance naked to earn her keep, anyway, why shouldn't she dance naked for hard cash in hand and earn enough to keep herself?' (ibid., 234).

In these passages, the body of the exotic woman – how she looks, how she moves – is paramount. For the women of 'Black Venus' and 'Master', it is their bodies that have value as a spectacle for the European male onlooker. Karayanni discusses the significance of the Orient for Flaubert, claiming:

> the Orient does not need Flaubert as much as he needs it, hence Flaubert's almost desperate attempt to unite with the Orient as it is condensed in this dancer's [Kuchuk Hanem] body. On her body he inscribes his physical desire, insatiably pouring himself inside Kuchuk as if to drown any other kind of ecstasy she is capable of experiencing. (Karayanni 2005: 52)

Like Flaubert, both Master and Baudelaire need the exotic woman far more than she needs him (note how Flaubert does not speculate very far into the possible thoughts and desires of Kuchuk Hanem). Duval provided Baudelaire with inspiration for some of his most well-known work and he supported her financially. Carter's story has Jeanne reflecting on the vagaries of morality, prostitution and promiscuity: 'prostitution was a question of number; of being paid by more than one person at a time. That was bad. She was not a bad girl. When she slept with anyone else she never let them pay . . . in these ethical surmises slumbered the birth of irony' (Carter 1995b: 234). For Jeanne, her exchanges with Baudelaire are strictly financial and because he is the sole man who pays her, this means she is not a prostitute. The fact that this man is Baudelaire in particular seems largely irrelevant to Jeanne. Master needs the girl as another outlet for his rage, but she does not need him – she has been bought and sold and removed from her tribe. Once he has imparted to her his only skill, killing, she becomes the better hunter and 'as she grew more like him, so she began to resent him' (Carter 1995a: 79). Both Jeanne and the girl come to resent the men who keep them. This resentment spurns them on towards escape through a combination of circumstance and transformation.

In order to better understand these textual transformations, I would like to draw on recent film theory to offer a model for how 'Master' and 'Black Venus' allow the reader the possibility of 'occupying the position of the other'. Charlotte Crofts writing on Carter and orientalism, notes that bell hooks: 'calls for the holders of hegemonic discourse to "de-hegemonise their subject position and themselves learn how to occupy the position of the other"' (Crofts 2006: 99). Although readers and spectators are theoretically distinct, shifting notions of literacy and the text allow us to consider the reader and spectator in a similar way and therefore the current arguments of spectatorship theory are relevant to an understanding of Carter's less examined work, such as 'Master'.

The notion of Deleuzian spectatorship in relation to cinema, particularly the idea of absorption has important implications for how we might therefore view the exotic woman as literary or cinematic object, and in turn how the reader or spectator sees and experiences this figure. She is no longer just the 'ambulant fetish, savage, obscene terrifying' (Carter 1995b: 241) as Jeanne is described in 'Black Venus', the object of the gaze via Carter's 'male ventriloquism' as we encounter it in these two stories. Instead, she is the being the reader is asked to absorb – we can occupy their space, we can become them through fiction:

This is one of the astonishing aspects of absorption: not merely that one can be looking in on another world, but also that one can have the sensation of bodily occupying that space in another world, the sensation of occupying the space of another being. To put it bluntly: one of the possibilities which absorption holds forth is the possibility of being another being. (Rushton 2009: 50)

In 'Black Venus' and 'Master' Carter opens up to the silent, exotic woman and gives her reader the possibility of experiencing absorption, of being inside the other: both exotic woman and the male bearer of the look – the white hunter/white artist. The hunter of 'Master' is intriguingly compared to the figure of the artist: 'his ferocity would attain the colouring of the fauves' (Carter 1995a: 75), as Carter describes him in the first few paragraphs. This comparison immediately likens the hunter to the 'wild beast' painters of the early twentieth century whose furious use of bright colour and sensual landscapes (such as Matisse's *Joie de Vivre* (1905–6)) were the scandal of the Salon d'Automne of 1905. This mention of the fauves aligns the anonymous white hunter closely with Carter's envisioning of Baudelaire as the white artist in 'Black Venus'. In these two stories, Carter is explicitly acknowledging the danger of occupying these powerful positions by equating hunter, artist and bearer of the male colonial gaze. In allowing the silent woman consciousness, the object returns the look, and the reader is absorbed and permitted to potentially occupy both positions: male and female. What is particularly exciting and significant about this idea is that it encompasses both the reader's intellectual and physical processes, which may include not only delight and relish, but also anxious or 'incorrect' pleasures.

This feeling of anxious, incorrect pleasure is particularly salient to the experience of reading 'Master'. Perhaps this anxiety is also reflected in the lack of criticism[4] dealing with 'Master' which is less obvious in its project of feminist rewriting and yet closer inspection reveals this particular story to be an example of Carter's radical technique for instigating complicity in her reader. 'Master' is in many ways a Sadeian fiction – 'the strong abuse, exploit and meatify the weak says Sade. They must and will devour their natural prey' (Carter 1998: 140), much like the girls taken by the native guide in 'Master':

His half-breed guide would often take one of the brown girls who guilelessly offered him her bare, pointed breasts and her veiled, limpid smile and, then and there, infect her with the clap to which he was a chronic martyr in the bushes at the rim of the clearing. Afterwards, licking his chops with remembered appetite, he would say to the hunter: 'Brown meat, brown meat. (Carter 1995a: 76)

Again, there are key parallels here with 'Black Venus', where Jeanne continues to infect her select clientele with the 'the veritable, the authentic, the true Baudelairean syphilis' (Carter 1995b: 243) in a kind of vengeful reversal of what occurs in 'Master'.

The women in 'Master' certainly fulfil the category of Sadeian prey. The hunter bites the girl and she, like de Sade's more corrupt heroines, eventually learns to bite back. In Carter's discussion of de Sade's fictions, there is often 'a dialectic of mutual aggression' (Carter 1998: 145) at work: the defiled will soon become the defiler. This is precisely what occurs in 'Master', where the wordless girl drives her claws into Master's back and when she finally kills him, worrying his flesh with her teeth – the exploited has become the predator. Aidan Day comments that Carter's use of the '. . . fantastic is entirely under conscious, rational control and is deployed in order to articulate issues concerning sexuality that occur in the actual, day-to-day world' (Day 1998: 7). But can this be said of 'Master', a brief and violent story that is little written about and that bears much in common with the scenarios Carter describes so vividly in *The Sadeian Woman*? Of de Sade, Carter claims 'the libertine chooses to surround himself, not with lovers or partners, but with accomplices' (Carter 1998: 146). The white hunter therefore becomes an analogy for de Sade's libertine (linking him even more strongly with the Baudelaire of 'Black Venus') who, by teaching the girl about his guns, makes her into 'death's apprentice' or the libertine's accomplice who is taught cruelty, exploitation and death by example. Margaret Atwood argues in her essay on Carter, 'Running with the Tigers', 'for de Sade, women can escape sacrificial lambhood (the "natural" condition of women, as exemplified by Justine and defined by men) only by adopting tigerhood (the role of the predatory aggressor, the "natural" role of men, as exemplified by Juliette and also defined by men)' (Atwood 1994: 119). 'Master' therefore represents an early interpretation of this idea that Carter was to develop later in *The Sadeian Woman* and in 'The Tiger's Bride', where the girl is transformed literally into the beast, covered in fur like her tiger lover although in this story she meets her lover on terms of physical equality, unlike the jaguar girl of 'Master'. The girl in 'Master' escapes her potential fate as 'meat' for the hunter who is likely to kill or discard her at any moment, who 'when he looked at her, he saw only a piece of curious flesh he had not paid much for,' (Carter 1995a: 77) by becoming the jaguar, the predator. The girl's eventual animal shape symbolically avoids the categories of human gender roles and she exits the story into nature, but potentially outside and beyond the symbolic social order.

Characters who do not conform to social roles and rules and who can even transcend traditional boundaries of gender or cross the human/animal divide is something that characterizes Carter's folktales, but can also be detected in novels such as *The Passion of New Eve* and *Nights at the Circus*. In *The Passion of New Eve*, the male protagonist undergoes a forced gender reassignment and must now cope with the consequences of being female in a harsh environment. Published only a few years after 'Master' was written, *Passion* is similarly radical in the brutality it visits upon Eve as well as the bizarre violence of the narrative world of the story. It also shares a remarkable similarity with the film by the Spanish director Pedro Almodovar, *The Skin I Live In*, which also deals with the subjectivity of the individual who becomes a woman and experiences physical and emotional brutality. In *Nights at the Circus*, the protagonist, Fevvers, represents a more joyful hybrid position as a figure that has profited from her unique anatomy – her wings – to transform herself into a star of popular theatre. Fevvers has been permitted to escape the realm of sexual subjugation and has attained a degree of freedom and independence which Eve never achieves and which the jaguar girl is permitted only by her complete animal transformation.

Atwood asserts 'lambhood and tigerishness may be found in either gender and in the same individual at different times. In this respect, Carter's arrangements are much more subject to mutability than are de Sade's' (Atwood 1994: 122). This demonstrates Carter's active engagement with the Sadeian scenario, rewriting and reimagining its positions through her fiction.

The absorbed reader of 'Master' and 'Black Venus' can foil the traditional pornographic structure used to confine the exotic woman. As Keenan observes 'the pornographic scenario . . . is always tripartite: the master/producer, the object (typically the woman/victim), and the onlooker (the producer's guest)' (Keenan 1997: 137). By having the absorbed reader occupy this triple space, Carter allows her reader to explore the anxiety-ridden position of master, object and onlooker simultaneously. To experience power and powerlessness through fiction allows for a greater understanding of the power dynamics inherent in pornography. Carter was certainly at work on *The Sadeian Woman* prior to the publication of *Fireworks*[5] and it precedes 'Black Venus' (published in 1985) by several years. As Sarah Gamble notes, Carter found the writing of *The Sadeian Woman* difficult and wrestled with the text considerably before it was ready for publication. It is therefore understandable that we would see some of the same themes emerge in the fiction she was writing before and while working on *The Sadeian Woman*. Sally Keenan asserts:

> The provocation in Carter's use of Sade is not her supposed validation of pornography, but her employment of his work to expose her female readers to their own complicity with the fictional representations of themselves as mythic archetypes. Such mystification of femininity amounts, in her view, to a complicity with the pornographic scenario on which the unequal gender relations of our society are founded. (Keenan 1997: 138)

'Master' and 'Black Venus' share this technique: by forcing the reader to recognize their complicity in the pleasure and eroticism of these representations of the exotic woman, but then also by becoming absorbed and thereby occupying each part of the pornographic triad (Jeanne/Baudelaire/the reader as voyeur; the girl/the hunter/the reader as voyeur), the stories go beyond the confines of that triad into an alternative political space. Just as Carter uses de Sade to critique the cultural function of pornography, she uses the power of the reader's experience and the traditionally hypnotic associations of the exotic, dancing woman's body to seduce her reader and then force them to question this experience of seduction.

Carter's work has always been concerned with representing the woman's subjectivity but the way the reader assumes the woman's role in 'Black Venus' and 'Master' and the way that the female protagonists of these stories reflect upon and regard their own bodies and subjectivities is both provocative and radical. Rather than being afraid to confront the position of the exoticized woman Carter writes boldly from this position and imbues the silenced figure with physical mastery and independent thoughts. Carter's simultaneous positioning of her reader as exploiter and exploited therefore renders her work invaluable in terms of coming to understand objectification through the lens of fiction.

Notes

1   She originally appeared in *The Artist's Studio* (1854–5) alongside Baudelaire but was later painted out by Courbet at Baudelaire's request.
2   See Dolan (1997) for a discussion of the portrait's history and critical reception.
3   For a history of the representation of the oriental dancer, see Buonaventura (1989).
4   Sarah Gamble confirms this in *Angela Carter: Writing from the Front Line:* 'With the exception of *Flesh and the Mirror*, this group of stories [Fireworks] . . . has received very little critical attention to Date' (Gamble 1997: 104).
5   Although *Fireworks* was published in 1974 and *The Sadeian Woman* in 1979, Gamble confirms '*The Sadeian Woman* took her five years to write, and she found it extremely hard work' (Gamble 1997: 99).

Works Cited

Almodovar, P. (2011), *La Piel Que Habito/The Skin I Live In. Spain*, Sony Pictures Classics.

Atwood, M. (1994), 'Running with the Tigers' in Lorna Sage (ed), *Flesh and the Mirror: Essays on the art of Angela Carter*, London: Virago Press, 117–35.

Britzolakis, C. (2000), 'Angela Carter's Fetishism' in Alison Easton (ed.), *Angela Carter: Contemporary Critical Essays*, St Martin's Press, 173–91.

Buonaventura, W. (1989), *Serpent of the Nile: Women Dance and the Arab World*, London: Saqi Books.

Carter, A. (1977), *The Passion of New Eve*, London: Virago.

—(1979), *The Bloody Chamber and Other Stories*, London: Victor Gollancz.

—(1984), *Nights at the Circus*, London: Chatto and Windus.

—(1995a), 'Master', *Burning Your Boats: Collected Short Stories*, Toronto: Penguin, 75–80.

—(1995b), 'Black Venus', *Burning Your Boats: Collected Short Stories*, Toronto: Penguin, 231–44.

—(1995c), 'The Bloody Chamber', *Burning Your Boats: Collected Short Stories*, Toronto: Penguin, 111–43.

—(1995d), 'Flesh and the Mirror', *Burning Your Boats: Collected Short Stories*, Toronto: Penguin, 68–74.

—(1995e), 'The Tiger's Bride', *Burning Your Boats: Collected Short Stories*, Toronto: Penguin,154–69.

—(1995f), 'Wolf-Alice', *Burning Your Boats: Collected Short Stories*, Toronto: Penguin, 221–8.

—(1998) [1979], *The Sadeian Woman: an exercise in cultural history*, London: Virago.

Crofts, C. (2006), ' "The Other of the Other": Angela Carter's "New-Fangled" Orientalism', in Rebecca Munford (ed.), *Re-Visiting Angela Carter: Texts, Contexts, Intertexts*, London: Palgrave-MacMillan, 87–109.

Day, A. (1998), *Angela Carter: The Rational Glass*. Manchester: Manchester University Press.

Dolan, T. (1997), 'Skirting the Issue: Manet's portrait "Baudelaire's Mistress, Reclining" ', *The Art Bulletin*, 79.4 (December) 611–19.

Gamble, S. (1997), *Angela Carter: Writing from the Front Line,* Edinburgh: Edinburgh University Press.

Kabbani, R. (2008), *Imperial Fictions: Europe's Myths of the Orient,* London: Saqi Books.

Karayanni, S. (2005), *Dancing Fear and Desire: Race, Sexuality and Imperial Politics in Middle Eastern Dance,* Waterloo: Wilfred Laurier University Press.

Keenan, S. (1997), '*The Sadeian Woman:* Feminism as Treason' in Joseph Bristow and Trev Lynn Broughton (eds), *The Infernal Desires of Angela Carter: Fiction, Femininity, Feminism,* London and New York: Addison Wesley Longman, 132–48.

Munford, R. (2004), 'Re-presenting Charles Baudelaire/Re-presencing Jeanne Duval: Transformations of the muse in Angela Carter's Black Venus', *Forum for Modern Language Studies* 40.1, 1–13.

Rushton, R. (2009), 'Deleuzian Spectatorship', *Screen* Spring 50.1, 45–53.

16

Seeing the City, Reading the City, Mapping the City: Angela Carter's *The Magic Toyshop* and the Sixties

Simon Goulding

Consider the role of the Thames in our understanding of London. On any map of the city the eye is drawn to it for two reasons: first, it divides the city into two halves; a northern and a southern and, secondly, we are aware of this because the river is highlighted in contrast to the landmass. This primary geographical feature is recognized as a cartographic sign (component) because of its differentiation in graphical form to the spaces around it; in its function as connotative symbol it serves to delineate the layout and boundaries of the landscape. It suggests that there are two Londons – a north and a south. In some respects this is a perfectly correct analysis, the river splits the city by a, roughly, east/west flow so the division must be north/south. The reality of London is of course not so simple. London is as much about the east/west division as the north/south divide. What constitutes the city may not be as simple as considering the Ordnance Survey maps, A–Z street guides or a listings magazine. The city for Jonathan Raban is not a fixed entity: '[t]he city as we imagine it, the soft city of illusion, myth, aspiration, nightmare, is as real, maybe more real, than the hard city one can locate on maps' (Raban 1998: 3–4). What we perceive is more important, argues Raban, than that which is offered us as representation.

Jacques Bertin notes 'for centuries the primary objective of cartography has been to provide representation of tangible points such as rivers, mountains, cities, and roads which can be used for human orientation' (Bertin 1983: 69). A map for him is a designed object, so when it fails to work in the manner intended, which is to aid us in our orientation, questions must be asked about the relevance and/or usefulness of the design. Which way then do we look at London, north/south or east/west, both or perhaps neither? Consider then Angela Carter's 1967 novel *The Magic Toyshop* as a representative example in its presentation of dislocation and reorientation. It employs the classic trope of the displaced orphans relocated to the city as foretext but beneath this lays a subtext of cultural, social and sexual misplacement. It combines styles – fairy tale, social realist, pantomime and English Gothic – each sufficient to itself and yet also part of the whole. It is a novel about the search for an understanding of the world around us. It is also a novel written during one of the periodic cultural fluxes when things seem to truly change. Yet, this is not a universal change and it is in some of the contrasts with the neighbouring area to the novel's (probable) location that we can see some of what motivates Carter's narrative and gives an insight into how she sees, reads and maps the city.

So what does *The Magic Toyshop* tell us of the way in which we are to understand the spaces in its text? One assessment of Carter's interpretation of the city is there on page one of *Wise Children*:

> Why is London like Budapest?
> Because it is two cities divided by a river. (Carter 1992b, 1)

She amplifies this in the next paragraph

> Once upon a time you could make a crude distinction, thus: the rich lived amidst pleasant verdure in the North speedily whisked to exclusive shopping by abundant public transport while the poor eked out miserable existences in the South in circumstances of urban deprivation condemned to wait for hours at windswept bus-stops. (ibid.)

Of course this is Dora Chance's voice and an adjustment must be made for that, but note how 'North' and 'South' are given capitals, not always the case. It is a tacit acknowledgement that these are two different entities, both as geographical and literary spaces. The image of the two cities is not new. For most of the twentieth-century writers were exploring the literary topography of the city pairing north against south. But the metropolis, and especially London, is not a matter of simple binaries. Raoul Vaneigem writes in 1967 that the modern city 'simply [has] no centre at all. It is increasingly obvious that *the reference point they propose is always somewhere else*. These are labyrinths in which you are allowed only to lose yourself' (Vaneigem 1994: 242; my italics).

The Magic Toyshop, is a novel written in the era of swinging London, and yet it is not about swinging London, at least not explicitly. The shadow of Carnaby Street and the King's Road is there, as I shall discuss below, but this is a novel of another London of the same period. This chapter is about one of those reference points that for Vaneigem are 'somewhere else'; for those who determine the 'swinging' image of the city and about those who live there and are not party to the 'party'. *The Magic Toyshop* is about the less fashionable parts of the city, the streets that did not appear on maps of smart London. What constitutes and occupies the space where we perceive the city to be is on closer examination a collection of smaller spaces, locations, settings and background. It is a vortex in which the characters interact, develop and simply live out their lives. The novel reflects this adaptation of the 'abstract space carved out by capital and planners, but to some degree reappropriated by those of the dérive; and a potential social space, based on psychogeographical possibilities' (Pinder 1996: 423). What follows is an examination of two such spaces: the neighbourhood and its relationship to the city, and the house in which the characters of the novel live, interact and develop. Through these I want to show how Carter's novel reflects another (and possibly more inclusive) city than the history of the 1960s, until recently, has suggested.

When discussing swinging London a certain set of images automatically come to mind: Carnaby Street, the King's Road, the boutiques 'Biba' and 'Granny Takes a Trip', photographers, dolly birds and pop stars. Of course much of this is exaggeration and media myth/hype, but there are certain elements to this period that are worth examining for their relationship to Carter's novel. In late 1966 the Royal Court Theatre in Sloane Square staged a production of Alfred Jarry's *Ubu Roi* with Max Wall in the lead, sets by David Hockney and with Paul McCartney and Jane Asher in the first night crowd. Further down the road Michelangelo Antonioni was filming *Blow-Up* and Michael Cooper opened his gallery with funding from Robert Fraser. By the spring of 1967 Richard Neville was selling the first issues of *Oz*, *IT* (International Times) was making, for it, regular appearances and *Blow-Up* was released – and it is then that the image or myth of the King's Road arguably takes off. *Blow-Up* is not really about plot or action. The idea that you can see more in a 'huge photographic print than you can see by looking at the 35mm negative with a decent magnifying glass' never really holds up (Décharné 2006: 203). *Blow-Up* is a combination of character, place, music, atmosphere and mood: the image of the young photographer with his harem of nubile young girls willing to take their clothes off for him, fast car, cash-on-hip, rock bands in the evening, immaculately cool neighbours, and a casual acceptance of hallucinogens (albeit at a fashionable party in Cheyne Walk) was less about experiments in cinematic narrative than with offering an aspirational magazine guide to what London could offer anyone willing to take the risk. It is the Dick Whittington myth rewritten for the twentieth century. Although films about the bohemian scene in Chelsea had been made before – notably Guy Hamilton's *The Party's Over* (1965, filmed 1962) – *Blow-Up* connected with the larger audience in that it reflected more frankly the scene in Chelsea at the time. Of course there is compression and exaggeration, yet it did not set out to expose the scene but to be an exploration. It also had the advantage, which the earlier film did not have, of artistic serendipity. Over the next few months Radio 1 would start broadcasting; the MPAA in America had a new President who would begin to review what was permitted on screen, changes which the British film censor John Trevelyan would watch and match; the role of the Lord Chamberlain as theatrical censor was to be reviewed; and the Beatles would release *Sergeant Pepper's Lonely Hearts Club Band*. Not to mention the legalization of homosexuality and abortion, rising protest about Vietnam and the devaluation of the pound. Truly, then, interesting times.

Of course most of London was, as the journalist and activist Mick Farren observes, much less glamorous: 'The light may have been on in Piccadilly and the West End undergoing its Swinging London face lift, but, just a few tube stations out, the city was the monochrome of an Ealing comedy, brown on grey, highlighted in sepia' (Farren 2002: 7). Iain Sinclair writing about the Michael Reeves film *The Sorcerers* (1967) remembers how Boris Karloff:

> Right from the start, cruising the pavements, arguing over advertisements with a news-agent, is an architectural creation: all greys and tired browns, homburg, long coat. The cheap set from which he operates with his wife belongs in the Thirties, in *Sabotage*. . . . It's salutary to be reminded, in those days of Dick Lester, *Darling* and *Modesty Blaise*, that such low-lit, suburban gravy tins could still exist. (Sinclair 1997: 300)

There were houses with a single toilet for 11 people, often too filthy to be used, reports of 19 children and 11 grown-ups in one house with nine rooms and no bathroom and cooking done on the landings. Farren notes of Wapping, where he lived at this time, with 'Granny Takes a Trip' at its height, *Bonnie and Clyde* at the Cinema and East End boys Michael Caine, Terence Stamp and David Bailey riding their Rolls Royce's around the city that:

> [T]he area had a large population of incredibly poor and fucked-up people. From the winos who made their home on the small and dirty tracts of grass next to Spitalfields Church known as Itchy Park, and the dully desperate hookers who took their lives in their hands turning grim and disconnected street tricks, to the struggling families whom the new affluence had failed to touch, a lot of folks were hurting. The daily contact could grow deeply depressing unless you took a firm grip and didn't go near the idea that there, but for the grace of God, went you. (Farren 2002: 56)

Let us assume then that *The Magic Toyshop* is located in the Clapham/Battersea part of the city, the area of Nell Dunn's *Up the Junction* (1965) and Jeremy Sanford's *Cathy Come Home* (1966). Cross over the Battersea bridge and you are in Chelsea, the heart of the 'swinging scene', don't cross it and you are in a part of London still blighted by the effects of the war 20 years on. This is the London that Cyril Connolly described in 1947 as 'the largest, saddest and dirtiest of great cities, with its miles of unpainted half inhabited houses . . . under a sky permanently dull and lowering like a metal dish-cover' (Connolly 1947: 151).

The landscape of Uncle Philip's shop is an aspect of its era. Its location is never given an explicit identification and could be anywhere in the late sixties metropolis outside of the west and west central postcodes. What really matters is that it represents a space that existed and represented the majority of the city. Sarah Gamble suggests that this landscape 'within which Melanie faces herself is distinctly reminiscent of the distinctively sixties landscape Carter has already evoked in *Shadow Dance*, situated at the point at which history has run out, leaving nothing but the wreckage of past glories' (Gamble 1997: 71). The city is failing and while the dance carries on in the more fashionable and better lit parts of the city, for Carter the focus remains on other streets.

However, Carter's description of the landscape is not based on any anthropological, social-realist model of description. The landscapes of *The Magic Toyshop* offer a kind of fairy-tale landscape, a place that Lorna Sage describes as a world 'which works according to the laws of demons, fairytales, folktales myth and magic . . . Here are no mirrors and no books *because it is the world you find in books and mirrors*, the region of copies and images and representations' (Sage 1994: 15; italics original). The cave with the troll and the woman struck dumb on her wedding day lie in a blighted landscape, a semi-suburban Mordor. There is an air of absence (or is it sadness) about in the square, the 'wedge-shaped open space' with a 'failed, boarded-up jeweller's and a grocer's displaying a windowful of sunshine cornflakes' (Carter 1992a: 38–39). Near it is a park, site of the 'National Exposition of 1852', now overgrown yet still with its monuments to the Victorian age present. Finn draws aside a fringe of branches to show Melanie 'a stone lioness at the mouth of a stone cave, guarding her cubs' (ibid.). There are statues of 'Dryads, slave girls, busts of great men . . . A handsome yet sylvan prospect' (ibid. 102). Finally there is an 'open plateau with a floor of chequered marble, white on black, and a wide stone staircase with balustrades running down to the dried bed of an ornamental lake, which the mist turned to a bowl of milk' (ibid., 102). In the middle there is the fallen statue of Queen Victoria, once dominant over the landscape and now prone, a middle-aged version of the Sleeping Beauty. In both *The Magic Toyshop*, and later in *Wise Children*, there is a sense that these areas of London are places set in contrast to the consumerist heart of the capital and offer, if not a more authentic experience of what London is, then at least a contrast to the more obvious West End and the city. If there is a fairy-tale quality to it then, why not; is the image created of the 'swinging' city any less of a fabrication, any less of an act of conscious mythologizing?

The Magic Toyshop is not a novel of swinging London but it is an absence that informs the text, a gap or a blank into which we provide what we feel is the necessary background information. Macherey writes that it is 'useful and legitimate to ask of every production what it tacitly implies, what it does not say' (Macherey 1986: 85). For example: the physical settings of the novel suggest something of the work of Don McCullin rather than David Bailey – a photographer happier to examine the rough, bombed-out and desolate parts of the city rather than the neon-lit aspects. His 2007 collection *In England* offers a record of the period that could serve as visual corollary to Carter's text. Even *Blow-Up* acknowledges this as David Hemmings' character is seen leaving a Salvation Army hostel where he has been taking pictures of low-life London. Yet, this is a not a theme that Antonioni dwells on. Thomas quickly moves on to more work with his models and trysts with Vanessa Redgrave and Jane Birkin; ugly and dirty London is soon left behind. The London of Victoriana as fashion accessory becomes the locus. As the film bypasses the landscape of the book, so the book does the same for the world of the film. Perhaps absence is the political objective of this text reflecting the shallowness and surface attraction of the King's Road or Carnaby Street through acknowledging the reality of this other London. What we perceive as the image of the sixties landscape is challenged by Carter's mapping of the other physical spaces, a challenging of cultural alignments and distorting the cultural hegemony that the classical idea of the swinging city did and has possessed.

One aspect of the cultural landscape in which *The Magic Toyshop* does resonate with the 'hip' elements of its period is in its ending. As Uncle Philip's house burns Finn and Melanie are trapped in the garden alone. It is an ending that provokes a variety of responses. For John Haffenden 'Melanie and Finn escape from the toyshop like Adam and Eve from the Garden of Eden, returning the reader to the biblical myth which is employed in the earlier description of Melanie's sexual awakening' (Haffenden 1985: 80). Or is Linden Peach correct when suggesting that Carter 'appears to imply, as she said, that the fall was fortunate, but also that Melanie and Finn are trapped by the Genesis myth' (Peach 1998: 84–5). Then again 'The theme of a new Eden and the human race reduced to an elemental pair was common in science fiction of the 1950s and 1960s. Carter's adaptation of it is ambiguous' (Crow 1996: 47). However, whether it is in film – for example the ending of *Fahrenheit 451* (1966); or fiction in *The Final*

Programme (1968); or music and the cover of *Sergeant Pepper* (1967); or pop culture with John Peel's Perfumed Garden; or the very name of flower power – the idea of the garden offers an image of rest and peace, an alternative to the commercialization of the capital and pursuit of capital. Finn's and Melanie's trip to the park is a suggestion of the peace that can occur within the city and reflects the calm within the soul of the individual. It allows Finn the opportunity to demonstrate that he is not quite as rough as earlier chapters may have indicated.

> 'You do talk funnily,' she complained because her feet were wet. He shot her a backward glance over his black gleaming shoulder.
> 'You mean I talk funny for an ex-bog-trotter slum-kid?
> She blushed.
> 'I read books from the library now and then. And living with your uncle is, God knows, an education. (Carter 1992a: 102)

Freed from the tyranny of the shop and the influence of Uncle Philip, Finn is freer outside to be himself. He can get it together in the country (or in this case a park) in a way he cannot in the house. As Jonathan Raban notes '[d]ecide who you are, and the city will again assume a fixed form round you. Decide what it is, and your own identity will be revealed, like a position on a map fixed by triangulation' (Raban 1998: 3). Carter's park and city square are not realistic shapes or locations but real spaces re-imagined and remade for the purpose of the text, psychodramatic theatres of experience, much like the magic forest or castle of the middle-European fairy tale.

In their 2005 book, *Geographies of Modernism: Literatures, Cultures and Spaces*, Peter Brooker and Andrew Thacker ask if 'material geography and the built environment operate as determining influences upon consciousness and conduct (Brooker and Thacker 2005: 5). I noted previously some contemporary accounts of London in the late sixties and it is worth remembering these when considering the interior of Philip's house. The bathroom as described by Carter is reflective of this period.

> There was a crack in the deep, old-fashioned wash-basin and a long, red hair was fixed in the crack and floated out in the water as the basin filled. The towel was on a roller; it fell off, tower and roller both when she tried to dry her hands . . . There was, she observed, no toilet paper next to the lavatory; but, hanging from a loop of string, a number of sheets of the *Daily Mirror* roughly ripped into squares. (Carter 1992a: 56)

Filth is a presence and character in this text. From the very first time Melanie sees Francie in his 'beige and brown shirt of the sort that is not supposed to show the dirt', to his final appearance as the house burns 'in his shirtsleeves [with] were black rings of sweat under his arms' dirt is a constant and levelling force within the narrative (Carter 1992a: 33–4, 198). For Mary Douglas, '[d]irt is the by-product of a systematic ordering and classification of matter, in so far as ordering involves rejecting inappropriate elements' (Douglas 1966: 2). Dirt separates Phillip from Finn and Francie; they are dirty so they are lesser than he is. By reducing Melanie to a similar level he can differentiate himself from her. For him cleaner equals better. It is dialectic representative of the period. Consider how Finn appears at first to Melanie: long hair, vaguely military jacket (but not of a contemporary cut) and corduroys. It is a combination of the fashionable for 1967 – hair and jacket – with the less so, that is, the trousers. There is an acknowledgement of the wider scene and a realistic assessment of the reality of the period; that not everybody could afford what constituted the fashions of the period. Military jackets from the boutiques on King's Road in 'Granny Takes a Trip' or 'Hung on You' cost around £20, the average labouring wage in the late 1960s which, although increasing above inflation throughout the period, would not stretch to such luxuries easily. On the surface Finn attempts to present himself as acceptable to the world outside of the house, inside he can be more relaxed: 'A ferocious, unwashed, animal reek came from them both; in addition, Finn sank of paint and turps on top of the poverty-stricken slum smell' (Carter 1992a: 36). The use of smell as a means of defining difference is a common element in Carter's work. One commentator describes the milieu of *Shadow Dance* as 'a British slum where streets smell of urine, vomit and stale beer' (O'Day 1994: 26) and the smell of cabbage never quite leaves 49 Bard Road, Brixton (Carter 1992b: 28). What is important in the context of *The Magic Toyshop* is that it reflects a 'slipping out of your precarious middle-classness into the house of (superficial) horrors but (libidinal) mirrors' (Sage 1994: 8). Dirt, subsumed in the country beneath a veneer of civilized aspects such as the neat house and the nuclear family is acknowledged in the metropolis as an inescapable aspect of life. Dickens for one understood this. As Peter Ackroyd notes:

> In the nineteenth century, the history of city refuse became part of the history of city finance. The dust-heap in Dickens's *Our Mutual Friend*, modelled upon a real and ever more offensive pile of the King's Cross Road, was believed to contain buried treasure and had already made a fortune for its owner. 'I'm a pretty fair scholar in dust,' Mr Boffin explains, 'I can price the mounds to a fraction, and I know how they can be best disposed of. (Ackroyd 2001: 340)

Philip's house is a place of resistance to the cultural ethos of the period. There is no white heat of technology here. The image is of 'old-fashioned charm' that an American visitor thinks 'kind of Dickensian'; its proprietor a real-life tyrannical Victorian patriarch that the heroine Melanie must escape (Duggan 2006: 164). This is the flipside to the swinging city so assiduously promoted in this period, the city with a landscape still reminiscent of a century before. Even the music-making of Finn, Francie and Maggie echoes this previous era; the culture of the Irish 'navvies' brought to the city in the 1850s, or escaping from the famine, still a present and defining aspect of their impression of London. It is not an impression that the text serves to labour, but then part of the attraction of *The Magic Toyshop* is that it is not a didactic text. Carter knows the value of standing back and allowing the reader to develop impressions and connections. Marc O'Day suggests that Carter saw herself as a 'social realist': 'She may have been joking, but there is no doubt that these novels work over the terrain of the emergent counterculture in a recognisably realist form' (O'Day 1994: 28). At the same time they offer an 'imaginative response' to known and experienced landscapes, a Lefebvre-type landscape of experienced, perceived and imagined places. How we experience the city is reshaped through acts of the imagination into a new perception of the cartographic and topographic landscape. There is no keen focusing on specific details so the lack of specificity saves the text from the fate that, for example, *Blow-Up* has suffered, in that it avoids becoming a museum piece, a picture of a period. Instead of being a sixties novel *The Magic Toyshop* remains a story that comes from the late sixties. A parallel can be drawn with Michael Moorcock's Jerry Cornelius Quartet which starts with *The Final Programme* published in 1968 which is soaked in the kind of period detailing that would make Antonioni blush, and ending in 1977 with *The Condition of Muzak* which, bar one or two references to dub parties and free concerts underneath the Westway, is far less time-specific.

Think again of that American visitor and what she means to Uncle Philip. For him she represents the world of the West End and the consumerism of the period. Placed against this landscape of the 'hip' and attractive sixties London, Philip could be read as a victim of the city. Consider his actions as those of an individual trying to protect himself against an alien environment he little understands. His lack of feeling and empathy for the others in the house is reminiscent of Nurse Ratched in *One Flew over the Cuckoo's Nest* (1962), another key sixties counterculture text. The troll in the cave is not always just an evil figure; it is sometimes the pathetic as well. Philip's character anticipates aspects of the Duke in The Bloody Chamber; uncertain of his ability to determine the outside world the control of the domestic becomes all. Placed in a landscape where he feels he does not belong, dressed in out-of-date fashion, frustrated at the commercialization of his world, control of the domestic space becomes an all-consuming passion because it is all he has left. He is a man out of time: his presence a throwback to an older idea of the artisan that the American tourist observes in passing. His identity is dependant on the shop and the house; he controls it and therefore he is it. The physical degradation of rooms such as the bathroom is matched by the moral and sexual humiliation he places on Melanie for 'the imprisoning house of Gothic fiction has from the very beginning been that of patriarchy" (Baldrick 1993: xiii-xiv). Melanie can resist because she is a recent refugee to this place.

This is a blighted landscape, physically, architecturally, spiritually and sexually. Philip cannot serve in heaven so he will reign in hell. Yet, there is a kernel of light – the relationship of Finn, Francie and Maggie is a 'yes' to life, a rejection of the negative that Philip offers. Similarly, Nora and Dora Chance never lose their belief that the next day will be better than the one before: '[W]e'll go singing and dancing until we drop in our tracks' (Carter 1992b: 232) is the penultimate statement of Carter's most optimistic novel. Like *The Magic Toyshop*, and *The Bloody Chamber*, *Wise Children* is a rejection of the dirt, not just the physical but also as a metaphorical presence.

However, this assumes that patriarchy is first an immediate and all-encompassing effect and, secondly, that it requires an unchallenged physical presence: Melanie resists. As Stephen Pile argues:

> Aspects of identity or self develop in relationship to place (people make their homes), but places set a brute limit on what individuals can make of themselves (homes make people). The home is not simply an expression of an individual's identity; it is also constitutive of that identity. (Pile 1996: 55)

This is not the only home that Melanie has known; there is the house in the country where she was born and grew up in that has served to develop and shape her. Also it is now 1967. Philip can pull up the drawbridge all he wants, the city outside is emblematic of a changing country just as Melanie is emblematic of the changing consciousness of women. In what conservative commentators describe as the beginning of the permissive era – the pill, abortion and divorce – the novel poses the question of how women place themselves, face up to and negotiate the modern cityscape.

What then is the fascination of these working-class locations for the bright young radicals of the sixties? Partly, it is a type of middle-class slumming, a search for authenticity in a period of consumerist and nationalist fervour. This is after all the height of the Wilson era and an English football team that is world champion. Carter's text transmutes the shop and the district from the traditional and everyday London experience into something fantastic and magical. It is a precursor to the work of Michael Moorcock or Iain Sinclair whose efforts in the following decade would take various London boroughs and reinvent them as theatres of drama, exploration and psychosexual exploration. So, is *The Magic Toyshop* part of the mainstream or does it belong to the emerging counterculture? It had a big name publisher (William Heinemann) and offers in overview and location what seems like a narrative of British social realism. But it is also reflective of the emerging counterculture in its appropriation of the mundane and every day, by the fantastic and magical and its opposition to the 'Man', quite literally in this case. That it seems somewhat outside of what we think of as the canonical counterculture is perhaps because it lacks much of the misogyny or sexualized representations of the period. Melanie is not Finn's 'old lady'; she is far more of a partner in the sense that they are sharing equally in the life that is before them when the narrative closes. *Blow-Up* bypasses characters such as Finn or Francie or employs them merely as background for the artfully dressed and repainted streets; for Carter they are the city. They are the people who made it and keep it functioning and they receive in *The Magic Toyshop* a little of their dignity back. The novel listens to the stories, appropriates the social signifiers and the cultural mores, the art, the music and the films as means of assessing the city, its boundaries and borders. From this Carter creates a map of the city outside of the canonical cartographic representation. We see the location of *The Magic Toyshop* as poor because we believe we 'know' that the city at that time was so much better. We now know better because we have far more sources from which to draw on in our understanding of time, place and person. A text such as *The Magic Toyshop* offers a beginning, a first step, in connecting the individual and the local to their time and broader cognitive spaces.

Works Cited

Ackroyd, P. (2001), *London the Biography*, London: Vintage.

Baldrick, C. (1993), 'Introduction,' to C. Baldrick (ed.), *The Oxford Book of Gothic Tales*, Oxford: Oxford University Press, xi–xxiii.

Bertin, J. (1983), 'A New Look at Cartography,' in D. R. Fraser-Taylor (ed.), *Graphic Communication and Design in Contemporary Cartography*, John Wiley and Sons, 69–79.

Brooker, P. and Thacker, A. (2005), *Geographies of Modernism. Literatures, Cultures and Spaces*, London and New York: Routledge.

Carter, A. (1992a) [1967], *The Magic Toyshop*, London: Vintage.

—(1992b) [1991], *Wise Children*, London: Vintage.

Connolly, C. (1947), *Horizon*, Vol. XV (April), 151–4.

Crow, T. E. (1996), *The Rise of the Sixties. American and European Art in the Era of Dissent*, London: George Weidenfeld & Nicholson.

Décharné, M. (2006), *King's Road*, London: Phoenix.

Douglas, M. (1966), *Purity and Danger. An Analysis of Concepts of Pollution and Taboo*, London: Routledge and Kegan Paul.

Duggan, R. (2006), ' "Circles of Stage Fire": Angela Carter, Charles Dickens and Heteroglossia in the English Comic Novel', in R. Munford (ed.), *Re-Visiting Angela Carter. Texts, Contexts, Intertexts*, London: Palgrave.

Farren, M. (2002), *Give the Anarchist a Cigarette*, London: Pimlico.

Gamble, S. (1997), *Angela Carter: Writing From the Front Line*, Edinburgh University Press.

Haffenden, J. (1985), *Novelists in Interview*, London: Methuen.

Kesey, K. (1975) [1962], *One Flew Over the Cuckoo's Nest*, London: Picador.

Lee, C. (1997), *Tall, Dark and Gruesome*, London: Victor Gollancz.

Macherey, P. (1986) [1978], *A Theory of Literary Production*, trans. Geoffrey Wall, London and New York: Routledge & Kegan Paul.

McCullin, D. (2003), *In England*, London: Jonathan Cape.

Moorcock, M. (2004a), *The Final Programme* (1968), London: Four Walls Eight Windows.

—(2004b), *The Condition of Muzak* (1977), London: Four Walls Eight Windows.

O'Day, M. (1994), 'Mutability is having a Field Day: The Sixties Aura of Angela Carter's Bristol Trilogy', in Lorna Sage (ed.), *Flesh and the Mirror. Essays on the Art of Angela Carter*, London: Virago Press, 24–59.

Peach, L. (1998), *Angela Carter*, Basingstoke: Macmillan.

Pile, S. (1996), *The Body and the City. Psychoanalysis, Space and Subjectivity*, London and New York: Routledge.

Pinder, D. (1996), 'Subverting Cartography: The Situationists and Maps of the City'. *Environment and Planning A28*, 405–27.

Raban, J. (1998) [1974], *Soft City*, London: Harvill.

Sage, L. (1994), *Angela Carter*, Plymouth: Northcote House.

Sinclair, I. (1997), *Lights Out for the Territory*, London: Granta.

Vaneigem, R. (1994), *The Revolution of Everyday Life*, trans. Donald Nicholson-Smith, London: Left Bank Books and Rebel Press.

17

Through the Looking Glass: Playing with Schizophrenia and Surrealism in *Shadow Dance*

Jane Hentgès

Written in the middle of the 1960s, *Shadow Dance*, Carter's first novel, presents us with a gallery of extravagant portraits of neurotic, and even psychotic characters all involved in a desperate search for identity. Carter observed at the time that she was 'interested in psychiatric illness' (Kenyon 1992: 29) and indeed, in her early novels she seems to be more interested in playing with psychoanalysis and mental illness than in deconstructing myths about gender. She refers not only to Freud, exaggerating his ideas in a typically postmodern way, but also to R. D. Laing,[1] whose work she read avidly as she underlined in an interview with Olga Kenyon, 'I'd just been reading Foucault and Laing, and was very much interested by them in the sixties' (ibid.).

Her interest in psychiatric illness is not surprising since, as a young woman, she suffered from anorexia and was very unhappy. She even declared that she 'was quite mad for quite a long time' (Clapp 1991: 26). Besides, she considered Britain in the 1960s to be divided and in *Nothing Sacred* used psychoanalytical terms to talk about this split in society, 'the pleasure principle met the reality principle like an irresistible force encountering an immoveable object' (Carter 1992a: 84), implicitly comparing the permissive society of the young and its 'irresistible force' with the weight of the old traditional society, 'an immoveable object', which was forced to confront its hidden face or shadow.[2] This can explain her interest in Laing and his work and theories.

First of all I shall show how all the characters in *Shadow Dance* seem to be decidedly neurotic before concentrating on Morris, through whose eyes we see the events, and who can be read as a case history taken straight from Laing's *The Divided Self* which serves as an intertext for Carter's first novel. After analysing how Carter plays with all the different symptoms of 'ontological insecurity' that Laing describes in patients suffering from schizophrenia, I shall show how she uses Morris and psychiatric illness to introduce a 'shadow dance', a new surrealist, subversive, inverted vision of the world; a dark, shadowy wonderland, both fascinating and frightening lying behind the looking glass of reality. To do so Carter manipulates time and space and Freud's theory of condensation, displacement and dramatization in dreams, in order to render 'the uncanny', entropic world of the unconscious visible, not only to destabilize accepted ideas on what constitutes reality but also to transform 'the valley of the *shadow* of death'

(Ps. 23, 4, emphasis added) into what Catherine Stott aptly names 'the black *jewels* of the subconscious' (Stott 1992: 9, emphasis added).

Playing with Neurotic Symptoms and Schizophrenia

The title *Shadow Dance* is significant since all the characters seem to be walking in 'the valley of the shadow of death'. Carter presents us with a gallery of portraits of characters suffering from more or less severe psychological problems. None of them seem capable of reconciling the pleasure principle and the reality principle, the *id* and the *superego*. In fact all the characters serve as Morris's shadows and form a sort of backdrop or 'shadow dance' in the valley of death which he frequents.

Many of these characters are also shadows or inverted images of each other. Morris's wife Edna, for example, seems to be stifled by an overwhelming superego and knows nothing of the pleasure principle. Submissive and mouse-like, like the colour of her hair, for her the sex act is disgusting and just a matter of procreation: 'Naturally, she resented contraception. Not only did she think it foiled the right, true end of love-making, which was making babies, but she constantly complained that she found the whole process undignified and disgusting' (Carter 1994: 46). The euphemism 'the whole process' and the childish expression 'making babies' underline the sexual immaturity of this woman who is, moreover, childless. On the other hand Emily, a younger female character, knows all about sexual pleasure but nonetheless also suffers from a repressive feeling of guilt expressed through neurotic obsession: she feels dirty and spends her time washing constantly to try and be as white as her cat:

> She disliked dirt. It offended her. One of the reasons why she liked her cat, Tom, so much was that it was always washing itself.
>   And so was she. . . . She consumed a great deal of Lifebuoy toilet soap in a week. Three times a day, she lathered and rinsed her face with her hands, eyeing herself non-committally in Honey's round, cracked shaving mirror and often she washed her arms and legs as well. She always had the faintly anti-septic spice of soap about her. (ibid., 100)

Sexuality is in fact often the cause of the neurotic and psychotic symptoms most of the characters suffer from. Many of them are even sexually ambivalent or perverse. Honeybuzzard, Morris's best friend and Emily's lover, is both. His name already suggests as much as it associates the feminine sweetness of honey, and the masculine cruelty of a bird of prey, the buzzard. His perverse ambivalence is also suggested by his appearance: 'His eyes were large and pale, with long fair lashes; huge eyes that blinked and stuttered in the light like shy children. His delicate pick-pocket hands dealt gracefully with his glasses; such pretty, pink and white butterfly hands. But they were extraordinarily, deceptively strong; Morris had once seen him tear a telephone directory in half with his pretty hands' (ibid., 74). Honeybuzzard's 'pretty' feminine hands are in fact strong and capable of tearing and destruction, as are his mouth and teeth. He is bisexual but he is above all a sadist and when kissing he literally turns into a bird of prey: 'It was an inexpressibly carnivorous mouth; a mouth that suggested snapping, tearing, biting' (ibid., 56). He rapes Ghislaine, his ex-girlfriend, in a graveyard slashing her face with a knife and transforming it into a mirror-image of his own, half-angelic and half-monstrous:

> She used to look like a young girl in a picture book, a soft and dewy young girl.
> . . . She had such a little face, all pale; and soft, baby cheeks and a half-open mouth
> as if she was expecting somebody, anybody, everybody she met to pop a sweetie
> into it. . . .
>
> The scar went all the way down her face, from the corner of her left eyebrow,
> down, down, down, past her nose and mouth and chin until it disappeared below
> the collar of her shirt. The scar was all red and raw as if, at the slightest exertion,
> it might open and bleed; and the flesh was marked with purple imprints from the
> stitches she had had in it. (ibid., 2)

Yet far from rejecting her former lover, Ghislaine in true masochistic fashion always comes back for more until Honeybuzzard finally kills her in a strange sadomasochistic ritual. The couple are obviously shadow, inverted images of each other since, as Carter herself points out in *Nothing Sacred*, 'Masochism and sadism are different sides of the same coin' (Carter 1992b: 38).

Carter exaggerates these cases of sexual ambivalence and perversion in a postmodern playful way to such an extent that she and her readers can distance themselves from them as the characters become more like case histories than real people and any feelings we could have for them give way to the pleasure of decoding Carter's references to Laing. Morris, however, cannot distance himself from such a group but is, on the contrary, attracted to it. In fact Carter makes him present all the schizoid symptoms Laing speaks of in *The Divided Self*. According to Laing, people suffering from schizophrenia suffer to varying degrees from a form of existential anguish which he calls 'ontological insecurity' and which he describes in the following terms:

> The individual in the ordinary circumstances of living may feel more unreal than
> real; in a literal sense, more dead than alive; precariously differentiated from the rest
> of the world, so that his identity and autonomy are always in question. He may lack
> the experience of his own temporal continuity. He may not possess an over-riding
> sense of personal consistency or cohesiveness. He may feel more insubstantial than
> substantial, and unable to assume that the stuff he is made of is genuine, good,
> valuable. And he may feel his self as partially divorced from his body. It is, of course,
> inevitable that an individual whose experience of himself is of this order can no
> more live in a 'secure' world than he can be secure 'in himself'. (Laing 1990: 42)

As we shall go on to demonstrate, this description fits Morris perfectly as he feels inconsistent, more unreal than real, more dead than alive and dreams of becoming 'a citizen of the real world, a world where there was black and white but no shadows' (ibid., 160).

This feeling of ontological insecurity has very destabilizing consequences. According to Laing schizoids feel that their identity is fragmented and unstable, and as they fear they could become non-existent, they spend a lot of their time trying not to lose themselves completely in the shadows. Indeed, to use Laing's term, they are even afraid of being 'engulfed' by other people. Morris, for example, is afraid not only of Ghislaine sucking his blood like a vampire, but even of being absorbed or 'engulfed' in the open scar on her face: 'It seemed to him that she was a vampire woman, walking the streets on the continual qui vive, her enormous brown eyes alert and ever watchful, and the moment she saw him she would catch him up and absorb him threshing into the chasm in her face' (Carter 1994: 39). However, as they feel they have no real substance, Laing argues that schizophrenics are also afraid of the opposite, of others entering *their* bodies; a phenomenon which Laing calls 'implosion'. Morris in particular fears this. Not only does Ghislaine 'engulf' him she also threatens to invade his body when he is drinking beer: 'He sipped cautiously at his beer. And was suddenly gripped with the nauseating conviction that it tasted of her. He was drinking her down sacramentally' (ibid., 5). No doubt Morris feels in some way responsible for Ghislaine's rape as he had willed it in his mind, and feels so much guilt regarding her that he imagines he is both figuratively and literally eaten up or invaded by her. As meeting others can therefore prove fatal to people suffering from ontological insecurity, they often cut themselves off from the rest of the world, and Morris, who often hides away in his studio or in the local museum, is no exception.

According to Laing, this flight into the shadows can be explained as well by the fact that, as they are convinced that they are worthless and do not really exist in the real world, schizophrenics also fear being turned into an object and depersonalized by others. Laing calls this fear 'petrification'. This points to why Morris goes as far as to say that Ghislaine has a 'Medusa head' (ibid., 41) evoking the famous Greek myth of petrification and why he overreacts when Honeybuzzard turns him into an object by making a paper puppet of him:

> The Jumping Jack was Morris. Honey pulled the string once more and Morris's cardboard self convulsed in its St Vitus' dance.
>
> 'Isn't it pretty? Isn't it funny?' said the exuberant Honey. . . .
>
> Did he not realize what he had done? Did he not realize how badly Morris wanted to hit him and to punch him and hurt him? (ibid., 80)

Faced with all these threats Laing believes that people suffering from schizophrenia set up several defence mechanisms, the first being to try and beat the others at their own game by petrifying them and turning them into objects or images before they themselves can be petrified. This explains why, in Morris's eyes, Henry Glass, a secondary character, becomes 'a Lowry stick man' (ibid., 114), Ghislaine a 'Francis Bacon horror painting of the flesh' (ibid., 20) painted by him, and Edna a painting of St. Ursula by Burne Jones: 'She would sigh and put on her martyred smile (St. Ursula, the virgin, smiling at the rapists; painted by Burne Jones, rather than Millais for in the heat she grew waxen and moist-looking at once)' (ibid., 120).

However, the second defence mechanism Laing believes schizophrenics use is far more dangerous for their own security as they divide themselves into two parts, which Laing describes as 'the embodied self' and 'the disembodied self'. In order to avoid being present in frightening circumstances Laing thinks they hide behind their body, which becomes a sort of empty façade, and dream of becoming an invisible 'disembodied self'.

He describes this phenomenon as follows: '*The body is felt more as one object among other objects in the world than as the core of the individual's own being.* Instead of being the core of his true self, the body is felt as the core of a false self, which a detached, disembodied, "inner", "true" self looks on at with tenderness, amusement or hatred as the case may be' (Laing 1990: 69). Morris very often dreams that he is disembodied, and this radical defence mechanism becomes more and more accentuated towards the end of the novel. He even uses his own name 'Morris' in the following dream and soars above his body as if he and his body were two separate entities: 'Morris would dissolve. Liberated – for somehow he associated invisibility with a lightness and airiness of body, so that he floated above the streets and soared with airy lightness from place to place' (Carter 1994: 121).

Dividing oneself into two separate parts can be tragic as the more someone splits themselves into two, the more cut off they are from reality. They lose the notion of a unified being and slip into a sort of chaotic non-existence which Laing describes as follows: 'In many schizophrenics, the self-body split remains the basic one. However, when the centre fails to hold, neither self-experience nor body-experience can retain identity, integrity, cohesiveness, or vitality, and the individual becomes precipitated into a condition the end result of which we suggested could best be described as a state of "chaotic nonentity"' (Laing 1990: 162). Paradoxically, according to Laing, through fear of nonentity someone suffering from schizophrenia chooses nonentity and, following the dream in which he floats above the streets, Morris quite justifiably wonders 'if he was becoming psychotic' (Carter 1994: 122). Indeed, at the end of the novel instead of calling the police after discovering Ghislaine's dead body and thus remaining in reality, Morris chooses to join Honeybuzzard and enters both literally and symbolically 'the valley of the shadow of death' as is proved by the final words of the novel, 'Morris vanished into the shadows' (ibid.).

However, in spite of the gravity of Morris's case, Carter manages to present us with what Catherine Stott rightly calls 'the black *jewels* of the subconscious' (Stott 1992: 9; emphasis added). Even if we set a foot in 'the valley of the shadow of death' with her gallery of troubled characters, Carter manages to keep both herself and her readers at a distance thanks not only to her exaggeration of different neurotic and psychotic symptoms but also and above all to her playful use of language. If she is fascinated by psychiatric illness, and in particular schizophrenia, it is above all because schizophrenics have a different vision of the world, a vision that enables Carter to question 'the limitations of what is normally taken as constituting reality' (Peach 1998: 164), and to go through the looking glass and create a new kind of surrealist wonderland.

Through the Looking Glass: A Surrealist Dream World

During the 1960s Carter was interested in reproducing Plato's 'shadow dance' and in experimenting with different visions of reality. This can explain why in *Shadow Dance* mirrors are absent or broken, and sight always seems to be blurred, indirect or distorted for one reason or another. None of her characters, either mad or sane, see reality in the same way. Emily for example is short-sighted and only sees 'the things she had decided she wished to see' (Carter 1994: 101), whereas Morris psychologically reduces what he doesn't want to see to miniature dimensions that he takes for reality. Thus his wife and her lover, Henry Glass, are made tiny and insignificant:

> He splashed his face with cold water. The chilly drops seemed to shock him into a sharp-outlined clearness of vision. He saw everything extremely distinct and very small, in brilliant miniature. He felt he could pick up the bed in his two hands, minutely examine its occupants, poke and finger every detail, like Gulliver among the Lilliputians' (Carter 1994: 129)

Ironically, Morris's 'sharp-outlined clearness of vision' does not correspond to a 'normal' perception of the world but to a different way of seeing. It was for this very reason that André Breton in particular[3] and the surrealists in general were fascinated by mental illness and madness and Carter obviously shares their interest.[4] She states this clearly in 'The Alchemy of the Word' in *Expletives Deleted* when she says, 'Surrealism created wonder, the capacity for seeing the world as if for the first time which, in its purist state, is the prerogative of children and madmen' (Carter 1992a: 67).

Carter often alludes to surrealism in *Shadow Dance* and many of its favourite symbols such as butterflies, birds, mirrors and floating 'disembodied' eyes abound. Even Morris's and Honeybuzzard's passion for anything second-hand makes one think of the surrealists for whom discarded junk represented the unconscious of capitalist society. As Sarana Alexandrine points out, junk was admired and cherished because of its oddness: 'The Surrealists loved junk, were regular *flâneurs* at the local flea market, always searching for the appropriate find, the object possessing an attraction as if never before seen' (Alexandrine 1991: 140–1). However, Carter goes further and alludes indirectly to surrealist works of art. For example, we are reminded of Magritte's *Le modèle rouge* (*The Red Model*),[5] when reading the following description of the old waitress's shoes: 'she waddled away on her creaking black shoes, moulded over the years to the shape of the horny, corny, nooks and crannies and lumps and bumps and crevices and promontories and fjords of her swollen and time-deformed feet' (Carter 1994: 161), and the following portrait of Honeybuzzard reminds the reader of Magritte's representation of the body as a cage, with Carter even throwing in a surrealist bird and disembodied eye for good measure: 'The lines of his ribs showed through his flesh like an elegant bird-cage where his trapped heart flapped its wings regularly, one, two, on the beat. You could see his navel peering like a surreptitious eye over the narrow snakeskin belt of his white levis, he wore them so low on the hips' (Carter 1994: 140). In fact, in *Shadow Dance* any stable vision of reality is shown to be an illusion as Carter uses her writing as a mirror which reproduces not appearances but the hidden side of things, a different, unexpected vision,[6] as in Lewis Carroll's *Alice's Adventures in Wonderland* and *Through the Looking-Glass*.

However, if Alice wakes up from her dream, Morris doesn't. He seems to live in a permanent dream world in which the first thing that is upset is the accepted idea of space and time. As Laing points out: 'Under usual circumstances, the physical birth of a new living organism into the world inaugurates rapidly ongoing processes whereby within an amazingly short time the infant feels real and alive and has a sense of being an entity, with continuity in time and location in space' (Laing 1990: 41). According to Laing schizophrenics lack this perception of 'being an entity with continuity in time and location in space' so, although *Shadow Dance* is set in 1960s Bristol, and although the novel begins in the spring and ends in the autumn, the narrative confuses things and chronological time is replaced by subjective time. For instance, instead of being a symbol of life and renewal, the month of May is synonymous with death. Indeed, Spring is associated in Morris's mind with a churchyard and white flowers (the traditional colour for wreaths in Britain), which are moreover not in bloom but pestilential and dead: 'The white lilacs in the churchyard where Honey said Ghislaine had been raped and hurt browned at the edges and reeked of halitosis and finally dropped down dead' (Carter 1994: 38). Such disconcerting imagery as lilacs which 'reeked of halitosis' and which 'dropped down dead' conveys Morris's confused state of mind. He obviously projects his depression on a world in which time is, like him, cut off from reality.

Indeed Morris's dreams and nightmares disrupt normal chronology in more than one way. Instead of being forgotten in the morning, they carry on in the form of day dreams and hallucinations which break up the narrative. There is a permanent oscillation between dream and reality in which time is not linear but fragmented and unstable, thus mirroring Morris's own instability and fragmentation. He seems to be a sleepwalker unconcerned by external reality. The 'real' dramatic events of the novel, Ghislaine's rape and disfigurement and her murder are not shown directly and surprisingly take up very little room in the text conveying the impression that it is reality which now and again invades Morris's dream world and not vice versa. Besides, his dreams are often about the past or the future. In this way Morris can avoid the present, which he finds threatening. Indeed, he refers to one of his dreams as, 'a memory of the future' (ibid., 157).

In fact some of Morris's dreams about the future are premonitory and thus disrupt chronological order. For example, he dreams that Ghislaine will cause his wife to leave him and this is indirectly the case. He also dreams of killing Ghislaine and it is his alter ego, Honeybuzzard, who does so at the end of the novel. He is so sure that his dreams are going to come true that, when he is going to the house where he is to discover Ghislaine's dead body, he knows in advance what he is going to find and projects all his morbid premonitions on the town: 'The muted and elegiac light seemed to be that filling a dead city. It was the light of a city of dream-come-true' (ibid., 174). This disruption of linear time, thanks to the importance given to dreams, confuses the reader who no longer knows if dreams are a *mise en abyme* of reality or vice versa. In fact Carter's observations about the work of William Burroughs could be applied to her own first novels:

> This constant derailment of the reader happens again and again, shattering the sense of cause and effect . . .
>
> You cannot hurry Burroughs, or skim, or read him for the story. He likes to take his time and to disrupt *your* time in such a way that you cannot be carried along by this narrative. Each time it tips you out, you have to stand and think about it; you yourself are being rendered as discontinuous as the text. (Carter 1992a: 40–41)

This derailment of chronological time is obviously a sign of Morris's ontological insecurity, but the loss of a sense of reality is also linked to the dissolution of space. It comes as no surprise therefore that in *Shadow Dance* Carter plunges the reader into an entropic, chaotic universe, a universe which reflects once again the chaos in Morris's mind and the apparent chaos of dreams. Like the surrealists Carter was fascinated by dreams and called Freud's *The Interpretation of Dreams* a 'key book' (ibid., 70). She goes on to clearly link together dreams, art and surrealism: 'When we dream we are all poets. Everywhere the surrealists left their visiting cards: "Parents! Tell your children your dreams"' (ibid., 70). In fact, Carter plays with Freud's ideas on dreams, particularly his concept of 'dramatization'. Freud claimed that in the psyche in general and in dreams in particular, thoughts, concepts and feelings are dramatized, that is to say transformed into visual images or pictures. This is evident in *Shadow Dance* through the allusions to paintings and the fact that Morris himself is a painter. As we have seen, Carter very rarely uses abstract words to express feelings but projects them on the setting, thus transforming psychology into images[7] and making the unconscious concrete. However, as in lots of surrealist painting, the most striking thing about the very visual dream world within the narrative is the overwhelming presence of objects which seem to have a life of their own. This blurring of boundaries between the inanimate and the animate[8] was one of the ways that Freud thought dreams could provoke a feeling of the 'uncanny' and corresponds to Morris's pathological vision of petrification.

Considering the importance of objects in *Shadow Dance* it is obvious that they play an essential role. For instance, the contents of Morris and Honeybuzzard's junk shop are described in detail and it is clear that some of the objects in the shop have a latent signification for the owners, who significantly do not even try to sell them.[9] Taken as a whole, the decaying junk symbolizes Morris's desire to return to a state of entropy, and his death drive. When he states that he feels 'a second-hand man' (Carter 1994: 19), he draws a clear comparison between himself and all the second-hand rubbish in the shop. In fact, in Morris's dream world one could say that one signifier, one object, can signify several things, a process which corresponds to Freud's idea of 'condensation'. Clothes for example are often more than simple clothes. They can be metonyms for people but also signify feelings. When Morris discovers Henry Glass in bed with his wife, Henry's shirt becomes a substitute for both its owner but also for his anger and his overprotective nature. Thus the sleeves of the shirt turn into arms which try and stop Morris from going to see what is happening in the bedroom: 'the white arms of Henry's flung off shirt wound round his ankles and brought him to a halt' (ibid., 156).[10] The inanimate becomes animate and is associated with verbs of action and even of intention such as 'bring someone to a halt'. In the same way Edna's knitting is compared to a snappy little dog trying to defend its mistress thus suggesting in a condensed form not only Edna and her repressed feelings of fear and hatred towards Morris, but also the latter's own feelings of guilt concerning his treatment of her which he tries to push aside: 'He kicked aside the knitting which caught at his feet as if it were a little black dog, trying to protect its mistress from him' (ibid., 53). In all these examples, thanks to metonymy, metaphor and comparison, things take the place of people and of feelings, condensing into one object several more or less hidden meanings.

However, there are also examples of hypallage, or transferred epithet; a figure of speech which corresponds to the process of 'displacement' in dreams.[11] Hypallage enables Carter to associate adjectives normally only used for human beings with objects, once again blurring the boundaries between the animate and the inanimate and obliging the reader to try and re-establish the real association and sometimes find the missing element in order to understand the sense. As in dreams this is not always straightforward. When the narrator uses hypallage it is usually an easy game for the reader to replace the adjective with the person that goes with it. For example when Emily leaves home and her father is broken-hearted the adjective broken-hearted is displaced onto his beer: 'Her father stared into his broken-hearted beer' (ibid., 98). It must be borne in mind though that both condensation and displacement are defence mechanisms set up to repress certain feelings and cover up certain fears. The father's broken-heartedness is no doubt displaced because it is related to his incestuous desire for his daughter.

When the displacement happens in Morris's mind the correct association is more difficult to establish as in the following example which is far more complicated than it appears to be at first sight. While he is on his way to the house where he is to discover Ghislaine's dead body, Morris sees a young girl passing by on a bicycle: 'A girl in shorts whizzed by on a beautiful, young bicycle' (ibid., 174). It is obviously the girl who is 'young' and 'beautiful' but we can wonder why Morris displaced these adjectives. First of all this displacement may show quite simply that Morris, who is a bisexual and really in love with Honeybuzzard, is not really interested in beautiful, young girls. However, it can also be linked to the context as Morris instinctively knows that Honey has disposed of or 'displaced' Ghislaine's beauty and youth by disfiguring her before finally killing her. He is afraid of what he is going to find and therefore doesn't want to see the girl on the bike clearly as her youth and beauty remind him of Ghislaine.

The world Carter describes in *Shadow Dance* may be chaotic but one thing is clear: Carter's use of language to reveal Morris's disturbed mind is 'playful'. Her use of comparisons, metonymy and hypallage rather than metaphor is significant in this respect. The surrealists prized the use of metaphor, as it allowed a complete change in the vision of reality, whereas they disparaged comparisons as they considered that when using them the writer remains too conscious of what he is doing.[12] The fact that the narrative seldom has recourse to metaphor therefore shows that Carter, while allowing a glimpse of what a schizophrenic's vision of the world could be like, remains in charge and stops short of entering Morris's chaotic world completely. There is always a sense of play in relation to psychoanalysis, and the figures of speech used help the reader to follow clues and read through the rhetorical devices and figures of speech that Freud thought corresponded to certain of the processes he observed in dreams.[13] In a word, *Shadow Dance* is a typical postmodern 'writerly' text in which the reader is led to participate and feel pleasure from deriving narrative meaning.

To conclude, it is the word 'playfulness' which best sums up Carter's use of surrealism and schizophrenia in *Shadow Dance*. Using *The Divided Self* as in intertext she plays not only with Laing's ideas on schizophrenia, but also with the dream processes described by Freud and with the rhetoric of dreams linked to these processes. The very idea of 'the rhetoric of dreams' is obviously interesting for a writer such as Carter. She loves playing with language and insists on her love of words in an interview with J. Haffenden.[14] It is this linguistic playfulness which allows her readers to distance themselves from schizophrenia. They participate fully in the act of reading and this prevents them from 'vanishing into the shadows' with Morris at the end of the novel. Although Carter was undoubtedly fascinated with psychoanalysis in the 1960s, and with Laing's work on schizophrenia in particular, we can't help feeling that this fascination had above all an aesthetic aim as it enabled her, like the surrealists, to go 'through the looking glass' and create a world of scintillating images, which Catherine Stott so aptly called 'the black *jewels* of the subconscious'.

Notes

1 R. D. Laing was part of the anti-psychiatry movement in Britain in the sixties. He developed the argument that it may be beneficial to let acute mental and emotional turmoil have its way, and tried to see the links between psychiatric illness and the social environment.

2 The idea of the shadow has always been linked with the idea of the double. In the past the shadow was considered to represent our soul but since psychoanalysis it has come to symbolize our unconscious, our dark hidden side, everything we want to repress but which nonetheless is part and parcel of us. Thus a person or society which denies its shadow or unconscious, denies its own reality.

3 André Breton says: 'Les confidences des fous, je passerais ma vie à les rechercher' (*Manifestes du surréalisme* 14).

4 In her interview with Kenyon Carter says, when talking of the sixties, 'When other people were reading Margaret Drabble, I was reading Alfred Jarry and the French surrealists' (Kenyon 1992: 24). However, in her article 'The Alchemy of the Word' she explains that she distanced herself from the surrealists in the seventies because of the way they considered women: 'The surrealists were not good with women. That is why, although I thought they were wonderful, I had to give them up in the end' (Carter 1992a: 73).

5 In this painting feet and toes can be seen through a pair of boots.

6 We can think of Magritte's *La reproduction interdite* (*Not to be Reproduced*). In this painting a man is looking at himself in a mirror which, instead of reflecting his face, reflects his back. Magritte called the artist's eye a 'faux miroir' ('false mirror') as it always gives a distorted or biased vision of reality.

7 Carter says in an interview with Moira Paterson that, 'I always think first in images, then grope for the words' (Paterson 1986: 45).

8 In *Shadow Dance*, the presence of stuffed animals, which are at the same time animate and inanimate, no doubt symbolizes this blurring of boundaries or the coming together of opposite states which interested the surrealists. There are stuffed birds, a stuffed carp and a stuffed badger in Morris and Honeybuzzard's junk shop (Carter 1994: 27, 61, 68,124).

9 The same thing can be said about Uncle Philip's toys in Carter's *The Magic Toyshop*.

10 This makes us think again of some of Magritte's paintings in which clothes suggest the hidden presence of the person who wears them. In *La Philosophie dans le boudoir* (*Philosophy in the Boudoir*) and *En Hommage à Mack Sennett* (*Homage to Mack Sennett*), breasts appear behind a nightgown and, as we have seen, in *Le modèle rouge* (*The Red Model*) feet can be seen inside a pair of boots.

11 This is how Freud describes displacement: 'l'accent psychique est transféré d'un élément important sur un autre, peu important, de sorte que le rêve reçoit un autre centre et apparaît étrange' (*Introduction à la psychanalyse* 158).

12 David Lodge explains this difference clearly: 'When we say that A is like B, we do not confuse what is actually there with what is merely illustrative, but when we say that A in a sense is B, the possibility of such confusion is always there' (Lodge 1997: 112).

13 'Les premières pensées du rêve qu'on développe par l'analyse frappent en effet souvent par leur habillage inhabituel ; elles ne semblent pas données dans les formes linguistiques sobres dont notre pensée se sert de préférence; elles sont au contraire figurées d'une manière symbolique par des comparaisons et des métaphores, en quelque sorte dans une langue poétique et imagée' (*Sur le rêve* 91–2).

14 When talking about words Carter says, 'Embrace them? I would say that I half-suffocate them with the enthusiasm with which I wrap my arms and legs around them. . . . It's the only way I can write. I'm not sure what beautiful writing is. There's a certain kind of flat, pedestrian writing which I know I don't like, but I'm cursed a bit by fluency, I think' (Haffenden 1985: 73).

Works Cited

Alexandrine, S. (1991), *Surrealist Art*, London: Thames and Hudson.

Breton, A. (1970) [1924], *Manifestes du Surréalisme*, Paris: Gallimard.

Carter, A. (1992a), *Expletives Deleted: Selected Writings*, London: Chatto & Windus.

—(1992b) [1982], *Nothing Sacred*, London: Virago Press.

—(1994) [1966], *Shadow Dance*, London: Virago Press.

Clapp, S. (1991), 'On Madness, Men and Fairy-Tales', *Independent on Sunday Review Supplement*, 9 June.

Freud, S. (1973) [1916], *Introduction à la psychanalyse*, Paris: Payot.

—(1998) [1901], *Sur le rêve*, Paris: Gallimard.

Haffenden, J. (ed.) (1985), *Novelists in Interview*, London: Methuen.

Kenyon, O. (ed.) (1992), *The Writer's Imagination*, Bradford: The University of Bradford Print Unit.

Laing, R. D. (1990) [1960], *The Divided Self*, London: Penguin Books.

Lodge, D. (1997) [1977], *The Modes of Modern Writing: Metaphor, Metonymy, and the Typology of Modern Literature*, London: Arnold.

Paterson, M. (1986), 'Flights of Fancy in Balham', *Observer Magazine*, 9 November.

Peach, L. (1998), *Angela Carter*, London: Macmillan Press.

Stott, C. (1992), 'Runaway to the Land of Promise', *Guardian*, 10 August.

Index